D1522150

Bureaucracy, Education, and Monopoly

Bureaucracy, Education, and Monopoly

Civil Service Reforms in Prussia and England

HANS-EBERHARD MUELLER

University of California Press

Berkeley / Los Angeles / London

University of California Press
Berkeley and Los Angeles, California
University of California Press, Ltd.
London, England
© 1984 by
The Regents of the University of California

Printed in the United States of America

1 2 3 4 5 6 7 8 9

Library of Congress Cataloging in Publication Data

Mueller, Hans-Eberhard.
  Bureacracy, education, and monopoly.

  Bibliography: p. 263
  Includes index.
  1. Civil service reform—Prussia—History. 2. Civil
service reform—England—History. 3. Education—Social
aspects—Prussia—History. 4. Education—Social aspects
—England—History. I. Title.
JN4533.M83 1983   354.42006'09   76-3877
ISBN 0-520-03209-8

OCT 2 0 1984

For Hendrika Mueller

Contents

Preface ix

Introduction 1

1. Conceptual Frames of Reference 5

   Shortcomings of Functional Analyses 5
   The Pattern Variables as Methods of Selection 13
   Status Groups and Classes 23

2. The Prussian Historical Background 37

   The Historical Pattern 38
   Militarization and Its Consequences 46
   From Patronage to Limited Competition 54
   The Social Structure of Education 82

3. The English Historical Background 91

   The Historical Pattern 91
   Patronage and the Unreformed Civil Service 96
   The Social Structure of Education 108
   The Redefinition of Gentility 118

4. The Prussian Civil Service Reform 126

   Stein-Hardenberg Memoranda 127
   The Crisis of the Aristocracy 137
   The Rising Middle Class 145
   Civil Service Reform and Reform of Education 155

5. The English Civil Service Reform   167

   The Trevelyan-Northcote Report   168
   Internal Pressures for Reform   173
   Political Pressures for Reform   178
   Civil Service Reform and Reform of Education   183
   Examinations in the Professions   188
   Dress Rehearsal: The Indian Civil Service Reform   197
   The Intentions of the Reformers   200
   Opposition to the Reform Plan   210
   From Limited to Open Competition   217

6. Summary and Conclusion   224

   Notes   235

   Bibliography   263

   Index   287

Preface

This book sprang from a concern that historical sociology advance beyond typological contrasts of "tradition" and "modernity" and beyond functional analyses in the direction of comparative, causal-historical interpretation of social change. I had gained the strong impression that sociological theorizing was too much given to generalize on the basis of limited experience. I had become convinced also that the tendencies to mechanism in sociological theorizing was a result partly of our waning sense of history and diminishing concern with the historical meanings and interests of the actors involved in social change. I had come to see "society" less as a system analogous to an organism and more as a set of arenas in which individuals and groups strive to realize their material and ideal interests by means of strategic social action. Simply to replace "functionalism" with "conflict theory" was not enough because any sociological theory of change must begin and end with comparative and interpretive historical research.

In writing the book, I learned the hard way that sociologists cannot rely on secondary materials but must be prepared to consult documents, letters, diaries, and the like in much the same way as participant observers of contemporary life must consult the understandings and opinions of their subjects. As I was spending more and more time with original communications between historical actors, I became more and more convinced that we must shed outdated notions of a division of labor between history and sociology.

We simply cannot assume that historians of "our" subject matter have worked up the facts from sources in such a way as to be free from their more or less explicit theoretical models. Nor can we safely assume that "authorities" on the subject have tapped all the relevant sources, especially after a new perspective on old data raises new questions and begs for data which an "authority" might have seen but not recognized as meaningful.

Historical sociology is more popular now than it was when the research for this book was started. There are more programmatic statements on "conflict sociology," more historical background chapters in otherwise unhistorical treatments of a subject matter, even more comparative-historical studies. But we are still far from that comparative-historical social science in which sociology and history would be partners in a common enterprise with many research traditions cutting across disciplinary boundaries. If I consider my work as a contribution to this end in the area of civil service reform, I do not wish to make immodest claims about the success of my work but rather to make tangible what I believe the general direction of sociological theory and research praxis should be in history or sociology. Nor do I wish to hide my sense of frustration stemming from the limitations of my disciplinary training and from the divergent disciplinary needs of the audience for which I am writing. I hope that someone will improve upon this work, expand its comparative scope, and find the perfect communication between the Scylla of historical narration and the Charybdis of analytical brevity.

As I deliver this study to the scrutiny of a wider audience, it is a pleasure to record my debts and express my gratitude to the many individuals who have taught me, inspired me, given me advice, or otherwise facilitated my research. The title of this study was suggested by the heading of the last section of Weber's chapter on bureaucracy in the 1968 edition of *Economy and Society*[1] and reflects my understanding of Weber's perspective as sketched in that programmatic section and elsewhere in his writings. My understanding of Weber's approach has been shaped during several years of my association with Professor Reinhard Bendix first as graduate student, then as a research assistant, and finally as a member of an editorial group that hammered out the intellectual orientation of a reader in comparative political sociology.[2]

Since then, this study has benefited from conversations and communications with many other individuals, including Professors Joseph Bensman, Leon Bramson, James Brow, Randall Collins, James Govan, Richard Schuldenfrei, and R. Stephen Warner, as well as with help from library staffs at the British Museum, Swarthmore College, the University of California, Berkeley, the University of Pennsylvania, and the University of Göttingen.

To all of them I wish to express my gratitude. Naturally, no one but myself is responsible for any defects in my scholarship.

H.-E.M.

The adjustment [of the aristocracy] to newly developing social forces and ideals . . . so far as it is voluntarily conceded does not aim at changing things, but rather at maintaining them. The decline of aristocratic prerogatives is the *conditio sine qua non* for saving the aristocratic regime itself.

GEORG SIMMEL

The role played in former days by the "proof of ancestry," as prerequisite for equality of birth, access to noble prebends and endowments and, wherever the nobility retained social power, for the qualification to state offices, is nowadays taken by the patent of education.

MAX WEBER

The possession of personal higher education . . . is the knighthood of modernity.

ALBERT SCHÄFFLE

Introduction

The purpose of this study is to explain the interrelationship of bureaucracy and education in two countries with different historical experiences. That bureaucratization means, among other things, the proliferation of civil service examinations, is of course well known and scarcely requires further demonstration.[1] Yet there is no agreement in the literature on how to explain this proliferation. Interpretations vary but seem to be informed by two basic explanatory models.

The first flows from a functional theory, according to which the introduction of educational standards and examinations in public employment was determined by expansion and intensification of public administration. Many history texts, as well as some recent works on the English civil service, use this model.[2] The civil service expanded and took on new functions; jobs became more demanding technically; and these changes forced a further change in the standards of recruitment. The old standards, based as they were on hereditary rights, informal connections, or political patronage, were no longer capable of selecting men with the qualifications needed in the new circumstances. Competitive civil service examinations solved this technical functional problem and, though only incidentally, enhanced access of social groups who had been disfavored by the old standards of recruitment.

The second model explains the introduction of civil service examinations as the outcome of struggles between conflict groups.[3]

Specifically, such groups attempted to capture the prizes held out by high civil service posts. There are essentially two versions of this conflict-group approach. The most widespread in the civil service literature links the introduction of civil service examinations to the rising middle class.[4] The educated middle class struggled against traditional methods of recruitment that loaded the dice in favor of the hereditary aristocracy and gentry. Middle-class professionals advocated merit, proven in examinations; and although they fought under the ideological banner of administrative efficiency, they were "really" interested in breaking the old elite's monopoly of advantageous positions. The less frequently encountered approach links civil service reforms to strategies of the traditional elites intent upon maintaining their preferred access to high civil service posts in changed social, economic, and political conditions.[5] Traditional elites, the argument goes, introduced high educational qualifications that might be expected to work in their favor, given the existing social stratification of higher education. Generally speaking, conflict theorists, whether or not they would link civil service reforms to the rising middle class, would view them in the light of strategies aimed at opening, maintaining, or closing access to civil service posts.

I shall argue that the comparison of Prussia and England bears out the conflict thesis. In both cases, civil service examinations are best explained as the outcome of strategic actions by historical groups enjoying a near-monopoly of higher education. In the Prussian case, civil service examinations were pressed by a middle-class intelligentsia anxious to expand its access to higher civil service posts. In the English case, they were a strategy of gentlemen to keep monopolizing the higher civil service.

The present study was conceived as a contribution to what is sometimes called "conflict theory," but which I prefer to regard simply as the distinctive approach of historical sociology. The first chapter deals with some of the conceptual underpinnings of this approach insofar as they bear on the thesis of this study. It begins with a critique of functional explanations of civil service reforms, proceeds to a critique of dichotomous typologies of recruitment methods, and finally takes a look at Weber's conceptualization of status-group and class formation, which offers an alternative to such dichotomies as Parsons' pattern variables.

The historical case studies are divided into four chapters. Chapters 2 and 3, devoted to Prussia and to England, sketch the divergent patterns of historical development in the two countries. Setting the stage for the analysis of the civil service reform, they provide profiles of the institutions to the eve of reform, especially methods of recruitment to the prereformed civil service; the structure and social composition of education; and the relationship of traditional ruling classes to professional groups rising with the new order of things. Chapters 4 and 5, finally, analyze the reforms in the light of other social and political changes. These linkages have given rise to many partial causal interpretations in specialized monographs, particularly in the English case. I will show that these partial interpretations add up to a consistent whole if the reforms are also interpreted from the point of view of the historical actors who propagated and pressed the reforms. In particular, I wish to show how technical-functional pressures for reform help to explain, perhaps, the abolition of the ways of doing things whereas a host of social and political considerations explain the shape of the new ways that replaced the old.

Causal-historical explanation, which augments analysis of functional connections with interpretations of the understandings and aims of historical actors, was realizable fully only in the English case, where documentary sources bearing on the thoughts and interests of the reformers flow more generously and where a richer monographic literature on civil service reforms exists. Since the Prussian civil service reform was but a sequence of seemingly unrelated events, each without the constitutional significance that the abolition of patronage and the introduction of open, competitive examinations had in England, it has not received the same attention by contemporaries and historians as the English civil service reform.[6] For these reasons, the Prussian case does not advance as much as I would like beyond an external analysis of relationships and constraints. In the English case, by contrast, we will eventually move to a more detailed, internal view of the group of men who propagated the reform, reacted to criticism, exchanged memoranda, and in doing so revealed their intentions. Such methodological limitations notwithstanding, the comparison of England and Prussia brings into high relief how divergent historical conditions determined the differential success of the Prussian and English aristocracies to adapt to the new social forces and ideas that undermined the old recruitment methods.

One might legitimately ask whether it is meaningful to compare and contrast Prussia and England given that the historical-political contexts and the timing of their civil service reforms were so different. Are we comparing apples and oranges? In answer to this question, I would like to point to Alexis de Tocqueville's rationale for comparing the status groups and classes as well as the institutions of the major states in Europe. In his study of the French Revolution, he was "struck by the remarkable similarity between the laws and institutions" of the European states. He recognized, of course, that they varied greatly, "almost infinitely on the points of detail . . . ;" but he found the historic principles everywhere the same.

> the administration of all three countries [Germany, France, England] derived from the same general principles; the political assemblies were composed of the same elements and invested with the same powers. The community was divided up on the same lines and there was the same hierarchy of classes. The nobles held identical positions, had the same privileges, the same appearance; there was, in fact, a family likeness between them, and one might almost say that they were not different men, but essentially the same men everywhere.[7]

These are, indeed, the reasons why the countries in this study may be compared meaningfully. If I seem to expend an extraordinary amount of space to highlighting the differences between them, it is because I wish to prepare the reader for the striking fact that the groups pressing for civil service reforms were interested in reform for divergent reasons. In Victorian England, it was a somewhat inclusive status group of gentlemen, oriented to the traditional ruling class, which was interested in educational qualifications so as to maintain its hold on the civil service. In Prussia, it was a bureaucratic intelligentsia, second in rank to the Junker aristocracy but briefly swept to power by the defeat of Prussia at the hands of Napoleon, which was most eager to change the rules of the game so as to improve its position vis-à-vis men of hereditary rank and privilege.

1. Conceptual Frames of Reference

Facts do not speak for themselves. Historical events and the utterances of historical actors reveal their relatedness and meaning only if interpreted in the light of concepts, models, and hypotheses. These conceptual underpinnings are the subject matter of the present chapter. Although the historical case studies stand on their own and may be read independently, I wish to lay bare the theoretical work that has shaped the comparative studies. In the first section I will discuss my claim that the functional model is deficient for explaining civil service reforms. In the second I will point out a number of pitfalls in the use of such dichotomous classifications of employment conditions as Parsons' pattern variables. In the third section, finally, I will take a look at Weber's "tendential" ideal types of group formation and strategic action. The dynamic aspect in Weber's concepts of status and class is not well understood in contemporary sociology but offers a fruitful alternative to functional analyses and dichotomous classifications of social structure, both of which have proliferated as sociologists have turned away from causal-historical explanation.

Shortcomings of Functional Analyses

Functional analyses of changing requirements for entry into the civil service tend to have three shortcomings. First, they tend to emphasize the technical aspects of changing job requirements, such as legal, professional, scientific, or technological expertise, and tend to obscure the political, ideological, and social considerations in the changing methods of selection. Second, insofar as the change from one method of selection to another is explained at all, functionalists tend to be preoccupied with the conditions causing the abolition of "traditional" ascriptive methods of selection and to neglect the reasons why some particular "modern" method, such as a civil service examination tied to a classical education, was selected by the reformers. Third, functional analyses tend to fall short of causal-historical explanation insofar as they often neglect to render explanations in terms of imputed and empirically verified interests of determinate groups and individuals in determinate social-historical conditions. For the remainder of this first section, I will address myself to these issues.

The functional approach suggests that traditional methods of recruitment were abolished because "ascriptive" methods, such as hereditary succession or patronage by notables with hereditary rights of nomination, became "disfunctional"—no longer able to meet the ever-increasing need for educated talent in the expanding bureaucracies. Now one might certainly cite a number of examples that would seem to make functional explanations quite plausible. For example, the Prussian monarchs of the eighteenth century certainly responded to a "need" for university-trained jurists to develop and administer the public law and for economists and practical men of business to run state enterprises, fiscal departments, and military procurement offices. The landed ruling class, it is true, often did not have the requisite expertise nor even the inclination for many of these new administrative functions in the royal bureaucracy. Similarly, the English aristocratic oligarchy in control of the unreformed civil service was challenged to deal with the consequences of capitalist industrial development. To carry out new governmental functions from factory inspection to public sanitation, they exercised their patronage so as to bring qualified professionals into a civil service that used to be a haven for ill-prepared spoilsmen with the right connections.

In both cases of expansion, different though they were, new administrative exigencies—here the expansion of monarchic dominance into the feudal sphere of influence, there the expansion of the state into a society dislocated by capitalist industrial development—induced the dominant interests to employ men with new qualifications for office. And in both cases, as we shall see, traditional recruitment methods were tempered with considerations of merit long before civil service examinations were introduced.

However, it is important to recognize that the new men were not only better qualified in a technical sense; they were also well qualified in a political and ideological sense. Indeed, once the changing methods of recruitment are examined in the light of the "politics" of the dominant groups, an additional reason for reform becomes apparent. In Prussia, for example, new employment conditions came to the fore when monarchs, bent upon destroying the feudal autonomy of the provincial estates, extended their dominance into aristocratic spheres of influence. In this struggle for supremacy, the "necessary" qualifications of the king's administrators included not only new kinds of technical expertise but also political reliability and ideological compatibility, which the members of the traditional ruling class could not be presumed to have. It is also, if not primarily, for this reason that burghers (and foreigners) were often preferred during the monarchy's struggle against a recalcitrant aristocracy. Similarly, the English aristocratic oligarchy may have brought in technical experts to man the expanding bureaucracy, but they were also careful in sponsoring politically reliable and ideologically and socially compatible gentlemen.

Functional explanations, as I have said earlier, emphasize the reasons why an old method of recruitment became obsolete and disfunctional and why it was eventually abolished. In practice, this means that the introduction of a particular new method is "explained" in terms of the reasons why an older method was abolished. Functionalists proceed from the assumption of a social state in equilibrium, move to a specification of some disturbing condition, and end up by depicting the change that has established a new equilibrium. Those who use this approach are not always clearly aware of the underlying assumptions though Parsons has stated them plainly in *The Social System.*

> We are assuming that the *continuance* of a stabilized motivational process . . . is to be treated as *not problematic.* This assumption, though seldom made explicit, seems to be of very general applicability in psychology. It may be compared to the first Newtonian law of motion, the law of inertia, which states that the *problems* for mechanics concern

not what makes bodies move, but what makes them *change* their motion, in direction or velocity. . . . Hence for the social system as well as the personality we will *not* be concerned with the problem of the maintenance of given states of social system *except where there are known tendencies to alter those states.*[1]

The logic of this position leads straightaway to the supposition that a sufficient reason for abolishing an institution (A) must also be a sufficient explanation why another institution (B) took its place. This mechanistic approach to things social masks the possibility that there might be a very great hiatus between explaining why a certain method of selecting candidates for office was abolished and why a particular other method was put in its place. One way of looking at the general problem may be to suppose that a whole range of functionally equivalent institutions (B1, B2, and so forth) might perhaps have solved the problem of institution (A). If so, it is obvious that we must search for additional reasons why the reformers preferred the particular solution (B) they introduced. It might be a sound methodological principle in the social sciences to assume that for any social problem there exists a range of technically adequate solutions. After all, the problem of an energy crisis can be solved by increasing production as well as by reducing demand to the level of supply, and there are different ways of accomplishing both of these ends. Hence, it is important to explain just why a particular solution was preferred at a particular time and place. This means explaining the particular solution in terms of the interests and situational conditions of the men who made the change. The choices of historical actors may be limited by moral, legal, political, and naked economic constraints in their situation. But however constrained and limited by situational conditions, the introduction of a new way of doing things can be fully explained only by reference to their ideas and interests.

This principle is easily forgotten, and historians and sociologists often explain the introduction of civil service examinations in terms of conditions that made older, ascriptive methods untenable. This oversight, I have argued, comes easily if structural change is conceptualized as reequilibration of a social system disturbed by new conditions. Since the reform evidently solved the problem of disequilibrium, why bother to explain exactly why and how the reformers hit upon the new arrangement they introduced? At best, one will merely fail to examine closely how a particular policy was selected from a range of functionally adequate solutions. At worst, one will be tempted to think that the policy that was picked was the only possible solution to the problem. Painstaking historical analysis may, indeed, reveal the latter conclusion to be correct. But in the absence of painstaking historical analysis of the interests and situation of historical actors, that conclusion is suspect as that fallacy of historical hindsight which is also known as "restrospective determinism."

In explaining civil service examinations, we clearly want to know not only that the new educational conditions of employment solved a personnel problem posed by the discarded "ascriptive" methods of recruitment but also why these educational requirements were set so high above a level of technically adequate preparation. As has been pointed out frequently, the high literary and classic studies required by nineteenth-century civil service examinations evidently provided not only adequately trained personnel.[2] In Britain, they also provided men with a socially exclusive education, which, to paraphrase a nineteenth-century critic, only the rich could afford. Were the educational requirements of civil service examinations significant also in terms of social and ideological screening? Indeed, were educational requirements deliberately inflated by status groups intent upon monopolizing administrative power? Questions such as these flow naturally from a conflict-group perspective but seem to be beyond the field of vision of the functional approach.

Collins recently raised similar questions with respect to the rising educational qualifications for most jobs in America over the last decades.[3] He challenges the functional interpretation according to which that educational inflation resulted from a rise of technical job requirements. He introduces some evidence to suggest (1) that only a small part of the educational inflation may be explained by a corresponding rise of educational job requirements, and (2) that the major part corresponds to deliberate strategies on the part of dominant status groups to exclude others by means of high educational conditions of employment. From there he proceeds to argue a theoretical point. "The construction of a general theory of the determinants of stratification in its various forms is best advanced by incorporating elements of the functional analysis of technical requirements of specific jobs at appropriate points within the conflict model."[4] Functional analysis, he implies, is but a subsidiary part of a more general conflict-group approach that explains social change in terms of interest groups struggling for advantages in and through social organizations.

Collins' point is well taken, but it seems to me that the greater generality of the conflict-group approach cannot be established by empirical data indicating that one variable (social screening) accounts for *more* of a certain educational "inflation" than another variable (technical-educational requirements of jobs). Even if the findings had been reversed, they could not have altered his contention that the conflict-group approach is more general than functional analysis in the sense that the conflict-group approach must necessarily include functional analysis, but not vice versa.

The greater generality of the conflict-group approach follows from the frame of reference of conflict "theory" and associated methodological considerations of historical sociology. As Collins suggests, in this frame of reference, society is conceived as an arena of interaction composed of many organizations—economic, political, social, religious, etc. The units of analysis are more or less coordinated groups, classes, status groups, and parties in Weber's sense, advancing their interests through strategic action in and across these organizations.[5] Generally speaking, in acting to advance their material and ideal interests, individuals and groups wittingly or unwittingly create conditions that are "functional" or "disfunctional" relative to the goals of these organizations and to the interests of the dominant groups who define those goals. Those who set organizational goals and make policy decisions, including decisions on employment standards, often solve deliberately the functional problems of "their" organizations once these impinge on their interests. Occasionally, functional problems get solved unwittingly—that is, as an unanticipated consequence of action intended to accomplish something else. And often deliberate short-run solutions create unanticipated problems in the long run. For all these reasons, it is clear that functional analysis is an indispensable aspect of sociological explanation if only because it identifies the significant interrelated social arrangements that need to be studied from a causal-historical point of view.

Functional analysis is certainly a part of every sociologist's attempt to orient himself in the realm of the interdependent institutions whose persistence and change he wishes to explain. In this sense, Kingsley Davis was surely correct when he suggested years ago that we are all functionalists now. But historical sociologists trying to explain the behavior of social groups in particular conditions regard functional analysis as a necessary preliminary to historical-causal explanations.

Explanations of the persistence or change of a social structure clearly involve something more than stating correlated conditions and more than analyzing the functional nexus between them. As Weber recognized long ago, functional analysis is a "highly important and indispensable preliminary task," though not the end of sociological explanation.[6] An explanation of why one social structure was abolished and another one took its place is not complete until a number of additional questions are answered. What were the historical determinants and conditions that moved men to action, individually or collectively? What material or ideal interest did they expect to realize? How did they assess and respond to the situational conditions that may have foiled or facilitated their objectives?

Of course, not every sociological analysis must necessarily be causal analysis in this sense. One might be content with merely describing social structures that tend to be associated in the long run of history, as when Weber, generalizing from many cases, points out that "the modern development of full bureaucratization brings the system of rational examinations for expertise irresistibly to the fore."[7] Note that he is not explaining examinations here; he is only depicting a strong historical affinity between examinations and other aspects of bureaucratization. One might go a step further, as Weber does in much of his work, and analyze the functional significance of this affinity. How do various institutional parts fit together to form a functional whole? But then, he cautions, one must be extremely careful to avoid pseudo-explanations in teleological terms that do not touch base with the strategic actions of historical individuals and groups. "Those who view the painstaking labor of causally understanding historical reality as of secondary importance can disregard it, but it is impossible to supplant it by any teleology."[8] To pretend that functional analysis is causal analysis leads straightaway to teleological reasoning and to the fallacy of retrospective determinism. Historical analysis may well reveal that individuals and groups were aware of and acted in terms of the functional logic of the situation, much as the analyst sees it. But then historical analysis may reveal that they did not and that the functional consequences of their actions were altogether unanticipated.

In the brief and largely programmatic section entitled "Bureaucracy and Education" in his *Economy and Society,* Weber follows these methodological considerations.[9] He begins by depicting the historical affinity between bureaucratization and civil service examinations, proceeds to an analysis of the functional nexus between them, and finally suggests the general terms of an explanation in the idiom of the conflict-group approach: examinations advance irresistibly because they are means by which university-trained status groups appropriate and monopolize social and economic advantages of bureaucratic positions.

> The role played in former days by the "proof of ancestry," as prerequisite for equality of birth, access to noble prebends and endowments and, wherever the nobility retained social power, for the qualification to state offices, is nowadays taken by the patent of education. The elaboration of the diplomas from universities, business and engineering colleges, and the universal clamor for the creation of further educational certificates in all fields serve the formation of a privileged stratum in bureaus and in offices. Such certificates support their holders' claims for connubium with the notables (in business offices, too, they raise hope for preferment with the boss's daughter), claims to be admitted into the circles that adhere to "codes of honor," claims for a "status-appropriate" salary instead of a wage according to performance, claims for assured advancement and old-age insurance, and, above all, claims to the monopolization of socially and economically advantageous positions. If we hear from all sides demands for the introduction of regulated curricula culminating in specialized examinations, the reason behind this is, of course, not a suddenly awakened "thirst for education," but rather the desire to limit the supply of candidates for these positions and to monopolize them for the holders of educational patents. For such monopolization, the "examination" is today the universal instrument—hence its irresistible advance.[10]

Naturally, strategies of monopolization by means of educational certificates and civil service examinations commend themselves only to those social groups who have access to the kind of education upon which civil service examinations may be based. Such strategies, moreover, can be successful only to the extent that opponent groups do not possess these educational qualifications to a large degree. How does this relate to the typical conflict interpretation in the civil service literature?

In this literature it is almost always the rising middle class who advances its interests against those of the hereditary aristocracy and gentry. As we shall see in a moment, this model fits the Prussian case tolerably well if only because German universities on the eve of reform were predominantly middle-class institutions, infrequently attended by nobles. But that situation was very different in the English case. Here the aristocracy and gentry were so strongly represented at Oxford and Cambridge that they could be expected easily to hold their own with higher educational standards of employment. This is only one of the significant differences between England and Prussia, but it raises the intriguing possibility that in England civil service examinations might have been used as a means of defending a threatened monopoly. Indeed, I shall argue that the comparison of Prussia and England provides a neat example of two cases where civil service examinations came in varying historical contexts to assume a different meaning to those historical actors who enjoyed a near monopoly of higher education: to the Prussian middle-class intelligentsia it meant gaining advantages; to the Victorian gentlemen it meant holding on to them.

The Pattern Variables as Methods of Selection

The sociological literature on bureaucratization and industrialization is replete with suggestions that the shift from tradition to modernity involved a shift from selection by family to selection by merit. "For hundreds of years," writes Michael Young, "society has been a battleground between two great principles—the principle of selection by family and the principle of selection by merit."[11] Smelser and Lipset echo the same theme. "As economic and social development proceeds, various criteria of achievement—achievement of wealth, attainment of political power, etc.—begin to intrude on ascribed memberships as bases for assigning persons to roles. . . . As the bases of role assignment and ranking. . . , ascriptive standards begin to give way to economic, political, and other standards. . . ."[12]

Statements such as these are unobjectionable in some respects. It is true that proponents of one method of selection have often been aligned against advocates of the other. As a result of such struggles, direct hereditary transmission of offices has given way to selection by some performance criterion, including also educational achievement, in many walks of life. However, statements such as Young's and Smelser's must be interpreted very carefully so as to avoid a number of pitfalls. Above all, the use of dichotomous classifications should not blind us to the fact that history does not divide neatly into unambiguous, mutually exclusive structural types. Although there has been a shift from selection by family and social status to selection by various performance criteria, the transition from tradition to modernity gave rise to many mixed types that cannot be described in terms of ascription *or* achievement. Nor does the introduction of a performance criterion such as education necessarily erode selection by family or social status. A new, seemingly achievement-oriented method of selection may turn out to be most interesting as a device for testing ancestors and, thus, as a method by which traditional status privileges are modernized.

In the remainder of this section I will explore several interrelated sources of confusion in the use of dichotomous classifications of "tradition" and "modernity." Some of the general problems I will call attention to have been pointed out by Bendix on several occasions.[13] My purpose in dealing with these matters in some detail here is twofold. First I wish to bring the abstract discussion of these matters down to the concrete concerns of this study, namely, the introduction of new methods of selection in the civil service. Second, I wish to focus attention on Parsons' pattern variables, which have become terminological commonplaces in discussions of changing methods of selecting individuals to occupational roles. These concepts, formulated in mutually exclusive terms, are especially conducive to viewing the rise of modernity as a progressive erosion of traditional ways. They are especially conducive to diverting the analyst's attention from historical conditions favoring strategies of maintaining traditional privileges by means of modern institutional forms. More generally, they tend to divert attention from the play of ascriptive tendencies in the modern context of achievement-oriented methods of selection. Although the disposition to view the rise of modernity as a progressive erosion of tradition is not confined to Parsons, his concepts provide an attractive target of critical comment not only because they have gained widespread currency but also because they are formulated so rigorously as to bring many pitfalls of dichotomous classifications of structural types into broad relief.

The two great principles, nowadays generally referred to as "ascription" and "achievement," are defined by Parsons as follows. "Achievement-oriented roles are those which place the accent on the performance of the incumbent, ascribed roles on his qualities or attributed independently of specific expected performances."[14] In some roles, in other words, it matters who the candidate or incumbent is; in others, the emphasis is more on what he can do. However, a single dichotomy, such as this, has not proved its usefulness for classifying the vast range of methods of selection. How is one to dichotomize the following assortment: selection by kin group and order of birth, selection by social status group and patronage, selection by lot or divination, selection by election or political patronage, selection by educational tests or proven merit, selection by seniority and sex, not to mention possible combinations? To solve this and related problems, Parsons has opted for a whole series of dichotomous concepts, the so-called pattern variables, said to represent an exhaustive set of decisions which all actors in roles must make, implicitly or explicitly, before they can relate properly to other actors.[15] Of course, actors do not normally have to make decisions at all because the pattern variables are institutionalized norms, internalized by the actors during their socialization. They structure the actors' cognitive, evaluative, and affective relations to objects and role partners.

Depending on the role he plays, an actor must "opt" for a number of alternatives. Is he to get involved emotionally, or is he to treat his role partner with the disciplined detachment of the bureaucrat (affectivity-affective neutrality)? Is he to give special consideration to a particular person, or is he to apply standards appropriate to everyone else in a general class (particularism-universalism)? Is some personal or social characteristic relevant to this relationship, or is he to relate only to the role partner's performance (ascription-achievement or, later, quality-performance)? Finally, does the role partner gratify a wide range of interests, or does he gratify only a single interest (diffuseness-specificity)? Thus, a traditional patron may be expected to appoint a kinsman to office (ascription), choose his favorite nephew (diffuseness), treat him warmly (affectivity), and judge him according to standards appropriate only to close kinsmen (particularism). A modern civil service commissioner, by contrast, is expected to look only at a person's past and likely future performance (achievement), take account only of such attributes of the candidate as may be relevant to the job (specificity), remain emotionally detached (affective neutrality), and judge the candidate's performance on the test according to standards applicable to all (universalism).

Having reformulated the many contrasts between tradition and modernity that may be found in the sociological literature as norms governing cognitive, evaluative, and affective relations between actors in roles, Parsons claims that he is now able to describe each role or each method of selection in terms of a particular set of dichotomous classifications. In this role-expectation frame of reference, a particular method of selection is described and classified either in terms of ascription *or* achievement, particularism *or* universalism, and so on. Both aspects may be present in a particular method, but it is impossible to maximize both. Hence, one aspect must be subordinated to the other if the situation is to be clearly and unambiguously defined for the selecting agent.

Since there is no reason to suppose that normative priorities are always clearly established or, if they are, that actual behavior always conforms to them, we should expect that many historical role situations and methods of selection are not describable in either-or terms. Indeed, there may be a long history of conflicting or ambiguous standards and much "deviant behavior" intervening between one period dominated by particularistic-ascriptive norms and another dominated by universalistic-achievement criteria. Parsons, of course, agrees that historical reality does not divide neatly into the unambiguous types of his conceptual scheme. He cautions that he has "not even begun to approach the difficult analysis of mixed and transitional cases, of which there are undoubtedly many." Similarly, he is quite aware that the pattern variables, applying to the normative aspects of action, rather than to actual behavior, can serve at best "for first approximations in comparative analysis."[16] All these caveats notwithstanding, his preoccupation with pure types of normative structure has often led him and his followers to exaggerate discontinuity in change. Confronted with a change from one ambiguous method of selection to another and approaching the analysis with pure types of "traditional" and "modern" normative patterns, one is tempted almost irresistibly to resolve the ambiguity by classifying the early method as particularistic, ascriptive, etc., and by classifying the successor as universalistic, achievement-oriented, etc. To succumb to this pitfall is not only to substitute mere labeling for historical analysis but also to exaggerate the change that may have taken place between one period and the next.

Those early civil service examinations in which we are interested in this study were typically divided into a written test, which gave some scope to achievement and universalistic standards, and an oral test, which, critics in England complained, gave much scope to ascriptive solidarities and highly particularistic judgments. Which method predominated here? One thing seems obvious. Just because a civil service examination was introduced does not mean that the actual practice of selecting candidates to office has changed at all. The old "ascriptive" method may have been so tempered with considerations of merit while the new "achievement" method may have been so compromised by ascriptive solidarities that the difference between the two might be negligible or nonexistent. Over the last hundred years or so, civil service examinations have of course changed. Successive regulations have narrowed the scope for ascriptive considerations and particularistic judgments, to be sure. But over long periods, as we shall see, the history of employment conditions was one of combinations and recombinations of opposing standards, notwithstanding the fact that achievement and universalism became more prominent in those combinations.

Turning now to the second, closely related, pitfall, suppose our analysis reveals that at time A the method of selection to the civil service was in fact particularistic and ascriptive whereas at time B it was universalistic and achievement-oriented. In other words, let us assume that the rules in both cases were unambiguous and that behavior conformed to the rules. Now it should be obvious that these two methods, though formally opposite, are not necessarily antagonistic with respect to the social results they achieve. In terms of access to the civil service, they may in fact achieve identical social results, owing to other conditions in the society.

Let us imagine, for example, that in the society we study a certain status group has preferred access to institutions of higher learning.

Members of that status group, we find, are recruited to the civil service on purely ascriptive grounds, that is, as members of their status group. Then this ascriptive method is replaced by an achievement method based on tests of higher learning. Given the prevailing social conditions in higher education, would we, and, for that matter, the historical actors, not have every reason to expect that the new method would select recruits from the same social circles as before? A complete identity of social results from different methods of selection is probably rare, but unequal access to education is not. If access to education is unequal, then any test based on educational qualifications must necessarily select individuals from a select social group. In the context of unequal access to education, achievement tests based on education necessarily must have ascriptive results.

In the recent literature on contemporary American education and testing, critical as it tends to be of the liberal faith (or ideology) that educational credentials are a sure-fire solvent of social inequality, reports of social biases in admission to education, selection to tracks, student-teacher relations, testing procedures, and the like have been forthcoming with increasing frequency. Such findings, as well as those reported in these pages, highlight the double meaning of Weber's felicitous phrase that today's certificates of education are what tests of ancestors used to be in the past. Weber wanted to suggest not only that one method of selection has replaced another but also and more importantly that tests of educational qualifications continue to function as tests of ancestors.

The second pitfall to avoid, therefore, is to "infer" opposite results from opposite methods of selection. The literature on civil service reforms gives ample testimony to a seemingly irrepressible urge to jump to the conclusion that access to civil service posts must have become more equalitarian just because a formally achievement-oriented method was introduced. Role analysis can establish only that a given method of selection was *formally* achievement-oriented or ascriptive, etc. To determine its characteristics from the point of view of its social effects, we must analyze it *contextually*, that is, in relation to other processes of selection in the society that might produce combined effects, and *historically* in terms of the interests and understanding of those who advocated it and those who opposed it.[17] As I am writing these lines, I am reminded of Morton White's characterization of antiformalism: To reach out into the entire space around a certain phenomenon, and to reach back in time in order to account for it.[18]

Turning now to the third pitfall, let us focus once more on Parsons' conceptualization of the pattern variables as *normative* patterns and on his classification of entire systems of roles and entire cultural systems in terms of pattern variables. Such classifications are subject to the same pitfalls as classifications of particular roles and, in addition, to a special intellectual trap. For example, take Parsons' classification of the modern industrial occupational structure as a "system of universalistic-specific-affectively neutral achievement-oriented roles."[19] Now this characterization obviously simplifies and exaggerates the behavior actually taking place. Indeed, the simplification and exaggeration is so blatant that Parsons must immediately qualify his every assertion. The gist of that qualification, if I understand it correctly, runs as follows. Universalism, specificity, affective neutrality, and achievement form really only the dominant pattern of value orientation in modern (American) culture. The occupational structure, which is governed by this value pattern, however, falls somewhat short of realizing those cultural ideals. Here, in his own words, is the reason why.

> We may then distinguish that part of the social structure which directly institutionalizes the dominant patterns of value-orientation of the culture; there is little doubt for instance that in the American case the core of this is the occupational system. But as a concrete sub-system of the social system even this cannot correspond exactly with the pattern-expectations of the value system itself. There will have to be adaptive aspects even of this structure, which may be interpreted as modes of adaptation to the exigencies of institutionalizing the value patterns in question under the given conditions, that is, to say in the light of the strains to which the population in question are subjected, in these roles themselves, and in combining these with the other roles in which the same people are involved in other aspects of the society. In the American occupational case, for example, the simultaneous involvement of the same individuals in both occupational and kinship roles is one of the key problems.[20]

In other words, role behavior in the occupational sphere, supposedly governed by the altogether consistent value pattern described above, is also affected by various exigencies of social life, including the interests of kinship and status groups, in which diffuse ascriptive solidarity, particularism, and affectivity are prominent characteristics. And so, various compromises are made in the intersection between the sphere of solidary kinship and status groups, on the one hand, and the occupational sphere, on the other.[21] These compromises amount to aberrations from the cultural ideals, but, unlike "deviant behavior," they are quite legitimate and socially sanctioned. Here and there, ascription, diffuseness, affectivity, and particularism are allowed to creep in to condition the rules of the social game. Parents are expected to pass their social status to their children; property laws and inheritance laws guarantee differential access to material advantages and their transmission from one generation to the next; families and status groups may purchase the right kind of education for their progeny to maintain the family's social position.

"Modernity," which Parsons associates with the consistent value pattern of achievement, universality, specificity, and affective neutrality, apparently reigns in a heaven of cultural ideals whereas social experience is composed of various compromises between "modernity" and the "tradition" of kinship, status, and class interests in given historical conditions. Thus, it would seem that history for Parsons is after all divided into neat patterns of ideals, the so-called central value system, even though rules and regulations (and actual behavior even more) may diverge from the perfection of those ideals.

Although the ideals do not exactly sweep everything before them, they nevertheless determine the rules and regulations within which kinship, status, and class interests are allowed to express themselves. A given pattern of cultural values determines the more specific norms of behavior in the sense that the latter must be compatible or consistent with the former. Parsons speaks of an imperative of compatibility or consistency. He thinks of the various societal types, labeled in pattern-variable terms, as systems of interrelated norms of behavior all the way from the most general values at the top to the most specific norms of behavior at the bottom, the interrelations being governed by some kind of immanent strain to consistency. Parsons likens that "pattern consistency" to the logical consistency of cognitive systems and art styles though he immediately cautions that complete consistency between cultural value pattern and social norms cannot obtain. "As an integral part of a concrete system of social interaction this norm of pattern-consistent integration of a cultural system can only be approximately realized, because of the strains arising out of the imperatives of interdependence with the situational and motivational elements of concrete action. . . ."[22]

Occasionally, the force of pattern-consistency that flows from the cultural patterns to the rules and regulations on the ground is even thought of as causal primacy of cultural factors in social change: the major social-cultural types, labeled in pattern-variable terms, "tend to emerge when major types of cultural development in the literate cultures have occurred, the emergence of religious systems, the development of science and the like, and these developments have a profound relation to changes in the structure of society itself."[23] Rather than dwell on the idealist implications of Parsons' work, which have become more pronounced as his system has developed from the voluntaristic action scheme in the early work to the evolutionary paradigm in the later work,[24] I wish to describe another temptation inherent in dichotomous ideal-type constructs—a temptation against which Weber has warned repeatedly.

When he classifies the normative aspects of behavior under dichotomous rubrics, Parsons states that he is formulating "ideal-type" constructs. Now ideal types, according to Weber, are indeed formed "by one-sided accentuation of one or more points of view and by synthesis of a great many diffuse, discrete, and more or less present and occasionally absent concrete individual phenomena, which are arranged according to one-sidedly emphasized viewpoints into a unified analytical construct."[25] Yet Weber immediately hastens to add that such mental constructs cannot be found in their conceptual purity in the empirical cases from which they are derived. These "idealizations" are merely heuristic devices for the purpose of analysis, for sorting out contradictory and ambiguous aspects of thought and action, and for identifying structural dimensions whose interrelations in time and space must be explained from case to case. Parsons, by contrast, suggests that his ideal-typical constructs may indeed be found in their purity in the cultural patterns of society though in their purity they might not be institutionalized in the social rules and regulations.[26] Unlike Weber's, Parsons' types are theories. They make claims about systemic interrelations between normative aspects of social-cultural wholes. Put another way, Weber's constructs are regulative ideas; Parsons' constructs are constitutive ideals.

This is precisely what Weber warned against when he cautioned sociologists and historians that they should not yield to the temptation to confuse ideal types with reality just because the logical classification of analytical concepts, on the one hand, and the empirical arrangements of events, on the other, appear to be intimately bound up with one another.[27] This temptation, he thought, becomes almost irresistible when the ideal-typical construct of an epoch also happens to contain terms referring to "thoughts and ideals which dominated the mass or at least an historically decisive number of persons living in that epoch itself."[28] Add to this a naturalistic prejudice—societies as self-regulating systems—and the temptation gets compounded many times. In Weber's words,

> Nothing, however, is more dangerous than the *confusion* of theory and history stemming from naturalistic prejudices. This confusion expresses itself firstly in the belief that the "true" content and the essence of historical reality is portrayed in such theoretical constructs or secondly, in the use of these constructs as a procrustean bed into which history is to be forced or thirdly, in the hypostatization of such "ideas" as real "forces" and as a "true" reality which operates behind the passage of events and which works itself out in history.[29]

At first thought, this third danger in dichotomous classifications in terms of general value patterns seems to be remote from the concerns of this study. After all, Parsons has not given us an interpretation of the introduction of civil service reforms in England and Prussia though his discussion of the universalistic-achievement pattern in *The Social System* contains the general terms in which a Parsonian analysis of civil service examinations might be made. Nevertheless, the notion of a strain to consistency and compatibility emanating from the central value pattern of a society is not confined to Parsons, nor is the notion of "ideas" as real "forces" ramifying from one part of the social system to another. There is a widespread tendency in the general historical literature to conceive of civil service reforms as somehow a "natural" consequence of the spread of democratic ideals, the values of equality and equity, which eventually informed the selection of candidates to positions in various spheres of occupational life as if by some supramundane logic operating behind the interests and strategic actions of individuals and groups. Or so it seems when "explanations" by-pass these strategic actions in specific historical conditions and, proceeding from a conception of structural arrangements associated with one another in the long run of "modernization," impose a spurious retrospective determinism on events in the short run.

Lest it be supposed that this fallacy of retrospective determinism is invariably associated with idealist leanings (that is, some conception of inherent strain to consistency in the normative aspects of behavior), it should be pointed out that there is also a "materialist" version. In the English case, the introduction of civil service reforms is almost universally related to the rising middle class. While bourgeois historians tend to give much space to the changing climate of opinion of the mid-Victorian reform era, in which the civil service reform is set, Donald Kingsley analyzes civil service reforms in the context of the changing labor process. Ultimately and in the long run, institutional arrangements associated with "modernity" are traceable to the changing labor process, that is, to the rise of the capitalist mode and bourgeois relations of production. From this premise he seems to "derive" the altogether spurious expectation that civil service reforms, a specific event in that long run, must have been a strategy of the rising bourgeoisie to displace aristocrats and to transform the civil service into a "representative" bureaucracy.[30]

I am arguing that contextual and historical analysis of the strategic actions of the British reformers reveals that the reforms were introduced for economic and associated political reasons and that these reasons, indeed, account for the *professionalization* of the civil service. But owing to conditions of restricted access to education, this professionalization did not and could not make the bureaucracy representative. I am going even a step further and suggesting that the old discarded method of selection—political patronage—might well have democratized the civil service owing to successive extensions of the franchise. In these conditions, tests of high educational qualifications were well suited to realize the strategic interest of gentlemen to maintain their near monopoly of higher civil service posts.

Status Groups and Classes

Nearly two decades ago, Homans argued that sociologists must take seriously the job of any science, namely, to provide explanations for the empirical relations they discover. For sociological theory, he argued, this means "bringing men back in."[31] Like others before and after him, he noted that in the conceptual scheme of normative functionalists, the human actor was transformed into an oversocialized role player. He might have added that groups were dissected into so many cross-cutting variables and functional subsystems fulfilling the imperatives of the social whole. One might disagree with Homans' view that the only general propositions of sociology are in fact psychological propositions and that sociological explanation devolves upon psychology. Yet he was surely correct that the analysis of correlated or functionally connected social arrangements do not constitute explanations but that the continuation as well as change of any of these arrangements can and must be explained in terms of the actors who participate in maintaining and changing them. Why is this so? "Institutions," says Homans, "do not mesh with others mechanically, like the parts of a machine. Institutions are the behavior of men; their relations are mediated by the behavior of men."[32]

Over the last twenty years, or so, the social actor has once again surfaced, if not uniformly, in the various branches of sociological theory. He has become the central concern in that quarter of the house of sociology in which symbolic interactionism, phenomenology, ethnomethodology, and related *isms* interact with one another. But in this quarter, the sociological vision has also shrunk to the *Lebenswelt* of the person, to the strategic actions of individuals, to the setting of the small face-to-face group, and even to fleeting encounters of strangers on the street.[33] In discarding normative functionalism and neoevolutionism, they have also abandoned macrohistorical sociology: status groups and classes, as well as the strategic actions of their more or less organized sectors in the institutional arenas of production, domination, and cultural life.

Historical sociologists of every persuasion would agree that we must "bring men back in" for the sake of historical explanation. However, since the perspective of historical sociologists goes well beyond the *Lebenswelt* of the individual, their "men" are typically collective actors.[34] The arenas of these actors are the institutions of production, domination, and intellectual life, as well as the marketplace. Industrial organizations, governmental bureaucracies, and cultural establishments are so many arenas in which interest groups engage in strategic action. What is the nature of these groups? How are they formed? How are the thoughts and actions of the members coordinated? How do they realize their interests? Although these are fundamental questions of sociology, they are still very much unsettled. In the Marxian tradition, classes come to mind at once. In the Weberian tradition, status groups compete for attention. What is the relationship between status groups and classes?

Not long ago, I discussed the findings of this study with a group of historians. Interested in the notion of strategies of monopolization, the participants in the discussion debated whether my repeated references to status groups reflect merely a propensity of sociologists to come up with new terms. Do I mean classes? Is there a difference between class analysis and status analysis? Will an analyst approach his subject matter differently if he draws a distinction between status groups and classes? The following discussion will, hopefully, answer these questions.

I will show that in Weber's sociology the distinction between status groups and classes, like the one between ascription and achievement in Parsons', is derived from an ideal-type contrast between traditional and modern society. In the discussion on ascription and achievement, I argued that the history of employment conditions in the civil service was a history of combinations and recombinations of opposing standards. Although the transition from one type to the other may have been long, sometimes ambiguous, and by no means linear, it might be said that in traditional society achievement comes to play within an ascriptive context whereas in modern society ascription appears within the framework of achievement rules. In other words, although rules have narrowed the scope for ascriptive considerations in the modern world, ascriptive tendencies continue to play a part in the achievement context. I will argue now that the same rationale applies to the dichotomy of status and class. This dichotomy, too, is an ideal-type contrast. It juxtaposes opposing and interacting *tendencies of group formation*. The tendency associated with class may be embedded in a status order. The tendency associated with status may be nested in class situations. Modernization, that is, capitalist development and bureaucratization, has shifted the context from status to class but has not eliminated the play of opposing tendencies associated with class and status.

In shifting the argument now from norms and regulations (pattern variables) to opposing tendencies of group formation (status and class), I have two aims. First, I wish to link the pattern variables to group formation and strategic action, which is the province of historical sociology. Second, I wish to frame conceptually the general topic of this study. What were the historical conditions which enabled the aristocracies of England and Prussia to adapt more or less successfully to the changing institutions of public administration? Why was modernity assimilated to tradition more readily in one country than the other? It will become apparent that Weber's ideal-type contrast between status and class makes one suspicious of the common assumption that bureaucratization implies the arrival of a new "class" and the eviction of traditional status groups. It raises the question whether civil service reforms might have been a "traditionalizing" strategy of monopolization.[35]

Weber accepted Marx's concept of class in a general way.[36] Class is bound up with economics. Transformations in the arena of production, mediated through the marketplace, create new life situations. These changing life situations may affect the social identity of individuals so as to weaken not only their interclass loyalty but also their loyalty to competing solidary groups within the class. In any case, this would be a necessary condition of class formation. Problematic life situations also stimulate receptivity to new ideas and unconventional thinking. Once these changes in the intellectual sphere are joined with organized action, then the necessary and sufficient conditions of a more encompassing class organization obtain. Unlike Marx, Weber did not link class situation directly to the changing capital structure of production. Instead, he linked class situation to market situation, assuming, however, that changes in market situation are a function of changes in the system of production. Like Marx, he emphasized that common class situation alone results neither in group solidarity nor in organized interest associations. Something more is needed for class formation to take place. "Every technological repercussion and economic transformation," writes Weber, "threatens stratification by status and pushes the class situation in the foreground. Epochs and countries in which the naked class situation is of predominant significance are regularly the periods of technical and economic transformations."[37] Moreover, Weber's "status communities" are the conceptual equivalents of the communal groups and "ranks" which block Marx's "class for itself." Finally, unlike Marx, Weber did not think that the final collapse of capitalism was imminent; and unlike some of Marx's interpreters, he did not think it inevitable in the long run. Since he rejected strenuously the notion of a necessary, ineluctable historical development, he was not disposed to regard status communities as necessarily residual phenomena that would be swept away in due course; instead, he conceived status-group formation and class formation as two opposing and interacting tendencies of group formation, varying with economic change and stability.

Class formation, then, is linked to economic, technological, and other transformations which alter the life situation of individuals and reorient their material and ideal interests. Status-group formation, on the other hand, means the formation of communities whose members share a style of life, social identity, sense of equality, and conventions of honorific, respectable, proper, acceptable ways of thought and action besides economic interests. Thus, the tendency to status-group formation is the advance of communities codifying conventions, enforcing a style of thought and action, discriminating against outsiders, and—within this context of convention—pursuing their interests by monopolizing opportunities for gain: wealth, power, and prestige.[38] The tendency to class formation, by contrast, cuts into these communities, conventions, and monopolies. It aligns individuals subject to a common, altered life situation according to unconventional conceptions of their interests and promotes interest associations along the lines of class or market situation.

Weber's discussion of class and status is set in a contrast between traditional societies stratified by endogamous kinship groups, castes, and, especially, the medieval estates, on the one hand, and "modern" societies stratified by class, on the other. This contrast yields two ideal types of society: "Status society" (*Ständische Gliederung*) and "class society" (*Klassengesellschaft*). It roughly parallels Marx's contrast between "feudal society" and "bourgeois society."

Status societies are characterized by a process of stratification in which exclusive, ranked social groups with distinctive styles of life and distinctive conceptions of honor or propriety appropriate and monopolize all sorts of advantages and opportunities for gain. As we shall see in the next two chapters, an aristocratic status group might have a monopoly on the ownership of manorial estates (lands with attached rights over peasants); it may also appropriate and monopolize official positions, turn them into freeholds, exchange them within a closed circle, or pass them down within the family. Thus, the stratification process characteristic of status societies works in the direction of regulating the market. It eliminates strictly economic and technical principles of calculation (marginal utility, functional adequacy) or, at any rate, pushes them into the background. Rational calculation is limited by imperatives of a style of life. Indeed, this style of life justifies the economic monopolies of the group. In order to maintain the military lifestyle and function of the Prussian Junker, eighteenth-century monarchs protected his monopoly of manorial estates. Conversely, Weber thought, the maintenance of economic monopolies provided also the most effective, though rarely sufficient, motives for the enforcement of a particular style of life for all new members admitted to the circle. Status societies, then, consist of hierarchies of social orders with conventionally, legally, or ritually fixed rights, privileges, responsibilities, and monopolized advantages.

Although closure is one of the essential characteristics, status groups are not as a rule absolutely closed. The closure of the aristocracy, as we shall see especially in the next chapter, was generally tempered with ennoblement of men who had distinguished themselves in the king's service. In some countries, like Russia, holders of a certain rank in the bureaucracy were automatically ennobled, as was Lenin's father. In most cases and most of the time, such changes in social rank were exceptions that proved the rule. They might be tolerated, with more or less success, so as to strengthen the aristocracy and to preserve its monopolies. Occasionally, as the English and the Prussian cases demonstrate, too much ennoblement might cause an "inflation of honors," lower aristocratic rank in the esteem of the public, and threaten the legitimacy of the entire order. Sometimes, as we shall see too, ennoblements were used deliberately by absolute monarchs to weaken a recalcitrant aristocracy. In any case, a typical status society obtained so long as socially mobile families were integrated into a fixed order of rights and duties, a traditional style of life, including a proper status education. So long as aristocracy meant a monopoly of tangible advantages, such as ownership of manorial estates or access to lucrative positions, a status order was secure. To the extent that aristocracy was reduced to merely an honorific title, status society vanished.

Class societies, by contrast, are characterized by a process of stratification which distributes life chances in and through the market. The advance of the market principle and a political-legal order making everyone formally free and equal are the preconditions for class formation. The status order of fixed rights and duties had to be swept away before the new market order of distributing life chances could predominate. This method of distributing life chances knows no personal distinctions, only naked property and mere technical-functional skills. It excludes all nonowners of property and of marketable technical-functional skills from competing for highly valued goods. Whatever advantages an individual may have in the impersonal market is decisive for his social fate and represents his class situation. The formal rationalization of the economy and the bureaucratization of public and private administration strips away impediments to free trade and free access to position. And along with the old status monopolies, it strips away the "irrational" social bonds that linked the members of a status group and even members of different status groups, such as masters and servants.

All this is, of course, reminiscent of that famous passage from the *Communist Manifesto.*

> The bourgeoisie, wherever it has got the upper hand, has put an end to all feudal, patriarchal, idyllic relations. It has pitilessly torn asunder the motley feudal ties that bound man to his "natural superiors," and has left remaining no other nexus between man and man than naked self-interest, than callous "cash payment." It has drowned the most heavenly ecstasies of religious fervour, of chivalrous enthusiasm, of philistine sentimentalism, in the icy water of egotistical calculation. It has resolved personal worth into exchange value, and in the place of the numberless indefeasible chartered freedoms, has set up that single, unconscionable freedom—Free Trade. In one word, for exploitation, veiled by religious and political illusions, it has substituted naked, shameless, direct, brutal exploitation.
>
> The bourgeoisie has stripped of its halo every occupation hitherto honoured and looked up to with reverent awe. It has converted the physician, the lawyer, the priest, the poet, the man of science, into its paid wage-labourers.[39]

The market tends to atomize status groups. It tends to individuate action in pursuit of personal advantages. Individuals tend to react similarly to given conditions in the market (mass behavior), but their actions are not coordinated by shared understandings. Indeed, their orientation to immediate personal advantage tends to impede group formation and coordinated, organized pursuit of group interests.

Weber draws these starkly contrasting ideal types of status and class societies to argue that in one type the tendency to status-group formation predominates whereas in the other the tendency to class formation predominates. In either case, the respective opposite plays a subordinate though not necessarily insignificant role.

In traditional societies status-group formation predominates. Economic, technological, and administrative structural changes, which might upset group monopolies and the associated styles of life, are assimilated to the traditional status order. As I see it, there are essentially two strategies of assimilation. The first I would like to call *adaptation* and the second *incorporation*. As an example of the first, consider the case of an aristocracy with a traditional monopoly on certain administrative offices, and suppose that the technical-functional qualifications for office holding change. If the aristocracy is able to assimilate the new qualifications into its style of life or if these lifestyles are already preadapted, then it can preserve its monopoly. As an example of the second, suppose that an aristocracy cannot readily adapt to the new situation, and therefore its office monopoly falls to new men with the necessary qualifications. In this condition, the traditional order may be preserved by incorporating the new men, raising them to aristocratic rank, or admitting them to the circle by expanding the definition of gentility. All of these forms of assimilation will be encountered in this study. They all aim at conserving the traditional order even though adaptation means some change in traditional lifestyle and incorporation means admitting new men into the social circle.

Aristocracies and, for that matter, other closed status groups in traditional societies have always faced the problem of conserving and renewing themselves over the generations. Traditional societies were not stationary. Apart from demographic fluctuations in the rate of reproduction, there were changes in the technology and organization of the economy, the military, as well as the sphere of administration. These changes created new situations to which lifestyles had to adapt. The transformation of the self-equipped knight into the officer of the standing army, the transformation of the manorial lord into the capitalist farmer, and the transformation of the owner of political, judicial, and administrative rights into the professional bureaucrat were the major lines along which adaptation and incorporation took place. Although, in the long run, these transformations destroyed the traditional status society, they have not dispersed the old status groups randomly into the new life situations of modern class society. The success of adaptation to new situations varied not only from country to country but also from one institutional sphere to another. Yet the old ruling class was not simply replaced by a rising class of bourgeois entrepreneurs and professional bureaucrats. Chapters 2 and 3 are devoted not only to an analysis of the prereformed administration and recruitment practices in Prussia and England but also to the historical circumstances which enabled the aristocracies of these countries to adapt, more or less successfully, to the changing civil service.

In modern class society, Weber's contrast suggests, class formation predominates. The "traditionalizing" tendency of status-group formation still comes into play but is nested in shifting class situations. Modern society undergoes rapid structural change and promotes social mobility. Capital, commodities, and skills are allocated according to principles of formal economic and technical-functional rationality. The market tends to atomize communities into so many families competing with one another. Individuals tend to react similarly to conditions and events in the market, but their actions are not coordinated by communal constraints. Special interest associations form but are threatened with opportunism, that is, the propensity of individuals *not* to forego immediate advantage in the interest of collective goals. If modern society does not match this ideal type of the war of all against all, it is because status-group formation communalizes individuals in similar situations and communalizes also interest associations spawned by fluctuations in the market. Indeed, in order to counteract opportunism, leaders of such organizations typically foster the spread of communal understandings, esprit de corps, and a sense of honor, which enjoins the members to live up to agreed-upon collective action. In this process of communalization, old lifestyles get adapted, and new ones are created to give form and symbolic meaning to new circumstances. To use contemporary terms, older "class cultures" change by dint of creative "adaptive drift" to catch up with new situational conditions, to stylize consumption patterns, occupational techniques, and interactions of people thrown together by the market.[40]

Where opportunism or naked self-interest is tempered with a communal ethos, and where it becomes a matter of honor or at least propriety to live up to communal ideals in everyday life, an individual's affiliation with a group ripens into membership. Status honor, psychologically a desire to rise in the esteem of the community and to maintain self-respect, is of course reinforced by social sanctions. Social honor and sanctions promote conformity and fortify the individual to sacrifice his "rational" self-interest in immediate advantage to the interests of the collectivity. To put it another way, they keep interests in the ideological grooves of the status group. Moreover, if a communal ethos develops in an association formed by rational agreement on interests and ways of realizing them—if such an association gets communalized—then it becomes a status group with social bonds stronger than means and ends rationally agreed upon.

It is not generally recognized that Weber's concept of "social honor" involves both a sense of honor to live up to communal norms by those included in the social circle as well as honor in the sense of a claim to prestige. While social honor in the first sense is easy to recognize among traditional status groups, it appears to become less salient among modern status groups. Thus, Bensman and Vidich argued recently that contemporary lifestyles are much less ingrained than the traditions of the old status groups. They are less exacting and less taken for granted; they afford less security and are often regarded as artificial and "spurious"; and they are more subject to calculated manipulation, experimentation, and emulation.[41] Perhaps, it is this real shift in the nature of contemporary status groups and their associated lifestyles which explains why contemporary sociologists and interpreters of Max Weber invariably equate "social honor" with prestige and individual status seeking and disregard consensual action based on a shared sense of honor or propriety.

Throughout this discussion I have wrestled with the English language. Transposing tradition into traditionalization, community into communalization, style into stylization is often awkward. I would have preferred to avoid the transposition had it not been necessary to overcome the static bias in the nouns. Like Weber, whose concepts stress becoming rather than being, I wished to emphasize the formative process rather than the outcomes of the process. *For status groups and classes are not so much distinct groups as distinct tendencies of group formation.* The groups which result from these opposed but interacting tendencies naturally straddle both dimensions. If yesteryear's aristocracy was a status group, it was also a class insofar as its members were recruited from a given class situation. And if today's businessman's club or trade union are class organizations, they are also status groups insofar as they develop a communal ethos, esprit de corps, status honor, and engage also in monopolistic practices.

We are now in a position to answer the question posed at the beginning of this section: What is the nature of the groups that are actors in the scheme of historical sociology? Individuals who react similarly to events and conditions in the marketplace may or may not act as members of a group. They may or may not be subject to utilitarian agreement or communal coordination. If not, then they do not constitute a group in the sociological sense. Although "mass behavior" (Weber) by individuals similarly situated but not bound by agreement or communal constraint is significant for the understanding of historical events, it would be incorrect in this case to say that the *class* acts. Weber insisted strongly on that point so as to redress "that kind of pseudo-scientific operation with the concepts of class and class interests so frequent these days and which has found its most classic expression in the statement of a talented author, that the individual may be in error concerning his interests but that the class is infallible about its interests."[42] Individuals who act similarly in the market or in any other arena of interaction may be subject to agreements or communal understandings, conventions, and imperatives of honor and propriety. In that case they are collective actors even in the absence of organization, that is, imperatives of a system of authority relations. As to more or less organized groups, they may range all the way from organizations based on rational agreement on common interests and ways of realizing them to thoroughly communalized organizations, in which the common interest is wrapped up in tradition, convention, style, honor, or propriety.[43]

We are now in a position also to argue that the approach by way of group formation and strategic action is a genuine alternative to Parsons' pattern variables and that it is, indeed, indispensable for explanatory purposes. The process of status-group formation may be nested in class situations, but the groups which result from or are affected by this process pursue their interests like the status groups of traditional societies—*in a monopolistic direction.* They try to maintain and expand access to advantages by eliminating competition, thus barring outsiders from access to values, utilitarian and ideal, which they regard as a status privilege. They temper and restrict the market with formal rules and conventions; achievement with ascription in the interests of kinsmen, friends, and other members of the circle; and universalistic norms with particularistic considerations alive to social distinctions. In other words, ascription and achievement as methods of selection are simply outcomes of class and status-group formation processes and the strategic action of conflict groups.

Next to his ideal types of group formation and strategic action, Weber elaborated his well-known *institutional* ideal types, such as "traditional administration" and "modern bureaucracy." These, too, are formulated in mutually exclusive terms but ought to be regarded as opposing and linked tendencies, as Bendix has argued on several occasions.[44] Thus, Weber formulated two kinds of ideal-typical tendencies—one on the level of group formation and strategic action (class and status) and the other on the level of institutional structure (for example, patrimonialism-feudalism and bureaucracy). The institutional ideal types, like Parsons' pattern variables, are *outcomes* of group formation tendencies, but they are stated, abstractly, as opposing yet interrelated tendencies in the rules of the game. As such, ideal types are markers of a broad historical change in the dominant principles of administration, recruitment, etc. Analysis of social change, however, always involves linking up tendencies of group formation and strategic action with normative tendencies in the institutional arenas of interaction—how may changes in, say, ways of office holding and employment conditions be explained in terms of group formation and strategic action?

I should like to conclude this discussion of the general conceptual framework of this study by highlighting two other features of Weber's "tendential" approach that mark his conceptualizations off from most of contemporary sociology. While Weber's ideal types refer to concrete historical institutions and groups, they avoid the difficulties of that extreme historicist relativity which requires for each historical period an essentially incomparable conceptual scheme. Weber avoided extreme historicist relativity by defining a "traditional status group" not as a concrete group but as an aspect of group formation ("traditionalizing status-group formation") dominant in traditional status society and subordinate in modern class society. By cautiously formalizing the "essential" structural principles of traditional and modern societies into "tendential aspects," he broke through extreme historicist relativity and fashioned concepts with some, if limited, historical continuity. The historical ideal types are thus no longer self-enclosed individuals or wholes but opposed and interacting tendencies. Although this approach represents a formalization from the point of view of extreme relativist historicism, the formalization never becomes so abstract or cuts so across historical structures that the concrete human actor, individual or collective, is dissolved conceptually into ahistorical variables of a general system of action. Weber rejected this sort of positivist formalism oriented on the model of mechanistic causality and organicist systems. Since sociological explanation ultimately means explaining the why, how, when, and where of social action, sociological conceptual schemes ought not be formalized to the point where "bringing men back in" becomes a problem. If every sociological analysis does not require "bringing men back in" (correlations and functional connections *are* useful and suggestive), no sociological explanation is complete until the social actions of individuals and groups have been *interpreted*.

Interpreting social action, moreover, means interpreting the meanings and intentions of social actors. This is a well-known principle of Weber's method. However, it is not generally appreciated that this also involves interpreting how group formation and strategic action *mediates* between changing life chances and situational ("class") interests, on the one hand, and communalization of lifestyles and conventional status ideals, on the other. Weber's concepts of class and status are formulated so as to keep these *opposing and interacting* tendencies from being linked in a reductionist way. If class formation and status-group formation are opposing tendencies because one may advance at the expense of the other, they are also interacting inasmuch as status-group formation elaborates situational ("class") interests into communal conventions and ideals.

It is for this reason that Weber severed the concepts of class and status from conceptions of a necessary, ineluctable historical development, especially some Marxist interpretations of this kind. He argued that the concepts of class and status should not be tied to a linear conception of history in which, come what may, class formation progressively erodes status groups nested in the shifting life situations of modern class society. Bendix is certainly correct that the study of social inequality and social structure will not advance much until modern social thought is cut loose from such mechanistic conceptions of history though, I might add, Western Marxists today do not generally interpret Marx as subscribing to such a conception.[45]

2. The Prussian Historical Background

Civil service reforms, like other controversial events in history, are fully comprehensible only if we know the chains of events leading up to them and understand also the historically grown meanings of the actors whose interests and political aims are in conflict on the eve of reform. To provide that necessary background is the purpose of this chapter and the next one, the first on Prussia and the other on England. How much background is necessary and how one chooses to provide it depend, of course, upon one's audience of readers. Historians require little historical narration because they will recognize scant references and mere allusions to complex processes that have shaped the politics of civil service reforms. They will be satisfied with, perhaps even grateful for, brief structural sketches of the relevant groups and institutions without much historical depth. Sociologists and political scientists, however, tend to ask for a good deal of background, so much so that a structural approach to exposition becomes awkward because more or less extended historical explanations interposed between structural passages tend to break the continuity and cohesion of the exposition. Since my audience includes social scientists with varied backgrounds, I have decided to divide the material into relatively self-contained topical sections, each of them elaborating a major component of the argument. Within each of these sections, I have decided to err on the side of historical narration, particularly in the Prussian case—not only because my fellow sociologists tend to be much less familiar with Prussian than with English history but also because I wish to correct a common misapprehension among historians that educational requirements were always prominent in Prussia and that the reforms of 1770 closed the higher ranks to all but university-trained men. In order to document the view that the Prussian civil service reform of 1770 was really a "reform before the reform" with respect to educational qualifications, I shall be quoting heavily from primary sources. If historians will find in this chapter much that appears familiar to them, I must beg their indulgence and invite them to pay close attention to the interpretation of these facts.

Both these historical background chapters open with sketches of the broad historical patterns of the two countries and are meant to outline the divergent contexts of politics and administration. In the Prussian case, the subject of the first section is the triumph of a monarchic military regime over the territorial estates (parliaments) and over a system of office holding akin to the English preformed system. This introductory sketch is followed by a section dealing in some detail with the militarization of Prussian social relations, the identification of the aristocracy with the military officer corps rather than the civil service, and the social-legal barriers between the status groups raised so as to preserve the military functions of the Junker aristocracy. This section has no counterpart in the English case because there is no counterpart to Prussian militarism in the English experience. The third section focuses on the dynastic bureaucracy, especially methods of selection, the emergence of a bureaucratic elite composed largely of nonnobles, the introduction of educational qualifications and in-service training, and finally, the civil service reform of 1770. Again, this "reform before the reform" is treated as part of the historical background because it did not yet specify university training as a prerequisite for entry into the higher civil service. The fourth and last section focuses attention on education and shows how the bifurcation of careers between the militarized aristocracy and the "bureaucratized" burgher intelligentsia in the dynastic service was duplicated by a bifurcation of educational patterns so that the social composition of higher education was tilted heavily in favor of the bourgeoisie.

The Historical Pattern

In the two countries examined in this study, the seventeenth century decisively changed the balance of power between the prince and parliament. Though the confrontations between the dynasties and the estates were similar in many respects, the political results were diametrically opposed. In England, Parliament limited the prerogatives of the crown and so insured the dominance of the aristocracy at the national center as well as in the countryside. In the Hohenzollerns' patrimonial lands, by contrast, the several estates or territorial parliaments lost in the struggle with the expanding dynastic power and had to leave an ever-widening circle of affairs to dynastic commissars.[1]

In the first half of the seventeenth century, Brandenburg and the other territories, many of which were falling to the dynasty at that time through inheritance and war, were scattered across northern Germany, not contiguously but with spaces of foreign territory between them.[2] Not yet a unified state and certainly not a society with a sense of unity and nationhood, these territories were held together by the House of Hohenzollern whose scions were Electors (*Kurfürsten*) of Brandenburg, dukes (*Herzoge*) of Prussia and Cleves, and counts (*Grafen*) of Mark and Ravensberg, and so forth. In each of these territories the estates had effectively limited the prerogatives of the dynasty. With a little exaggeration one might say that they were the real rulers, holding as they did the power of the purse, the right of nomination, if not of appointment, to virtually every important office and benefice in the realm.

In Brandenburg, for instance, the Electors had, in return for money grants, solemnly promised to consult the estates on matters affecting the commonwealth, had in fact transferred the collection of tolls and taxes to committees and officials of the estates, and had confirmed repeatedly the exclusive right of the indigenous nobility to occupy and exploit positions and places of consequence, except in the military where foreigners might be employed if suitable natives could not be found. It was, perhaps, a measure of the limits of dynastic power that the first military contingents in Brandenburg during the Thirty Years' War, all of them native noblemen nominated by the estates, were sworn to duty by an oath of allegiance to both the prince and the estates. Besides, the aristocracy, ever anxious to expand its revenues at the expense of the prince, had appropriated the management and in some cases the titles of the Electors' heavily mortgaged domains.

In Prussia, which fell to the Brandenburg Hohenzollerns in 1618, the indigenous nobility, too, had gained exclusive access to important positions and benefices. As in Brandenburg, it was understood that they had preferred access to cheap leases of ducal domains, and they were in fact appropriating most of the surplus from these lands.[3] Much of the same general picture obtained in the rest of northeastern Germany at the beginning of the seventeenth century. Territorial governments, though shared between the prince and parliament, were on balance dominated by the landowning aristocracy, which had also managed to raise agricultural production by redistributing land in its favor, by reducing the free peasantry to serfdom, and by expanding large demesne farming under a feudal manorial regime, which was already beginning to break up in western Europe.

Unlike the nobilities of southern and western Germany, the East Elbian Junkerdom had enjoyed generations of prosperity, untroubled even by the depression of the middle of the sixteenth century. But this period of profitable expansion of the manorial system came to an end as the depression attendant upon the Thirty Years' War caught up with the Junkers and, together with the dislocations and instabilities of the war and postwar years, weakened their grip on territorial institutions. Ruling the territories with an overriding concern for local tradition, that is, their own vested interests in local economic and political arrangements, they were loath to think and act according to the more encompassing, supraterritorial considerations which were beginning to motivate the dynasty. Any development from territorial particularism toward a unified state, in which the resources of one territory might be used for the benefit of another, was vigorously opposed. Had it been up to the estates, the whole of the Hohenzollerns' lands would have remained but a loose federation of territories with no other bond between them than a shared prince kept at arm's length. Nor could the several estates see their way to convening an Estates General to oppose the expansion of princely prerogatives and thus participate in a unification of Brandenburg-Prussia that might have preserved the representative principle of government. Instead, the dislocation and instabilities of the war and, especially, the general European development toward militarily powerful unified states, relative to which Prussia was lagging behind, favored a dynastic political entrepreneur who was not reluctant to shed old customs, to disregard vested interests, and, seizing the initiative, to develop, little by little, a new system of domination which unified the scattered provinces by means of military-administrative institutions. In doing so, Prussia was not only to catch up with absolutist developments in the West but even to overtake them in the eighteenth century.

Frederick William, the Great Elector (1648–1688), was no mere imitator of France, however, nor did he have an overall plan as he embarked on the journey to royal absolutism. He had simply grasped the lesson of the Thirty Years' War that the political independence of his lands, buffeted as they were by foreign armies, could be maintained in the new conditions of Europe only if he developed the military potential of his entire realm. But the maintenance of a standing army required getting control of the territorial purses, that is, the power to introduce regular taxes and tolls as he saw fit. That, in turn, meant the forging of a military-fiscal administration apart from the offices controlled by the estates. Finally, a loyal and successful dynastic service depended on his power to appoint officials unencumbered by the right to indigenous placement (*jus indigenatus*). All of these interrelated claims naturally entailed confrontations with the estates. Each in its own territory, they naturally resisted these encroachments, and so one confrontation leading to another spawned a strategy to crush the estates or at least limit them to local affairs.

Little by little, the estates were stripped of their political prerogatives, and little by little, many functions of the old administration were "nationalized," taken over by a new military and fiscal commissariat loyal to and controlled by the prince. Still, this new dynastic service did not completely displace the offices of the estates. The latter retained some of their functions as local governmental agencies and as jurisdictions carefully separated from the growing public law monopolized by the new dynastic agencies. It was an essential feature of the new arrangement that the aristocracy lost its political status in the central affairs of state—diplomacy and military-fiscal affairs—but was confirmed in its local, economic, and political preeminence. The Brandenburg rulers did nothing to alter the status system with its legal boundaries among the aristocracy, the bourgeoisie, and the peasantry but confirmed and even extended it. They did nothing to undermine the aristocracy's privileged ownership of manorial estates, their virtually autocratic power over the people settled in the environs of the manor, or their economic rights over the labor of manorial serfs. The aristocracy was to remain a privileged and unquestionably the first estate, free from the taxes and customs charged to ordinary folk. It was a compromise in which the aristocracy became a sort of private corporation of landlords with local governmental powers over "their" peasants as a matter of hereditary right. If this compromise did not incline the aristocracy to embrace the new system cheerfully, at least the Elector's struggle with a recalcitrant nobility was no struggle to the death. His grandson, building on the politics of his ancestor, not without new concessions, managed to win the first estate over to serve him in a new kind of dynastic officer corps forged along with a thoroughgoing militarization of Prussian life.

From the beginning of that hundred-year period of centralization spanning the reigns of the Great Elector Frederick William (1648–1688), Frederick I (1688–1713), and Frederick William I (1713–1740), the military was the heart and soul of dynastic absolutism. It was not only the instrument of the Hohenzollerns (kings of Prussia since 1701) in diplomacy and in their becoming a power to be reckoned with in Europe. The military was also the motor of all the distinctively Prussian administrative developments. For these were all tied to the maintenance and expansion of a standing army; they were to provide the financial and manpower needs for the army and in such a way as not to exhaust the society altogether. Finally, the military was also the "school of the nation," an expression coined in the nineteenth century but eminently applicable to the eighteenth century when the military shaped the distinctive culture of the Prussian Junker and his peasant soldiers.

Frederick William I "nationalized" the territorial military contingents of the Thirty Years' War. As elsewhere in Europe, these contingents had been private enterprises put together by war leaders of the *condottiere* type—contingents leased to the prince for profit for the time being.[4] The new standing regiments, by contrast, were organized and equipped by the prince, who also appointed the regimental commanders. However, for the rest of the seventeenth century these commanders continued to be fairly independent. They recruited the field officers, who in turn recruited the soldiers. There was no unified officer corps, and it was several decades into the eighteenth century before the relatively self-contained units and their officers could be fitted into something approaching a modern command structure. Nor was the Elector's army very large, ranging in peace or war between 7,000 and 15,000 men and, with foreign subsidies, even numbering as many as 30,000 men in the latter part of the seventeenth century.

The dependence on foreign subsidies in the expansion of the army points to yet another characteristic of this early phase of state building. The army, much as in the modernizing countries today, tended to exceed the financial resources of the new state. Yet Prussia's independence, much less her expansion, could be insured, her rulers realized, only if the state's administration would become more intensive so as to meet the requirements of the military. This circumstance, then, was the motor of administrative change in fiscal affairs and dynastic domains. Eventually, intensive administration had to go beyond exploiting resources such as they were and aim at social-economic expansion so as to raise the productivity of the society. As Hintze put it succinctly, "an enormous *cultural* effort to catch up was needed to raise the economic capacity of Prussia to the level of her politics, so as to adapt her economy somewhat to the level of her political power position."[5] As her bureaucracy was indeed catching up with the military pacemaker, initially perhaps more exploiting than cultivating resources, Prussia was on her way to becoming that peculiar social system which a nineteenth-century writer once characterized in these striking words, "Prussia was not a country with an army, but an army with a country which served as headquarters and food magazine."[6]

Matters of organizational detail are clearly beyond the scope of this study, but in order to frame policies of recruitment and social composition, it might be helpful to sketch, however briefly, the bare outlines of the expanding administrative system.[7] The reorganization begun in the second half of the seventeenth century brought about a peculiar bifurcation of the new state into a "civil" and a military administration. As elsewhere in Europe, the civil administration grew out of the quasi-feudal councils of the various territories, the so-called *Regierungen*. By dint of specialization, these councils had developed via subcommittees, boards, or colleges into a supreme court and into a business administration, the function of which was to manage the domanial bailiffs, audit their accounts, and coordinate such regalia as the coinage, licenses, monopolies, tolls, and the like. Most of these functions were carried out by the so-called *Amtskammern*[8] in the various territorial *Regierungen*. Centralization of these "civil" functions barely emancipated from household administration of the prince meant, on the one hand, to impose the hegemony of the Brandenburg *Hofkammer* on the *Amtskammern* of the territories, thus reducing them to provincial offices, and, on the other, to wrest the territorial *Amtskammern* from the grasp of the territorial estates. Naturally, the territorial *Regierungen* resisted the alignment of their territorial boards under a superior Brandenburg board, as did the estates, realizing that local *Amtskammern* responsible to Brandenburg would halt and reverse the tendency of the nobility to appropriate mortgaged domains, acquire cheap leases to augment their revenues, and regard regalia as so many spoils of local cliques and coteries.

The central *Hofkammer,* a subcommittee or board of the Brandenburg privy council, became the coordinating agency directing the various territorial *Amtskammern,* thus centralizing the management and accounting of domains and regalia. A sort of exchequer of accounts, facilitating the drafting of a general budget, it pressed to convert the business of the domains to a money economy so as to gain fluid resources for expansion, including the payment of money salaries rather than payments in kind to the new officials.

Next to this domains and exchequer administration arose a system of administration geared rather more directly to building and maintaining a standing army. Even more than the new domains and exchequer administration, the new military administration, the so-called war commissariat, became the instrument for gathering the several territories into a unified state. Its function was not only to provide manpower, supply, provisions, transportation, and quarters for the army but also to develop and administer a new tax system as well as to regulate economic activities in agriculture, trade, mining, communications, and population settlement—all for the benefit of the expanding army. It developed an entire financial administration side by side with the one that grew out of the administration of domains and regalia. In the eighteenth century, finally, these two administrative branches were fused. The General Directory in Berlin, composed of a number of administrative boards, became the central bureaucracy directing the so-called Boards of War and Domains in the provinces.

The old war commissars had been agents of the prince who mustered and inspected the troops put together by war leaders, furnished provisions and quarters on the march, and otherwise coordinated the movements of the army and the necessary services of the civilian population.[9] With the development of a standing army, the general war commissar in Berlin, the chief commissars in the provinces, and the many commissars on the regimental district levels became a standing organization permanently charged with recruiting and mustering functions, pay and quartermaster functions, including the acquisition of food, forage, quarters, munitions, stores, cartage for artillery and supply trains, etc. Initially, these more nearly military functions predominated, but little by little as we approach the turn of the seventeenth century, the economic and fiscal functions aimed at maintaining and enhancing the army's tax and manpower base became more prominent. As this tendency preponderated, the war commissariat was transformed from a sort of military supply administration to the highest tax and economic policy administration of the land. In this form, it epitomized the new military, bureaucratic, mercantile state which had overrun the estates, had taken over its former tax functions, and was about to reshuffle economic arrangements in every nook and cranny of the realm. Everything was regulated, from prices, wages, and labor services to long-distance trade, municipal markets, and local fairs. Forests and meadows, mills and foundries, manufactures and mines, universities and schools—all were harnessed to the military-bureaucratic state.[10]

Still, there were limits beyond which the tentacles of bureaucratization could not spread easily. As the estates were removed from the center of political and administrative affairs in the provinces, the aristocracy was retreating to the corporations of local landowners and the administration of local districts. The highest official in this retreat of local self-government, which had been part of the bargain between the crown and the aristocracy, was the district director, like the English justice of the peace a representative of the noble landowners in the county. However, in these districts, too, the expansive military machine wrought enormous changes. In the Kurmark the district directors had been used as local war commissars, and this pattern became the model for drawing the district directors in other parts into the war commissariat. Called *Landräte* once Prussia became a kingdom, they assumed a peculiar pivotal position—half representatives of local landed interests, half officials of the dynastic service. As the *Landrat* himself was harnessed to the expanding military machine, his office diverged more and more from that of a J.P., who bears a family resemblance to the old district director.[11]

Militarization and Its Consequences

Between the middle of the seventeenth century and the middle of the eighteenth century, the entire social structure of Prussia became thoroughly militarized.[12] The peasantry was organized to serve the recruitment needs of the army, and the landowning nobility was transformed into an officer corps. These sociological changes ossified the feudal manorial system of agriculture and raised the legal barriers between the status groups. This circumstance also affected the culture of the Junker aristocracy. Barred from the professions, which were the province of university trained burghers, gentlemen, if they did not neglect their studies to start soldiering early in life, received an education geared to a military career and set apart from the ladder leading to the university. Thus, when university studies in law and cameralistics became increasingly significant in a civil-judicial career, the nobility, subscribing to the educational ideals of the military *galant homme,* was unable to furnish many officials with the necessary qualifications.

In the latter part of the seventeenth century, the ranks of the army were increasingly replenished with forcibly inducted peasants. The new war commissars, who took over much of the recruitment, were to round up a certain number of men in each district and deliver them to a given regiment. As these involuntary recruitments (*Aushebungen*) became more frequent and widespread, they began to affect agricultural production adversely, and before the century was up, the Elector recognized that this form of recruitment would depopulate the country and ruin agriculture.[13] However, conditions were to become a good deal worse under the Soldier King (Frederick William I), who made soldiering a life-long "damn duty and liability" imposed on serfs and lords alike "according to their natural birth and the order and command of the highest God."[14] They were to serve the royal master with devotion and "with possessions and blood" in war as in peace. Now the regimental commanders themselves became responsible for replenishing their units, spawning complaints and reports of cruelty and violence as never before. Fear in some areas became so overwhelming that entire villages decided to emigrate.[15]

The new system that eventually emerged so as to preserve the agricultural base of the army recognized an old practice used by many regimental commanders to save recruiting costs and forestall depopulation of their own estates. Since they were responsible for the numerical strength of their regiments, yet not disposed to pay the high cost of recruiting foreign mercenaries, commanders recruited their own and their neighbors' serfs but furloughed them for most of the year so that they might bring in the harvest. To keep other regimental recruiters out of their own bailiwick, they began to "enroll" adolescents as future recruits, duly certified and partially uniformed as furloughed members of the regiment. Each regiment was thus appropriating a district as a sort of recruitment base. This system was so widely used in 1733 that the king only needed to divide the realm into military districts (*Kantone*), distribute the regiments without overlap, and decree the enrollment of all young people into regimental lists.[16]

If every peasant thus became a regular or at least an enrolled soldier, his master on the manor or someone like him became his officer in the regiment. Until the accession of Frederick William I, however, the aristocracy on the whole was not favorable disposed toward the army. After all, it was the chief instrument of royal absolutism. To most nobles, the army of the Brandenburg rulers seemed as foreign as the many foreign armies they might join when they were seeking an occupation suited to a gentleman.[17] Frederick William I wanted to nationalize the army in the sense of integrating it with the social structure, and this meant forcing not only peasants into the ranks but also noblemen into a stable and permanent officer corps.

In 1722 he instructed his heir apparent that the first principle of his policy should be "that all nobles and counts from all his provinces be pressed into the Corps of Cadets."[18] However, he lived long enough to accomplish the feat himself. He prohibited service in a foreign army, even travel abroad, on pain of confiscating the violator's property and branding him as a deserter.[19] His son, who didn't think much of the Grand Tour anyway, also expressly forbade attendance at a foreign university, academy, or school, causing Sir Charles Wenburg Williams, the English ambassador, to remark, "The entire Prussian territory is a literal prison: no one may leave it without the King's knowledge."[20]

District officers were ordered to register noble youngsters and convey them to Berlin. There they would be placed in the corps of cadets or directly in some regiment so that they may learn to "serve His Royal Majesty as it is appropriate for honest vassals."[21] The king was anxious to have young noblemen early in life, and he found ways to recruit them. He kept pressing the provincial *Kammern* to press the district commissioners: "We are ordering you . . . to instruct immediately all of the *Landräte* under you to give more attention than before to young nobles, to see them and get acquainted with them, and to send annually a certain number of them to the Corps of Cadets in proportion to the size of the district." The king added that he was especially interested in "boys who look good and healthy, have straight legs, and might be expected to grow." Nothing was to stop the commissioners so that "those nobles who are not yet adults will learn something in the Cadets."[22] Parents and even the estates complained that youngsters were taken away before they had received an education that might have enabled them to serve in a civilian job.[23] But that is precisely what the king didn't want, ever suspicious as he was that young nominees to civilian posts were somewhat less than loyal vassals. "A man of status who is not a soldier is a wretch," wrote Frederick II, and his father would certainly have agreed.[24] In order to meet the objections of those parents who feared that their son would get improper care and education, the king had a suggestion.

> In order that parents be more willing to send their sons, the district commissioners should best insinuate that, although in the past this or that may have been wrong with the Cadets, everything has been redressed and provisions have been made that youngsters may be instructed in Christianity, in the essential sciences and spiritual exercises, as well as in writing and arithmetic, mathematics, fortification, French language, geography and history, fencing and dancing. Twenty-four of them at a time will have an opportunity to learn riding without charge, in addition to which they will be lodged in clean rooms and will be well supplied with healthy and good food and drink. Besides, all care will be taken to bring them up so that they will be capable for useful service in the future.[25]

The nobility may have been reluctant at first, but eventually the royal taskmaster prevailed by hook and crook and sometimes with the help of mounted police sent from estate to estate to gather young gentlemen for his cadets.[26]

Within a remarkably short time, a generation or so, the Junker nobility embraced the military values of the royal drillmaster. Coerced and victimized, but also induced and rewarded with an aristocratic monopoly over the officer corps, that nobility began more and more to identify with a military career as officer—a career regarded as the *métier des gens d'honneur,* from which all low-born men should be purged. Frederick II approved of his father's policy, namely, that "the officer corps in each regiment was purged of those people whose conduct and birth did not at all correspond to the profession of gentlemen . . . ," and he appreciated that ever since that time, "the refined sentiments of officers tolerated as companions only people without reproach."[27] In building this aristocratic monopoly and injecting into it that esprit de corps and status consciousness, Frederick William I was guided by practical reasons: the nobility was most qualified to command peasant soldiers because nobles were the born masters of peasant serfs. The patriarchal relations and the harsh punishments of the manor might be infused into the army to lend it a unique cohesion and discipline. The enlightened Frederick stated the principle simply enough: soldiers should "fear their officers more than any danger to which they might be exposed" on the battlefield.[28] In any case, this fusion of the authority relations of the manor and the regiment was the sociological basis of the militarization of Prussian life. In both spheres, the same uniformed men, oriented from childhood to military values and discipline, faced each other as commanders and subordinates. This condition became ever more general as the army and the officer corps multiplied several times in the course of the eighteenth century.

Between 1713 and 1806, the army increased from about 40,000 men to 235,000 men. Similarly, the officer corps increased during that period from less than 3,000 men (3,116 in 1740) to 7,000 or 8,000 men.[29] This expansion, combined with the social exclusiveness of the officer corps, meant that in some areas like Pomerania, almost the entire nobility was or had been serving in the army.[30] Unfortunately, few data are available for most of the eighteenth century. Around the turn of the century, some 60 to 70 percent of the nobility of the Mark Brandenburg and East Prussia seemed to have served at one time or other.[31] Among the sons and relations of owners of manorial estates in the Mark, more than 80 percent were or had been serving in the army. This, certainly, is an extraordinary proportion by any standard.[32]

Were the crown and the Junker nobility successful in forging that aristocratic monopoly which they hailed throughout the eighteenth century? The answer is, undoubtedly, yes. From Frederick William I onward to the end of the eighteenth century, nobles accounted for some 90 percent of the officer corps.[33] Very few nonnobles may be found in the higher rank. In 1734 all generals were nobles, 200 out of 211 staff officers were nobles. At the end of Frederick's reign, 667 out of 689 officers from major upward were nobles. Finally, in 1806, when the old military system collapsed, only 695 out of the entire officer corps of more than 7,000 men were nonnobles.[34] Nonnobles were typically segregated in the garrison regiments or technical services, such as artillery or engineers. In these distinctly low-status services, nonnobles predominated even on the staff level though some of them might eventually be raised to nobility.[35]

Although the proportion of burghers was low in the nontechnical services (the lower the higher the rank), it should not be supposed that the preponderant noble majority was entirely composed of nobles of descent. Frederick II, even more than his father, preferred noble officers and, especially after the Seven Years' War, subscribed to a conception of honor which, by definition, would seem to have excluded nonnoble men. Yet low as his opinion of burgher aptitude for command might have been, he was not above recognizing merit when he saw it and raising a man to noble status as a reward. And so quite a number of nobles in his officer corps were in fact nobles of ascent; indeed, some of the highest officers and generals of his reign had been ennobled from humble backgrounds.[36]

If the king did not mind raising a nobility of military heroes or men with obvious aptitude for command, he emphatically denied that men should be ennobled for any other reason. "Noble status," he declared, "must be acquired only by means of the sword and bravery or other extraordinary conduct or merit. I will also have no other vassals than those capable at all times to give me useful service in the army."[37] The status society with its ascriptive links between families and positions of consequence was to be maintained even if it meant that the recognition of extraordinary merit would have to entail a change in social status. Such a change of status was important in an officer corps whose code of conduct and conception of honor was based on the principle of fundamental social equality among its members regardless of service rank. This fundamental social equality was symbolized by the fact that all the way from the king at the top down to the lowliest ensign, all officers wore identical uniforms without insignia of rank. In the language of the time, it was a "caste," not altogether closed, but one over which a royal gatekeeper watched, ever mindful to preserve that Junker spirit which was the soul of the old regime.

It naturally became a matter of urgency to preserve the economic foundation of that "caste," especially since the pay was slight below the rank of a company commander and the manorial economy thus had to furnish most of the income to brothers, sons, and nephews who were officers. Yet up until the latter part of the soldier king's reign, Prussia's agrarian policy was dominated by the rising crown reclaiming and expanding its domains, involving the domains administration in extensive litigation with the aristocracy and dictating also a personnel policy discriminating against aristocrats. One by one, noble bailiffs were evicted, and by 1732 nobles were debarred legally from leasing crown lands. Moreover, bourgeois administrators all but monopolized the domains administration from top to bottom. Now that the officer corps needed protection, the expansion of domains at the expense of the nobility had to be stopped. And since it would no longer be possible for a nobleman to augment his income with a cheap lease of crown lands, it was imperative also to keep financially hard-pressed Junkers from selling their manors to wealthy burghers. A landless nobility, according to leading opinion, would be much less effective than a landed Junker class in combining the roles of officer of a regiment and lord of a manor. As to bourgeois landowners, they were altogether unsuitable, according to Frederick II. "Most of them think lowly and are bad officers."[38]

Thus, the state's policy shifted to one designed to keep aristocratic income and landed wealth from being threatened either by the crown or by a moneyed bourgeoisie ready to cash in on mortgaged estates. When Frederick II ascended to the throne, he quickly instructed his administrative boards to "stop fiscal officials from harassing the nobility—on pain of hanging." They should no longer err on the side of the crown, as they had been instructed to do, but on the side of the nobility, for "what is a small loss to me, is a large advantage to the nobleman whose sons must defend the land and whose race is so good as to deserve to be conserved in any way."[39] In order to "emphatically maintain the nobility in its possessions," the king also thought it imperative that manors not be bought up by burghers lest "one by one the number of nobles in the country decline . . . thus finally depriving my army of officers with noble backgrounds."[40] It is strikingly apparent from these documents that ownership of manorial estates, nobility, and the existence of a cohesive and effective officer corps, indeed, the very integrity of the state, were all insolubly bound up with one another in the ruler's mind. Change one part, and the whole system will surely come apart. To forestall so awesome a contingency, the exclusive right of the nobility to own manorial estates, written into the law of the land, was augmented also with a prohibition against nobles entering the learned professions except serving on the bench. These measures amounted to an ossification of feudal property relations throughout the eighteenth century, when elsewhere in Europe they were breaking up. When the agrarian crisis of 1760 brought many estates to the brink of ruin, their owners were yet legally barred from selling them to wealthy burghers, temporary exemptions and royal exceptions notwithstanding. Instead, the state established credit institutions and low-cost mortgages to prevent bankruptcies and the emergence of a "nominal aristocracy," which "would not have power and lively interest enough to fulfill its constitutional function in the state."[41] Perhaps the most important consequence of these measures for the purpose of this study was the segregation of the status groups. Instead of creating a border zone of near-gentry country and professional families, as in England, Prussia at the same period in history widened the deep chasm between the major status groups, thanks to the legal wedge which Frederick II inserted between them to protect his officer corps.

Finally, the militarization of the aristocracy also shaped the education which young gentlemen were to receive so that they might become loyal, devoted, and effective officers. For this purpose, the Latin schools and universities of the bourgeois sphere of life were not thought adequate, nor, might I add, did most nobles think they were appropriate institutions for young gentlemen. Nevertheless, there were some who sent their sons to universities, perhaps in anticipation of a career on the bench. When one of their number, General Count zu Dohna, asked Frederick II in 1777 for permission to send his nephew to the University of Geneva, he received the following answer.

> As I see it, this won't do at all. For if you want him to become a scholar, then everything he must know to serve the fatherland he can learn in this country, for example, at Halle. At Geneva, however, he will learn only to become an affected French preacher. If, as I believe, he is to become a soldier, then all the Latin and other speculative things, which he will bring back from the university, will not help him; instead it will be better for him to enter the service immediately and concentrate on the *métier*. In that case, you should, the sooner the better, take him into your regiment and instruct him under your own eyes.[42]

The education of the young officer was to be practical, oriented to the *métier des gens d'honneur*; it might include mathematics, geography, and natural science as an adjunct to such military subjects as artillery, fortification, map making, tactics, field engineering but not the "pedantic Latin" of the grammar schools or most of the subjects taught at the universities. In the last section of this chapter we will survey the educational institutions which were catering to the nobility and have a look at the evidence on where, how, and to what degree the aristocracy was educated. At this point, I wish to suggest only that the militarization of Prussian life in the eighteenth century did nothing to encourage nobles to turn to the education of bourgeois scholars, yet much to foster a quasi-professional, military education embedded in highly status-conscious, separate institutional settings. The majority did not attend any school but might have been instructed at home before they were placed in a regiment as Junkers; others were educated as pages at court, in the corps of cadets, or at a military academy; and an indeterminate, probably small, minority, including also those who were constitutionally unfit for military service, attended grammar schools and universities.

Among the majority who did not attend any school were also those whose parents could ill afford an expensive education and who welcomed the opportunity to place their sons in the military, where educational qualifications of entry and promotion were very modest indeed, or who welcomed the opportunity to have them educated at the expense of the state in the corps of cadets. Many parents were evidently anxious to have their son accepted as *Fahnenjunker* (cornet) at the tender age of eleven to thirteen, anticipating that in a few years' time he might rise to a higher rank and be provided for as an adult with a professional, if modest, living.[43] The basic problem was the seniority system of promotion. There was an incentive to send boys soldiering in their early teens when they might have learned their letters. Frederick II was not entirely happy with the youthfulness of so many of his officers, but he preferred those "youths snatched from their mothers' breasts," as he described them, to bourgeois officers.[44] His expanding army needed officer replacements, and so he condoned the corps' ideology that education was scarcely a recommendation for military life, or even that education, if too learned, was tantamount to conduct unbecoming a military gentleman.

From Patronage to Limited Competition

The system of limited competition in the eighteenth-century Prussian civil service grew out of a system of patronage akin to clientage, family jobbery, and parliamentary placementship which spread in England as an aristocratic oligarchy forged a parliamentary government dispensing civil office under the crown for the benefit of family and faction. A nascent system of this kind, similar in all but detail, obtained in the several territories of the Hohenzollern realm in the seventeenth century before and for a considerable time after the Elector Frederick William embarked upon the journey to royal absolutism. In England, the patronage system lasted with some modifications until the middle of the nineteenth century whereas in Prussia it was surpressed by the rise of royal absolutism and changed into the varied eighteenth-century practice of limited competition. Since this system of limited competition forms the background of the Prussian civil service reform, only a most general outline of the old patronage system will suffice for our purposes. In the next chapter, however, we will dwell at some length on the English system of patronage.

The offices of the territorial governments, the *Regierungen,* and even to some extent the domains and regalia, were regarded as so many spoils of the estates, that is, of the leading aristocratic families and their coteries of friends. The *jus indigenatus* was a political institution, to be sure. It limited the prince's discretion of appointment, thus furnishing aristocratic interest groups with the wherewithal to build political alliances. However, it was also an institution meant to keep within the circle of the provincial aristocracy the bounty of office which the East Prussian estates correctly perceived as "the indigenous nobility's greatest benefice."[45] At a time when places under the crown were everywhere regarded, not so much as a public trust, but as a private sphere of profiteering, the crown's benefices were subject to literal appropriation, transformation into freeholds, inheritance from one generation to the next as any piece of property, even lease or sale to the highest bidder. This proprietary conception of government was the norm of what Weber called the "politics of notables," and contemporaries perceived no essential difference between ownership of a landed estate and an office under the crown, or between drawing revenues from one and emoluments and fees from the other. Governmental functions were attached to both of them and in either case might be discharged by a low-paid deputy. If the holder stooped to handle these functions himself, he always remained an amateur who did not regard himself as a professional bureaucrat. If there were any professionals at all, they might be found largely as trained jurists, drawn mostly from the urban patriciate, and beholden to a patrimonial rather than a bureaucratic conception of service.[46]

In any case, it is this system of patronage which had to be abolished along with the political prerogatives of the estates, if the crown was to realize its interest. But raising a bureaucracy turned out to be a rather more protracted struggle than political subjugation of the estates. Up to the middle of the eighteenth century, appropriation, nepotism, venality, amateurism, and rugged independence were still very much in evidence although political loyalty, probity, ability, expertise, diligence, and discipline in observing regulations were encroaching on the old patronage system. For a century or so, there was a pulling and hauling between opposing principles, interests, and customs, and it would be difficult to type that system of limited competition which emerged ever so slowly as ascriptive or achievement-oriented even if it were possible to reduce the clashing forces to a single dimension. It was a mixed type, oscillating to and fro at the same time that it moved, perceptible in retrospect, to the form and substance of a bureaucracy.

There can be little doubt that the prime qualification of the new breed of royal servants in the first thrust of bureaucratization was not so much a matter of "achievement" or expertise as political reliability pure and simple. In order to be well taken care of, the relatives and friends of the big patronage dispensers had, according to a contemporary in 1690, "to worship the Herrn *Hauptman* and the Herrn *Landrat* like a god."⁴⁷ A report from Cleves in 1710 hinted at the same circumstance, especially the closed circles of jobbing friends and kinsmen against which an outsider had no chance at all.

> The *Kammer*-councillors, the chief treasurer, the customs director and the other officers are very friendly with the bailiffs, the treasury officials, and the customs men and will advance no one to these positions who will not ally himself with them; the sons of the *Kammer*-councillors are bailiffs, whose sons are married to the daughters of treasury officials; one *Kammer*-councillor and customs director has a brother who is a customs collector, and the rest are their relations; they have doled out to one another the best leaseholds and have favored each other in everything.⁴⁸

To break the back of some of these cousinhoods and coteries, Frederick William I envisioned servants loyal only to himself and his purposes. "One has to serve his sovereign with body and soul, with goods and chattels, with honor and conscience, and to commit everything but salvation: that is God's, but everything else must be mine."⁴⁹

One way of achieving these ends was to employ the ancient method of appointing officials not in their native territory but systematically in another—in other words, to disregard the *jus indigenatus,* to insist on royal discretion in hiring and firing and to establish sovereignty "like a *rocher de bronce*," as the young king put it early in his reign. He instructed his provincial agencies, about to be fused into the Boards of War and Domains, "that no one shall be recommended who is born in a province where a vacant position is to be filled again."⁵⁰

Another way of achieving those sovereign ends was to give attention, ever sharpened by suspicion of intrigue, to details of every single nomination of appointment, down even to the lower ranks; indeed, especially the lower ranks, for in the days of the patronage system, appointment of lower officials was traditionally in the gift of the higher. An important asset, this practice was politically valuable in building trains of clients and financially lucrative as well since tenure turned on kickbacks, gifts, and other lubricants of favor. This, too, had to be stopped. All subaltern officials—we would call them intermediate civil servants today—were as a rule appointed by the king himself; all should feel dependent on and responsible to the king alone; and as to kickbacks—well, these too were centralized by mandatory payments to the royal recruiting chest. Thus, the General Directory was instructed, "When low and subordinate positions are filled in our provincial boards and commissariats, the candidates must properly come to terms with the recruiting chest, and the position shall go to him who is the most qualified and offers the most."[51]

These and other devices were primarily a matter of politics rather than of efficiency in the ordinary sense of that word. Aimed at defeating the aristocratic opposition to "Prussification"—an opposition whose cliques and claques were attached to the offices of the territorial governments—they were to make the world safe for expanding absolutism. As the dynastic commissariat seized the new "public" or "civil" functions, the opposition entrenched itself largely in the *Regierungen* which were losing all but their judicial functions. Forging its own administrative jurisdiction and litigating on behalf of the crown as judges and prosecutors, the new commissariat encroached on the traditional prerogatives of the *Regierungen* and reduced them to private (traditional) law jurisdictions opposed to the new public law spawned by expansive dynastic politics and administration. And so well into the eighteenth century there was a deep cleavage between two opposing groups, one associated with the retreating institutions of the territorial state, the other with expansive dynastic absolutism. It was a struggle between "power groups," as Rosenberg puts it, at the same time that it "was a contest for administrative influence, social preeminence, pecuniary profit, and the ultimate control of civic life."[52]

If the centralization of patronage was essentially a political matter, the imposition of codes of conduct, rules of procedure, and all the other regulations of behavior we associate with bureaucratization were also part of a social-cultural effort at harnessing a heterogeneous officialdom into a cohesive and servile instrument of dynastic policy. This harnessing by means of material and status incentives as well as by coercive pressures and occasionally harsh penalties—this struggle against insubordination, intractibility, cavalierly independence and

nonchalance typical of the traditional amateur style—this forging
of a servile, diligent, honest, militarily disciplined and almost pu-
ritanically conscientious workforce has been described in much colorful detail by Rosenberg, whose study is by far the best that has
been written on the subject.[53]

When the founders of Prussian absolutism wanted meritorious
men, they wanted more than political loyalty and capacity for vo-
cational discipline. They also wanted men with the know-how and
skill necessary in the jobs they were called upon to perform. In
cabinet order after cabinet order, they specified the general qualifications: "agile and open minds," also "good common sense," a
"lively spirit," and "smart, honest and clever *subjects*." They also
stressed "*capacité, droiture,* and aptitude" or "*activité, diligence,*
and *accuratesse*." But, above all, they wanted "hard-working, lively,
and sensible people" with "good knowledge, insight, and routine
in matters of taxation, commerce, and manufacture." In the domains
administration, they wanted men "who had themselves been farmers
and leaseholders and who had themselves operated large leaseholds,
are skilled also with the pen, knowlegeable in accounts, and vigilant
and healthy people." All, according to Frederick William I, must
be "the most skilled people as might be found the length and breadth
of the realm, evangelical-reformed or lutheran, loyal and honest,
capable of writing, open-headed, and born subjects." Or, in the
words of Frederick II, they must be men "who possess the necessary
capacity, talent, and experience and, at the same time, are honest,
diligent, and incorruptible."[54]

No weight was to be given to whether the candidate was "the
brother, cousin, brother-in-law, or any other in-law or client of the
sponsor," and to a suggestion that the son of Judge Pestel of Herford
owned a fortune, the king replied "that a fortune of 30,000 thaler
is no significant recommendation for someone to be placed in a
Kammer, considering that he might nevertheless be a bad booby
with no special aptitude."[55] At the same time, he was not loath to
give his loyal servants every fair encouragement and "to take care
of them and their relatives and to miss no opportunity to extend
indeed special favors to them."[56]

Similarly, Frederick II, in a communication to the whole service,
encouraged his higher civil servants to train their sons for a career
under the crown and held out the prospect that the former might

be succeeded by the latter.[57] Hoping that service families would cultivate a tradition of loyalty to the dynastic state, he was willing to compromise. Yet when an official asked that his son-in-law succeed him as war and tax councillor, the king declined "because the same Highness does not wish that places be made heritable and be given to daughters in lieu of a dowry."[58] If the eighteenth-century system was one of limited competition, it was also one of limited nepotism— a system in which political, social, and personal considerations might from case to case make a considerable difference in the balance of ascription and achievement.[59]

Until the latter part of the eighteenth century, qualifications for office were spelled out in no greater detail than the above specifications. No special education was required. Frederick William I, certainly, wanted practical men of business, who were experienced in commerce and agriculture, skilled in management and bookkeeping, and clever in promoting dynastic interests. He believed that university-trained men were not especially suited for these purposes. When the *Kammer* of Cleves suggested that a university-trained chief burgomaster be set over two burgomasters who had served well but had never attended a university, he snapped back at the insinuation, "Are the people who have not studied at a university idiots—hence I am an idiot, too?"[60] As we shall see presently, the "civil" establishment, like the judicial system, accepted in-service trainees since the twenties, and although in this context references to university studies were becoming more frequent, there were no well-defined standards or regular examinations until 1770. Even then, the new civil service regulations, establishing a standing commission to examine candidates, did not recommend, much less require, particular academic studies. Besides, examinations, though mandatory now, were often disregarded. The Freiherr vom Stein, to mention only one example, entered the Prussian service after 1770 and apparently passed without so much as lifting a pen.

The servants of the Prussian rulers were drawn from heterogeneous backgrounds. During the hundred years preceding the accession of Frederick II, the political struggle with the proponents of the *Ständestaat* was, perhaps, the prime factor in the choice of personnel. The Great Elector drew officials from the reformed nobility, which was weakly integrated with aristocratic cliques and coteries opposing the expansion of the crown's prerogative; from French refugees, even more disconnected from the estates and much more dependent on royal favor; from other nobles who for one reason or another linked their fortune with the crown; and, most importantly, from the bourgeoisie, which was the most dependent group and also offered special qualifications. Low-born men were likely to remain more pliable than nobles with independent landed wealth. They were not likely to merge with the aristocratic opposition *in the short run*. If their low social station was sometimes a liability in their dealings with status-conscious aristocrats, they were likely to compensate that shortcoming with diligence, experience, and professional skills required by the king's antiaristocratic business. This influx of commoners, recruited from the universities, the urban patriciate, the professions, the trades, and even from subaltern secretaries, transformed the old system, which had placed a premium on birth and what the English called "connexion." Already during the Great Elector's reign it became proverbial that "in Brandenburg the emphasis is placed on pens, not ancestors, for one can't tell whether some business is negotiated with noble or bourgeois blood."[61]

During the reign of Frederick William I, the advance of bourgeois councillors continued, as did the administrative pressure on the nobility, even though by now the estates had been reduced politically to registering formal protests.[62] The king, who is sometimes called a bourgeois king on account of his personal style, regarded much of the nobility with great suspicion, hurling at them some of the choicest epithets of his less than tactful, if colorful, vocabulary. At the same time, he recommended to his heir apparent that he might find it expedient to indulge the class as a whole.

An era was drawing to an end. The expansion of monarchic absolutism at the expense of the estates was giving way to a policy of winning the nobility to serve the dynasty with devotion in return for which it might expect the protection of the crown. During the reign of Frederick William I, this shift became noticeable in his forging of the officer corps. In the "civil" service, however, the king kept leaning on low-born men from whom he expected to receive the loyalty, devotion, diligence, and expertise that the continuing expansion of dynastic administration required.

Given the fact that administration developed so much in the orbit of militarization, it is not surprising that there was always a generous dash of generals among the soldier king's secret councillors and commissioners, for example, Prince Leopold von Dessau, the Duke von Holstein Beck, the Imperial Knight von Wylich and Lottum, and the Counts von Dohna, Wartensleben, Degenfeld-Schönburg, Bork, and Grumbkow. Indeed, this rise of generals had been common since the Thirty Years' War not only in Prussia but also elsewhere on the continent. Chancellor von Ludewig at the University of Halle thought it remarkable that "in almost all places the highest generals are nowadays sitting at the desk, for which purpose they had not been used in past times because few of them would have had the training and aptitude for such work."[63] Yet even more remarkable, perhaps, was the fact that civilians like Kraut, Creutz, Görne, Happen, Boden, and Fuchs, Jr., should rise to the top of the General War Commissariat without so much as a drop of blue blood or military rank. Although Frederick William I was rather contemptuous, probably with very good reason, of the scholastic pedantry of academics in his time, he nevertheless called upon such professors as Thomasius, Gundling, J. H. Böhmer, Heineccius, and the aforementioned von Ludewig to fill positions and write legal briefs on matters of public law. For the most part, however, the king wanted practical men of business, and he took them wherever he could find them, provided that they were loyal subjects. He raised his secretaries and subalterns in the royal secretariat, every one of them a commoner, to the highest ministerial posts. Among them were sons of merchants and former managers of royal domains; similarly, elsewhere in the higher civil service were men who had gained practical experience in the sort of work which aristocrats were inclined to leave to low-born men. It was indeed "a golden age of select men of common origin" whose chances of advancement were, as Rosenberg points out, "unmatched in Prussian government employment until the 1920s when the Prussian state was the stronghold of the Social Democrats."[64] The officer corps was now closing to men of common social origin, but in the civil service they were enjoying the incomparable advantage.

On the ministerial level, nonnobles held a small majority over nobles.[65] Although in 1723 noble privy councillors of the General Directory still outnumbered low-born men nine to eight, by 1740 commoners held a sizable majority of eighteen to three.[66] Of the twenty councillors appointed to the General Financial Directory between 1713 and 1723, eleven were commoners whereas of the twenty-eight councillors appointed to the General War Commissariat between 1700 and 1723, eighteen were commoners and several more of recently ennobled stock.[67] In the provinces the picture was much the same. Of the 118 councillors and directors of the provincial Boards of War and Domains in 1737, only thirty-six were noble.[68] A few extant samples from various provinces at different times round out the picture. Between 1714 and 1723, eighteen out of twenty-two appointments to the *Kammer* of the Kurmark were commoners. Magdeburg in 1721 had one noble president and six nonnoble councillors in the *Kammer,* as well as three nobles and four nonnobles in the commissariat. On the Board of War and Domains in Berlin in 1735, sixteen out of twenty-seven councillors were commoners. On the board in Küstrin in 1739, six out of ten councillors were commoners.[69]

Still, the nobility was not losing out everywhere. Of all the presidents of the Boards of War and Domains, only one was a commoner. As heads of the provincial administrative boards, these presidents were charged with spearheading the expansion of dynastic administration into the provinces, negotiating with the local aristocracies, and coordinating the *Junker Landräte* who now as then had a dual function. On the one hand, they were the nominees of the nobility in the districts (*Kreise*) and, thus, representatives of local interests; on the other hand, they occupied positions at the end of the chain of command of the dynastic bureaucracy and were, thus, also local commissars of the crown. It was a matter of expediency to have as presidents men of old lineage, capable of negotiating with local aristocrats and directing the *Junker Landräte.* A low-born official, efficient and knowledgeable though he might have been, could not have functioned adequately in this important position, which made many a president the equal or even superior of ministers in point of influence, power, and prestige.[70] With the militarization of life in the districts, the *Landräte* were increasingly recruited from former officers who were expected to bring to the job that distinctive military loyalty to the commander in chief (*Königstreue*), which was the hallmark of the officer corps. On the high courts, as we shall see presently, the nobility prevailed, too. Finally, as elsewhere in Europe until the demise of monarchy itself, the diplomatic corps was a haven of the old nobility simply because commoners and *nouveaux arrivés* would not have gained entry in many royal courts. It was thought to be essential that ambassadors and diplomatic secretaries could associate with the best of international court society. When the director of the public textile corporation (*Lagerhaus*) in Berlin, the Privy Councillor von Eichmann, nominated his son for one of the newly established councillorships in the diplomatic corps, Frederick II replied in 1749 that he could not appoint him "because most of the foreign courts are very *pointilleux* with respect to old lineage and will accept only people of well-known *naissance*."[71] Although he suggested that young Eichmann might perhaps be acceptable as a diplomatic secretary, it would appear that the diplomatic service held out slim prospects of advancement even to a member of a recently ennobled family.

Under Frederick William I, the civil service, unlike the army, emerged as a career in which low-born men had a considerable advantage. But the crown's sponsorship of a career in which commoners might rise to the very foot of the throne created awkward problems in a society in which so close a proximity to the throne was still generally accepted as the prerogative of gentlemen. Popular opinion, not only among the status-conscious aristocracy, still equated high administrative function with noble birth. Since the two parts of the equation were drifting apart as low-born men were lifted to positions conceptually bound up with aristocratic rank, Frederick William I reconciled the dissonance between the ideal and the real by ennobling those commoners who had risen to the highest ranks.

While "achievement" was encroaching on "ascription" in the dynastic service, achievement also became the basis for ascription. For the men who were thus raised to noble status spared no effort to become acceptable to nobles of descent. If they did not always succeed in becoming themselves gentlemen of high standing in aristocratic circles, their offspring generally bridged the social gap, particularly if their acquired landed property and title were suitably amalgamated through marriage with families of old lineage. Marshall, son of a merchant and former cabinet councillor, married a von Schwerin and later a von Münchow, both families of old lineage. He arrived in his own lifetime. His son, unlike von Eichmann's son, was accepted in the diplomatic service, moved in the best society, and married the daughter of his boss, the minister von Podewils. If this was a particularly striking success story, it points out how the new upstart nobility became linked with the nobility of descent. In this process of incorporation, the sharp distinction between claims to preferment based on merit, on the one hand, and social status, on the other, became constantly mitigated as did the sharp distinction between nobles of ascent and nobles of descent. During the reign of Frederick I, the noble top administrators were rather *nouveaux arrivés*. So long as the door to ennoblement remained open and the noble elite was constantly infused with low-born men, complete merger of the new bureaucratic nobility with the aristocracy of old lineage was impossible.

Ennoblement in Prussia remained a matter of the king's discretion. Unlike in Russia, a patent of nobility was not automatically granted once an official reached a certain service rank. Nor was ennoblement always an act of grace. Suspicious of the nobility and contemptuous of the status pretentions of old-line nobles, Frederick William I was occasionally motivated by uncharitable motives to slight aristocratic rank. When he gave his court jester a seat on the nobility bench of a court and raised him to the titled nobility, granting him a string of noble caricatures as ancestors to boot, or when he issued a patent of nobility to an official because he had built "such a beautiful, magnificent house," he was giving symbolic, if trenchant, expression to his contempt for claims of status unaccompanied by merit or social pretense devoid of achievement. If he intended to devalue aristocratic rank in the esteem of the public, it is far from clear, however, that he succeeded in lowering aristocratic rank in the estimation of his low-born officials.

His son, Frederick II, was an aristocrat at heart. He set out to make peace with the nobility, aiming to draw even the last holdouts into the dynastic fold. The major battles with the aristocracy were now history; there were fewer reasons for preferring burghers as a matter of political expediency and more for giving qualified support to the claims and prejudices of the high born. He called the aristocracy "the fairest jewel in my crown"[72] and thought he recognized in noble rank those sterling qualities—"they are able both to obey and to command"[73]—which made his men of honor especially suitable as pillars of the state. The nobility was to be preserved not only in its possessions but also in its glory, and this meant stopping the practice of ennobling low-born civil servants, whatever their desserts. "One may become a nobleman by means of the sword, not otherwise," was the new royal maxim.[74] If possible, civil offices under the crown were to be moved closer into the orbit of the aristocracy and were to be infused with gentle blood. It was part of the grand scheme to win the aristocracy for the dynastic civil and military services. Indeed, Frederick II would have liked to place nobles in all positions of consequence had it not been disagreeably difficult to find gentlemen with the requisite education and experience.

Although the king intended to keep the "nonnoble riffraff" down, he did not wish to sacrifice merit to status. On one occasion he rejected a suggestion that noble students be dispensed from public disputations; on another he wrote that "everything would be lost in a state if birth were to rise victorious over merit."[75] Besides, his expanding army was so much in need of noble officers that it became a matter of concern not to divert too many young noblemen by making the civil establishments attractive to them. For this reason, the king did not wish "to fill the *Kammern* with too many nobles," and more than once he requested examining officials to see whether a noble nominee for the civil service was able-bodied so that he might be transferred to the army.[76] On one such occasion the king ordered, "If von Gellhorn, who wants to enter the *Kammer* of the Kurmark as an in-service trainee, is tall and intelligent, then I wish to place him in the army; if however he is small and not bright, then I will be content to have him accepted as a trainee in said *Kammer*."[77] The army and its needs still ranked above all else.

As a result of all these contingencies—the functional requirements of talent and expertise, the shortage of duly qualified nobles, and the preponderant requirements of the army—the actual shift in the social composition of the civil service was much less dramatic than the shift in ideology. The trend toward employment of middle-class careerists was not altered in all but the highest ministerial posts. To this level, it is true, Frederick II advanced only one commoner and refused to ennoble him. The presidencies of the provincial administrative boards continued to be reserved largely to the nobility and for the same reason as before. "Presidents of the *Kammern* should be from good, old, noble families and also have the necessary ability and capacity"[78] Since it was difficult to find men with this combination of qualifications, the king had to resort to such commoners as Lenz, Colomb, and Domhardt. The latter was even awarded the especially high-status title of *Oberpräsident*.[79] Below these ranks bourgeois bureaucrats predominated and advanced proportionately in some areas. Low-born privy councillors of finance in the General

Directory held a two-thirds majority over their noble colleagues, and much the same situation obtained in the *Regierungen* and *Kammern* of the provincial administration.[80] In the words of Rosenberg,

> The logic of growing "bureaucratization" and the continued drive for the improvement of efficiency, combined with the unplanned, stubborn facts of social mobility, proved strong enough in real life to prevent the hierarchy of hereditary estates and royal wishful thinking from blocking the social ascent of commoners and the downgrading of a sizeable section of the nobility. Many nominating top officials, increasingly concerned with raising the standards of admission and promotion, recommended commoners rather than titled aristocrats for appointment in the higher grades.[81]

Finally, this raising of standards in the second half of the eighteenth century gradually moved higher education to the foreground of attention.

The reader will have noticed not only that I am going over some of the same ground as Rosenberg but also that I am setting the accents somewhat differently. It may be well at this point to highlight briefly this difference. Unlike most of the older German literature, Rosenberg avoids overemphasizing the achievements of the eighteenth-century monarchs in terms of "moral purification." He gives considerable space to exploring the tenacious continuity of "corrupt," traditional practices. He also argues that the very methods used by Frederick William I and Frederick II enhanced struggle and strife within the bureaucracy. For example, the collegial form of administration, that is, administrative boards with joint responsibility, enhanced "steadiness, greater uniformity, cooperation, and accountability"; it reduced "graft, favoritism, and personal arbitrariness"; and it "did much to make administrative management more scientific by basing decisions on facts and the critical examination of information rather than on loose personal opinions, preconceived notions, and individual fancy."[82] Yet combined with the rulers' policy of "divide and rule," that system also

> fostered *esprit de parti*. . . . The royal tactics turned the administration hierarchy into a hothouse of disharmony, suspicion, animosity, and underhanded plotting. The kings inadvertently encouraged the very paralyzing intraservice strife against which they often thundered. In fact,

they converted the bureaucracy into an informer- and spy-ridden association.[83]

This aspect has to be kept firmly in mind along with the facts concerning the social composition of the service. For all the social cohesiveness and shared consciousness of superior social status that linked noble and nonnoble bureaucrats, the eighteenth-century civil service remained ridden with social conflicts not only among the elites of the several branches of the dynastic service but also between aristocrats and burghers. Moreover, commoners of high-service rank might aspire to nothing more than to be accepted into the circle of nobility; they might take on the mentality and manner of their social superiors and, in doing so, facilitate "the diffusion of a sense of aristocratic status within the bureaucratic elite as a group."[84] However, to recognize that there were forces tending to override the differences between aristocrats and burghers should not lead us in the end to forget persistent cleavages. Rosenberg's study, aiming to show how a relatively cohesive bureaucratic elite managed to emancipate itself from royal tutelage, deals with these cleavages but always ends up stressing cohesion and communalization within the bureaucracy. Thus, civil service reform is regarded as a strategy of emancipation from royal tutelage—a strategy emerging from a shared collective consciousness between aristocrats and burghers. Aiming to show that the persistent conflict between aristocrats and burghers was significant in the civil service reform, I am more alive to the persisting social cleavages within the bureaucracy.

In the remainder of this section we will complete the analysis of Prussia's system of limited competition by focusing on the series of reforms that culminated in the civil service reform of 1770. One might well treat the reform of 1770 as the first in a series of changes culminating in the reform period of the early nineteenth century. I am arguing, however, that the reform of 1770 was really a "reform before the reform": although formal education became more prominent than ever before, it still played second fiddle to practical experience; and for all the lip service paid to the importance of a good education, the reform did not require specific educational requirements for entry into in-service training. We will first examine the pioneering reform in the judicial service and then focus on the circumstances surrounding the adoption of the judicial model in the civil service.

I am arguing that the judicial reform was part and parcel of a scheme aimed at bringing the judiciary under dynastic control whereas the civil service reform was meant to *keep* the bureaucracy under the control of a king no longer able to pay attention to every single appointment. Forced to delegate authority by the sheer growth of the dynastic establishment, the king opted for standardization of employment conditions so as to limit the delegated authority of his bureaucratic chiefs. In practice, largely because educational requirements were vague, the examination system of 1770 provided ample opportunity for the bureaucratic top echelon to screen out socially incompatible candidates, thus frustrating the aspirations of the educated middle class.

Frederick William I issued a series of decrees regulating examinations for all types of judicial servants. In 1713 already he specified that judges be examined and not be placed until they had demonstrated their ability by writing a sample legal brief (*Proberelation*). Inexperienced men fresh from the university might be accepted without the test but only as unpaid trainees without voice or vote on the judicial boards. Ten years later, prospective advocates and judges were warned that they must not only have attended a university but also have completed their disputations and be duly certified by the university.[85] In 1737, finally, an edict once more codified the basic conditions of employment. Although the details are unimportant for our purpose, the opening paragraph of the edict is worth quoting in part.

> As ordered already in Our General Judicial Regulation, Our judicial boards and courts shall be staffed entirely with university-trained and experienced servants, yet . . . up til now many judicial servants were lacking the necessary qualifications and were thus a burden to the boards as well as to the country. Hence We were motivated to resolve that henceforth better attention be given to the placement of judicial servants and that they shall not be appointed without a strict prior examination and ability demonstrated by a solid sample legal brief.[86]

The king's resolve was perfunctory, to say the least. During the rest of his reign, no serious examinations were held, and the prerequisite of legal training was disregarded in many appointments, particularly of nobles. Despite Minister Cocceji's protests, the king continued to sell places on the bench for thousands of thalers irrespective of a noble candidate's education or professional experience.[87] As a result, the judiciary fell deeper into a state of ignorance, abuse, and venality and was regarded as corrupt even by the less exacting standards of the time. The king might thunder against the proponents of the traditional system, entrenched as they still were in the judiciary, that "they attempt by all sorts of ways and methods to make profits or gain means of support at the expense of the public."[88] He might bemoan the fact that his judicial servants did "not have the proper qualifications."[89] But he was not quite ready to move against them in their stronghold and enforce his decrees. Indeed, he contributed in no small measure to the venality of the system by selling places for so high a price that, naturally, the investors, too, had to inflate the take from fees and fines and favors. In any case, here was another institutional sphere spawning disinclination to pursue a higher education. Like the reformed army, the unreformed judiciary did much to depress the education of the aristocracy. If the army appealed especially to less well-to-do nobles, the choice posts in the judiciary drew the wealthy who were able to afford the finest education but who did not need it to make their way in the courts.

The reform of the system of training and examination of judicial personnel was completed early in the reign of Frederick II and found its culmination in the inauguration of a permanent Judicial Examination Commission two weeks after Cocceji's death in 1755. The judicial examination, also known as the great state examination, was designed to test a candidate's theoretical and practical knowledge of the law. It was administered in three parts. The first part, an oral test of legal theory, was administered to a candidate fresh from the university before he was accepted as an unpaid in-service trainee. Then followed an apprenticeship of roughly four to five years, upon completion of which a candidate for a judgeship had to take the other two parts of his examination. One of these was a sample legal brief (*Proberelation*) to be written on a case pending before a court. The other was another oral test combined with a defense of the brief. If the candidate passed, he was placed on a waiting list as an active candidate for a regular, paid appointment.

Two social results of Cocceji's reform are important for the purpose of this study. First, the combination of university studies and unpaid in-service training for a period of four to five years limited candidates to men from relatively well-to-do backgrounds. Second, the social structure of higher education gave the middle class a considerable advantage over the nobility and, in fact, resulted in a marked increase of judges drawn from the bourgeoisie.

The first social result was in fact anticipated. In a royal rescript of 1751 to the high courts in East Prussia, the king warned parents against preparing their sons for a judicial career unless they could afford to support them for many years after completion of their son's university training.

> Since we . . . have noticed that many parents who have neither the means nor the subsidies . . . to let their children study [the law] and who are even less able to support them four to five years as . . . in-service trainees, nevertheless send them to the university. We wish to give them the well-meant counsel to save time and expense by urging their children to prepare for commerce or agriculture or some other art, especially since We have serious reservations anyway about employing in the Justice Department councillors who lack financial means whatever.[90]

The general regulations of 1755 were even more explicit.

> It will not be appropriate that in-service trainees be poor and unable to afford the expense of travel [to Berlin, where they will be examined]. This should be considered in advance, so that they may devote themselves to military service, business, commerce, or to training for another art or the clergy. Besides, we have reservations to entrust to the Justice Department poor people such as this.[91]

This warning applied to poor noblemen as well as to poor burghers. As to the well-to-do nobility, the new regulations were spiked with warnings that noble birth alone was no longer sufficient qualification for judicial office.

> Although We will always prefer Our nobility, it is self-understood that noble subjects must also have the necessary qualifications; hence they should emphasize solid studies in legal theory rather than the so-called gallant studies they have emphasized up til now. For if there is an opening and we find someone from the bourgeoisie who has achieved greater capacity because of diligence, application, and experience, We shall not be bound to the nobility nor to the proportion of nobles but will consider only merit. Therefore parents will henceforth remind and admonish their children to make good use of their time at the university.[92]

It is difficult to assess whether these admonitions bore any fruit at all inasmuch as we do not have a series of statistics on the social composition of student bodies in the law faculties of the Prussian universities. But considering the fact that the reform changed the social composition of the judiciary to the detriment of nobles below the top echelons, that is, the presidents of the courts, it would seem that the royal admonitions went largely unheeded.

Although in one place Rosenberg suggests that Cocceji's reforms "refrained from seriously attacking the aristocratic social structure of the legal system," in another he explains that "Cocceji carried out a purge of the judiciary by checking the credentials and by personally testing the professional performance of numerous judges." He goes on to say, "For all prospective bench members he introduced, as a matter of principle, prescribed university training. He also stiffened entrance examinations."[93] Cocceji, in fact, did not attack the social-legal inequalities between the status groups but wrote them into the Prussian code. However, his reform of training and appointment of judicial personnel did change the social structure of the judicial administration. The reform and subsequent policy may not have drastically changed the social composition of the highest echelon in the judiciary. But below the presidents of the courts, the proportion of bourgeois judges increased sharply. Why was this so?

There can be no doubt that Frederick II would have liked to fill all vacancies, of judges and presidents alike, with nobles if only he could have found qualified men. Although favoring the nobility, he reiterated that there were limits to the priority of social status over professional qualification.

> If a court presidency, directorship, or judgeship falls vacant and we cannot find anyone among the nobility who has the required capacity for the position, then we will consider merit rather than noble descent and consequently prefer those from the middle class; therefore it will have to be impressed upon those children of the nobility who intend to follow a judicial career that, if they do not apply themselves to their studies and acquire a solid background in jurisprudence at the university, they can have no hope of being promoted.[94]

When Cocceji promoted a qualified commoner to the presidency of a high court and the nobility protested to the king that the appointment should have gone to a nobleman, Frederick II replied that this was neither the first nor the last time that merit ranked above social status.[95] The king pressed Cocceji constantly to fill vacancies with noblemen to a larger extent than he managed to do, and Cocceji almost pleaded with the estates "to propose to His Majesty a few *Subjecta* who have sufficient experience *in theoria et praxi,* such as is required in the new regulations."[96] On one occasion he wrote,

> In order that the youth of the nobility henceforth have an opportunity to enter the service upon coming from the university, His Royal Majesty has ordered that several of them might be employed as in-service trainees. But to this hour no one has come forth. Since the gentlemen of the noble estates are concerned that young noblemen be drawn to the king's service in the judiciary, I will leave it to the kind consideration of my most honorable lords whether they will deign to select a few capable *Subjecta* for the purpose.[97]

On this occasion, he was lucky. A young nobleman, said to have studied jurisprudence for three years at Halle, was nominated, and Cocceji, replying, asked that he be referred to an examiner. On that occasion, he, too, stressed how important it was "that young nobles be admonished to study the law in a solid manner and not only take up the so-called gallant studies."[98] On another occasion the king expressed doubt whether two noble nominees for presidencies were sufficiently qualified for the job. In his reply to the king, Cocceji summed up the basic problem. "Your Royal Majesty cannot believe how difficult it is to find the kinds of presidents nowadays demanded by Your Majesty. For thirty years, the nobility has neglected its studies because it has devoted itself to military service."[99] Loath to fill the presidencies with commoners, the king was often forced to disregard his policy and in fact prefer status over merit.

Finally, Rosenberg suggests that Cocceji's reform of the judiciary was a sort of negotiated settlement with the aristocratic defenders of the old system. Co-opted into the bureaucratic fold, the estates retained considerable influence over appointments, even footing part of the salary bill for the new bureaucratized judiciary. In his view, the significance of the reform was that it maintained the ideological, political ties between the judiciary and the landed nobility even though its personnel might be largely bourgeois. The new judicial officers might henceforth be "royal servants and *mostly nonnobles*," but the reform "maintained the traditional, intimate alliance with the landed interests."[100] This view has considerable merit. The judiciary as a whole, change as its social composition might below the noble top echelon, remained a guardian of conservative landed interests down to the reform period in the beginning of the nineteenth century, when the conservative "party" opposing the reform "party" was drawn heavily from the judiciary.[101] Yet it is interesting to note that commoners might hold rather liberal opinions when their own interests were at stake even though they might be serving in a rather conservatively oriented branch of the Prussian service.

Cocceji never abolished the ancient division of the courts into two benches, one for nobles, the other for nonnoble, "learned" jurists. Nor did he abolish the traditional rule giving occupants of the nobiliary bench precedence over occupants of the "learned" bench. Cocceji, asserting the crown's absolute discretion in appointing judges, asserted also the prerogative of the crown to appoint bourgeois judges to the noble bench and nobles to the "learned" bench. This circumstance led to a protest by nonnoble judges who interpreted the crown's practice of appointing commoners to the noble bench as a de facto abolition of the segregated benches and, hence, also of the ancient rule which gave nobles, as occupants of the noble bench, precedence over "learned" bourgeois judges. Cocceji's successor (the case came up in 1763) rejected this interpretation and reaffirmed the crown's discretion to appoint judges to either bench regardless of social status. That fascinating exchange between the justice department and nonnoble judges of a provincial court made clear that noble colleagues were indeed more equal in the judicial service; yet it also would seem to indicate that nagging social antagonism might erupt in an otherwise cohesive and, on the whole, conservative interest group.[102] In a way, this minor skirmish of bourgeois judges against the top echelon of the justice department is a paradigm of the civil service reform of the nineteenth century; from the point of view of the middle class, the issue of reform was at best a matter of equality of opportunity within the service, and that point of contention was eminently compatible with a whole range of social and political interests which noble and nonnoble bureaucrats might share.

While Cocceji's reform of the judiciary in the 1740s and 1750s made university legal studies a requirement in the judicial service, the civil service retained its emphasis on practical experience. In the 1760s, however, there was a noticeable shift to an emphasis on education, but even the civil service reforms of 1770 did not make education an indispensable prerequisite for appointment.

So long as higher education was not a prerequisite for appointment to the higher civil service, it was possible for subaltern officials to rise to executive positions if they had distinguished themselves in the administration of domains, the collection of taxes, in military quartermaster functions, and, of course, in the king's secretariat, the so-called cabinet. Both Frederick William I and Frederick II liked to promote men who had shown diligence, competence, and loyalty in positions which became a distinctly lower career rung once university training became more common after 1770 and, in fact if not in yet in law, a prerequisite of many positions in the higher civil service.

In the first half of the eighteenth century already there is evidence of concern that the expanding higher civil service might not be staffed entirely with men coming up from the ranks. The civil service, it was felt, ought to establish a sort of executive training program in order to create a pool of competent and loyal candidates for councillorships in the General Directory and provincial Boards of War and Domains. During the 1720s and 1730s, the king instructed provincial boards to take in two noble and two bourgeois in-service trainees who, serving without pay, would learn the business of the boards under the eyes of experienced councillors. They would be considered eventually for paid positions as war, tax, or domain councillors.[103] It was not supposed that these executive trainees should have attended a university. The king merely wanted "young people" with "agile and open minds" and some experience in agriculture or commerce. Although a cabinet order of 1743 recommended some studies in cameralistics, lectures which were open to men who did not have the educational qualifications for matriculation at a university, the chief requirement was still practical experience.[104] In 1748 an instruction concerning the employment conditions of in-service trainees required one year of prior service at a domain, where the candidate was to have learned all aspects of agriculture. He was to be examined by the president of the board in which he wished to be trained, and presidents were to send annual reports of the progress and prospects of in-service trainees as well as subaltern officials. To indicate that these regulations were no departure from existing personnel policies, a significant comment was added. "Since the best people are generally those who serve from the bottom up, His Royal Majesty is not disinclined to advance those secretaries who are able people, who worked hard, conducted themselves well, and have done their duty faithfully and honestly."[105]

In the first half of the eighteenth century, it seems to have been difficult to attract in-service trainees with the proper qualifications. There were relatively few trainees, and some boards had none at all.[106] Concerned to expand the pool of candidates for higher civil service posts, the king instructed all provincial boards in 1738 to find out whether there were any suitable subjects in their provinces.

> The list of nobles sent to me suggest that here and there some noblemen might be useful in Our service at this time or in the future. Hence We command you herewith to investigate thoroughly and without delay what kinds of young noblemen who are military officers neither in Our service nor in a foreign one are presently residing in your province and what kinds are presently residing in foreign lands. What is their capacity and conduct? Are they devoting themselves to education or to what else are they inclined? Not least in what position in Our service might they be employed? You are requested to send information of this kind to Our General Directory as soon as possible and to continue sending it each year because We wish to have the best possible knowledge of the nobility in your province. . . . We also wish to be informed whether there might be persons of bourgeois status, including leaseholders of domains, who have talent in matters of cameralistics and the commissariat, and who have the capacity to be usefully employed in the Boards of War and Domains in the near future. . . .[107]

In the 1750s in-service training became popular—also with university-trained men for whom the institution provided a welcome opportunity to acquire the practical experience needed for a career in the higher civil service. Rather than serving as subaltern officials or secretaries, they preferred in-service training, if they could afford it, inasmuch as there was a presumption that promotion to a higher position would be forthcoming in a few years' time. Yet this popularity of in-service training was no cause for satisfaction. Frederick II complained repeatedly that the boards had altogether too many in-service trainees. He even rejected the application of a young noble who had attended the university of Königsberg "because there are already so many in-service trainees and because they are asking His Royal Majesty for promotions to positions as war councillor the moment they are accepted."[108] He also expressed repeatedly his dissatisfaction with the performance of young men fresh from the university. "The experience of the past few years has taught me," he wrote, "that people like that succeed rarely, that most of the time they catch on badly, yet, whether able or not, they demand to be placed as councillors once they have served a few years at a board."[109] He tended to think that university men, especially if they were nonnobles, ought to serve as secretaries or subaltern officials.[110] On one occasion he suggested that a young applicant be placed as a secretary. If he proved to be able, he might be promoted to a higher post at some future date.[111] On another occasion he wrote to the president of a provincial board.

> As to the young people you wish to recommend as in-service trainees at the board, I will answer you that they would do better if they were sent to a domain and a capable leaseholder to learn the basics of the entire economy as well as its praxis rather than to an administrative board where they can be used only for a few tasks, and therefore get habituated to a kind of laziness, which afterwards stays with them almost for the rest of their lives. Moreover, I do not like to see the boards filled up with such young people, for that deprives me to a certain degree of the opportunity to place able, experienced, and mature regimental quartermasters and auditors who are already used to work and who may be useful immediately, whereas not much may be expected of said young people for many years to come.[112]

By the 1760s Cocceji's reform of the judiciary was bearing fruit. The caliber of the judiciary improved markedly as the system of university training, in-service training, and examinations was raising a new generation of competent judges. And so by the middle of the 1760s the civil service administration was looking to the justice department as a model. In 1765 the General Directory recommended that the educational qualifications of prospective in-service trainees be examined more closely. The civil service, it suggested, was in great need of "subjects who have a good education and who possess natural ability, ambition, drive, and honesty to become useful to the state." They should be given thorough knowledge and experience during in-service training so that they might be placed following an examination "as it is done with success in the Justice Department." It suggested again that in-service training had fallen short of expectations in the past, but the reasons given were somewhat different. The shortcomings were blamed partly on insufficient attention given to prior education and ability and partly to insufficient instruction during in-service training. Hence, the General Directory instructed the provincial boards to select candidates, nobles and nonnobles, more carefully, to "examine them regarding their capacity and education," to keep examining them semiannually while in training, and to send protocols of the examinations to Berlin.[113] This rescript signaled a shift in emphasis toward educational qualifications, which was to mark the civil service reform of 1770.

In Minister Hagen's reform plan, submitted to the king in 1770, the shift in policy was clearly expressed. The civil service, Hagen argued, needed "subjects who already have a good education and knowledge of the law, of mathematics and practical physics, of mechanics as well as of the whole and parts of agriculture." In the past,

> appointments in the financial and cameral fields were not made in a manner serving the purpose and solid interest of the prince (*Landesvater*) and of the conservation of all status groups because many servants, nobles as well as burghers, were lacking the above-mentioned knowledge and ability and were thinking that the deficiency might be compensated with routine in actual service.[114]

From now on, administrative boards "must work harder to recruit young, able, and lively people as in-service trainees, and to examine them thoroughly before they are recommended for appointment to determine whether they have acquired a basis of scientific knowledge."[115]

The reforms of 1770 were aimed at improving not only examinations at the point of entry into in-service training but also examinations at the point of entry into a regular employment. For the latter purpose, the reform established a standing civil service commission, which was to administer the major portion of the civil service test much as the Judicial Examination Commission administered the great judicial state examination. Candidates for positions as war, domains, and tax councillors were henceforth required to write two sample briefs on cameral matters and draft a complete assessment of a domain. In addition, an oral examination before the civil service commission was to "test thoroughly their knowledge of all parts of finance, of natural law, and other sciences related to finance." It was ordered "that no one who has not passed the examination in the prescribed manner will be admitted . . . and no one, regardless of status or background, shall be dispensed from taking the examination."[116]

In a rescript to the newly appointed civil service commission, the king and his ministers noted that now and then people had been admitted to the civil service who were lacking the necessary ability, scientific knowledge, and judgment and that the new commission was to remedy such deficiencies "in the same way as it was done successfully already in the judicial service."[117] The ministers von Fürst and von Münchhausen received a copy of this rescript with a letter asking what other measures might be employed to upgrade the civil service and "to motivate young people to attend universities, gymnasia, and schools."[118]

Although there can be little doubt that the emphasis in appointment was shifting to educational considerations, the reform of 1770 did not establish precise educational qualifications nor a determinate course of prior study. It merely required "a good education" and charged the new commission to test candidates in subjects which were in fact taught at the universities but which might also be studied independently, with a tutor, in a nobiliary academy or by attending a few public lectures in cameralistics. The reform, though critical of the emphasis on in-service routine and the exclusively practical orientation of the past, was still beholden to the older view that the necessary "scientific knowledge" might be acquired by a candidate during in-service training. It was not until the final phase of Prussian civil service reform, which will be the subject of Chapter 4, that a university education became an indispensable prerequisite of access to the higher civil service. Nevertheless, it appears that the shift to educational considerations inserted a wedge between subaltern careers and careers in the higher civil service, for the latter was staffed increasingly with former in-service trainees who had attended a university.

The reforms of 1770 resulted from a number of interrelated conditions. First, the royal bureaucracy, like the army, expanded considerably during the eighteenth century, and it became increasingly impossible for the king to give attention to every single appointment. In reading the documents pertaining to appointments over the decades, one gains the impression that in the first half of the century, the king was rather well acquainted with the men nominated for appointments. Many of them were, in fact, sons and relations of royal servants. In the second half of the eighteenth century more background information is provided by department heads, and by 1770 lists of proposed appointments sent to the king for approval were considerably longer and might have a marginal comment suggesting that approval was given even though "of all these proposed subjects I do not know a single one and therefore must rely entirely upon your testimony concerning their ability."[119] Nor was the civil service the only dynastic sphere in which the staff became too large for the king to be personally acquainted with it. When Frederick II inspected the regiments of his growing army, it happened occasionally that he did not know this or that young officer. To the consternation of the young lieutenants, he assumed that any officer he did not recognize must be a burgher and sometimes ordered on the spot that he be transferred to a garrison regiment.

The days of patrimonialism in hiring and promotion were coming to an end. Now that the king had to rely on the judgment of his ministers and they on the judgment of their subordinates, it became imperative to develop universalistic standards of judgment in place of the king's discretion and a permanent method of examination in place of the traditional ad hoc referrals to this or that examiner. Indeterminate standards of judgment, such as the king had applied—as often as not to frustrate patronage nominations by his subordinates—would no longer do. For if the growth of the dynastic establishment decentralized decision making, it also threatened to give the patronage system of appointment a new lease on life. Educational attainments, though not in themselves a guarantee of a candidate's likely success in the civil service, promised at least a degree of standardized decision making, which might compensate a little for the loss of the king's ability to counteract the force of family and faction by means of royal discretion. Besides, had the reforms of the judicial service not done much to upgrade the caliber of the judges and bring the judiciary under dynastic control? Perhaps this remarkable change in a service which had been a hotbed of nepotism and venality, cavalier independence and professional ignorance evoked second thoughts in Frederick II, who, like his father, was generally inclined to value practical experience above theoretical knowledge.

The civil service reform of 1770, as Rosenberg points out, "was a landmark in the process of growing corporate independence of the bureaucracy."[120] Yet it is far from clear that the reform was a strategy of the bureaucratic elite aiming to wrest the power of appointment from the king. The scant documentary evidence is consistent also with the view that the king, no longer able to exercise that power and forced to delegate it, opted for standardizing employment conditions and for more "objective," educational qualifications. This view is supported by Rosenberg's own account of the pressure brought to bear on the bureaucratic leadership by Frederick II, who blamed his chiefs for the decline in discipline, loyalty, efficiency, and morale during the Seven Years' War.[121] Thus, when he taunted his chiefs for their "vile disposition," "criminal indolence," "obdurate trickery," and "infamous interests," or when he pressured them to raise the professional caliber and reliability of the civil service along the lines of the judiciary, the king might have wished not only to raise the efficiency of the service but also to limit the discretion of his chiefs in making appointments—to limit that discretion in order to check the tendency to patronage appointments, nepotism, and faction-building, which decentralization of hiring and promotion was likely to enhance.

Whichever interpretation one prefers, one thing is clear, however. The new examination system gave much scope to the new civil service commission precisely because employment conditions remained rather indeterminate. Since educational requirements were not very well specified and since the "scientific" subject matter areas in which candidates were to be tested were stated only in vague terms, the new system of examination might indeed be used by the bureaucratic leadership as "a wonderful device for consolidating its control over personnel recruitment and for gaining greater freedom from royal molestation in this crucial area."[122] Indeterminate standards apart, the new system enabled examiners to discriminate against a candidate with superior educational credentials and to favor one who had better social and political qualifications. This was so because the new system tested only whether a particular candidate was minimally qualified for the job. It did not establish an open, competitive test of a large number of candidates at a time and a rank order among them according to their relative achievement on the test. Besides, as in the judicial service, unpaid in-service training and sizable examination fees discriminated against the vast majority of university students who might have had superior educational qualifications but who were lacking the independent means necessary even to contemplate a higher civil service career. The new system had a competitive ring; yet in practice it allowed competition to be severely limited by social considerations, thus giving nepotism and favoritism a new lease on life.

Finally, this circumstance enhanced the existing friction between nobles and nonnobles. The advantages enjoyed by men with the proper social qualifications in the new examination system, dominated as it was by the noble top echelon of Frederick's regime, enhanced also the resentment of burghers who often surpassed their noble superiors in education and professional skills and who were wont to feel that they were doing the real work while their superiors were taking the credit for it.[123] In the years after 1770, especially after Frederick's death in 1782, it was not unusual, according to a defender of the superior claims of noble status, "to appoint bourgeois councillors with the prudent intent to make work easier for noble councillors so that the latter will have time for more important matters," that is, for "governing" rather than departmental routine.[124] In the light of this practice, it is no paradox that the minister von Hagen, who boasted that he never read a printed line, should be the author of the civil service reform of 1770.[125] After 1770, some men advanced primarily because of their social status whereas others, whom the former needed, advanced because of their professional qualifications. In any case, the examination system of 1770, designed to standardize employment conditions and raise the caliber of the civil service profession turned out to be an effective device for social and political screening. As we shall see in Chapter 4, social considerations became even more salient during the noble reaction in the era of the French Revolution, as did the resentment of qualified, low-born men who were held back by a system that was said to favor merit over status.

The Social Structure of Education

The efflorescence of court life after the Thirty Years' War signaled a new cultural orientation at variance with the scholastic traditions of the universities. German territorial princes, great and small, were modernizing on the model of the French court. They promoted French as the language of polite society, and they patronized the arts and such "modern" disciplines of learning as mathematics, science, engineering, architecture, and history. All of these were strangers in the world of the old universities. Only political-constitutional theory and cameralistics were gradually introduced into faculties of law. Establishment intellectuals, who would have nothing to do with the old universities, derided their sterile, "medieval" scholasticism. Aware of the contempt of princes and polite societies for "pedantic scholars" and anxious to promote schemes for the education of mankind, they wrote convincing tracts showing that universities, utterly useless remnants of the past, were beyond reform.

The well-known cleavage between the cultural preferences of eighteenth-century court society and the preferences of the old universities was accompanied by a bifurcation of educational institutions. For as the new royal academies were established primarily to promote "useful" scientific inquiry, so new teaching institutions were established to promote an education more modern and useful to dynastic designs than the instruction offered in municipal grammar schools and universities. Aside from specialized academies for the training of military doctors, engineers, architects, and so forth, the new institutions included also princely boarding schools offering a general, modern advanced education. Although some new princely boarding schools in other parts of Germany might accept select young men of middle-class origin, the Prussian equivalents were from the start reserved for nobles. Universities and grammar schools, on the other hand, were regarded as institutions mostly for the bourgeoisie. Although Frederick II encouraged young noblemen to attend universities after the reform of the judiciary, the military pattern set before his time and, indeed, the military values of the enlightened Frederick himself continued to impede the flow of nobles into "bourgeois" educational institutions.

In the present section we will survey first the new institutions for the education of the aristocracy and then turn to the institutions of learning in the bourgeois sphere. The purpose of this survey is to highlight the educational ramifications of that social-legal cleavage between the status groups which, as suggested in the second section, was largely a function of the militarization of the Prussian aristocracy.

Around the turn of the seventeenth century, a number of nobiliary academies were established in various German principalities. Princes were interested in cultivating their company by raising the indigenous nobility to the standards of international gentle society. They were interested in diffusing among their nobles some of the "scientific" knowledge related to changes in military technology. They may have wished also to indoctrinate young gentlemen in the ways of absolute monarchy. At the same time, European noblemen were occasionally complaining that there were no schools for the education of gentlemen and that it would be decidedly improper to send them to Latin grammar schools. After all, these were schools for socializing academics, clergymen, and learned jurists—all occupations which were of no interest to the landed nobility. Although a nobleman might attend a university to acquire some legal knowledge, it was thought that he should have received a proper status education to begin with. Much of the Prussian nobility, however, was either unable or disinclined to educate their children expensively. Many of them were unable to afford the private instruction and foreign travel which was prescribed by the ideal of gentlemanly education, and many of them, most likely, had little taste for learning. Demeter suggests that the new nobiliary academies mushrooming around the turn of the seventeenth century were part of a broader European effort at buttressing a gentry threatened with decline owing to economic depression, changes in military technology, and the exigencies of absolutist statecraft, which drew many new men into offices under the crown.[126] I suspect, however, that the rulers of Brandenburg-Prussia from the Great Elector to Frederick William I were especially attracted to a form of noble education that might be supervised so as to generate nobles loyal to the dynastic cause.

Whatever the motivation, the new institutions of higher learning exclusively for nobles were meant to be a good deal more than military academies or finishing schools of courtly manners. Aside from military subjects and "gallant studies" such as riding, fencing, and dancing, they were to offer courses in modern language, mathematics, natural science, political theory, history, and cameralistics by the best teachers of these modern disciplines. In fact, they were to provide an alternative to the education of the universities—a useful, modern education for gentlemen destined to be employed in the service of the government. Frederick II carried the idea so far as to think his nobiliary academy might eventually train the bulk of a new breed of scholarly (*gelehrte*) noble official. Yet the new nobiliary academies were not very successful, least of all the Prussian ones. Scholarly education fell regularly behind military education and "gallant studies"; students did not take to the new schools enthusiastically; and in many cases it took the fringe benefits of the court, in the vicinity of which the schools were located, to get them to attend at all. Announcements typically described the amenities of the court in the most enticing terms. The new academy at Wolfenbüttel, for example, promised that the young gentlemen scholars would be invited "to frequent the princely court" and attend "*divertissements,* balls, and the like so that they might learn *honnêtes conversations.*" Besides, they would have access to horses and riding arenas, dancing and fencing masters, and other facilities of the court.[127] Although it is not clear whether these promises helped admissions, it became painfully clear that students were too ill-prepared to follow lectures held in the manner of the university. Masters, expecting to be associated with institutions of higher learning, found themselves teaching the basics of reading, writing, and arithmetic.

The first Prussian nobiliary academy was established in Pomerania the moment the Swedish occupation was withdrawn. The Great Elector evidently regarded the new school as a welcome instrument for welding that newly acquired territory to his hereditary lands. Although the school seems to have been successful initially, it declined shortly thereafter, certainly in the area of higher education, and was closed in 1701. It was replaced by a unit of the corps of cadets, which did not pretend to offer much more than elementary education. However, the idea of a higher nobiliary academy was not abandoned, and four years later a new one was established in Berlin. The bulletin of this new academy suggested that admission was confined to "princes, counts, and gentlemen, though of no lesser status than nobility." Since the prince wished to do something about "the great shortcoming" of the education of young gentlemen, instruction was to go considerably beyond riding, dancing, and fencing.

His Royal Majesty has ordered most graciously to call upon the best and most famous professors to teach the fashionable youth all decent sciences, namely Studio Morali, Politico, Jure Naturae, Jure Publico, Arte Heraldica, Noticia Genealogiae, and Praetensorium Illustrium; also Philosophia as well as Experimenta Physica; moreover, all parts of Mathesi such as Arithmetica, Geometrica, Mechanica, Optica, Gnomonica, Fortification and Architecture; furthermore, Drawing and Perspective . . . Languages, too, shall be taught, in particular Latin, French, Italian, Spanish, and also pure German.[128]

Once again, the program was extremely ambitious and entirely in keeping with the modern educational orientation. Yet once again, the project was a failure almost from the start. Asked to submit opinions in 1711, the few remaining professors and masters suggested some of the problems. Teachers, whose salaries were apparently paid most irregularly if at all, had left in a hurry or were forced to make a living on the side. Students found galant studies and gentle pastimes more interesting than science and simply refused to learn. Everyone was bitterly disappointed: professors because they had been degraded to common schoolmasters on account of their students' deficient elementary education; students because they had not been invited to court as frequently as promised in the invitation. Two years later the school was closed. Still another one was established to take its place, but its future was scarcely brighter. In 1723 the director had to inform the king that the academy had unfortunately degenerated into a riding school.[129]

After the Seven Years' War, still another attempt was made to found an institution of higher learning exclusively for aristocrats destined to serve the state. The school, variously referred to as *Académie des Nobles, Académie Royal des Gentilhommes, Académie Militaire,* and even *Ecole Militaire,* was to train students not only for the military but also for the civil service and, especially, for the reorganized diplomatic corps. Young gentlemen were to learn Latin (at a closeby municipal grammar school) and the whole spectrum of modern science, philosophy, and art from a brilliant faculty composed primarily of Frenchmen who had been recommended by D'Alambert and Condorcet. Once again, the great expectations were not fulfilled. The exorbitant costs dwarfed the educational payoff, which came largely in the coin of military education. Frederick William II (1786–1797) was most dissatisfied and, resigned to the purely military character of the school, placed it under the command of the General Board of War. Scharnhost, the future reformer of the Prussian officer corps, thought that from its inception the institution had been saddled with an irreconcilable conflict between "academic" and military functions. Frederick II, he suggested, "intended to train [in the academy] the main force of scholars (*Gelehrten*) as well as military men," though it seems obvious that "few people are able to excel in both branches of learning."[130]

The corps of cadets, ranking below the nobiliary academies, were more significant for the education of the aristocracy. While the nobiliary academy graduated only five students per year from 1765 to 1786, the cadet corps graduated approximately seventy corpsmen per year during the reign of Frederick II.[131] Although the corps attempted to furnish a general education, the instruction was in fact confined largely to elementary education. Elementary education might be augmented by subjects like mathematics, engineering, and geography, which were considered relevant to the military arts of artillery, fortification, and tactics; it might be augmented also by French and the gallant studies of fencing, riding, and dancing; but there was no question that military education and training had priority. Tharau, a recent defender of the culture and education of the old Prussian officer, suggests that the corps of cadets offered "a solid foundation for the acquisition of a personal intellectual culture" to any prospective officer "who wished to educate himself further."[132] Yet the evidence he gives is also consistent with the view that prominent, well-educated officers, who had graduated from the corps of cadets, acquired their "personal" education despite rather than because of their experience in the corps.

Finally, most of the eighteenth-century Prussian nobility attended neither a nobiliary academy nor the corps of cadets. The majority were educated at home and were trained as enlisted men or Junkers of a regiment. Only a small proportion turned to Latin grammar schools and universities. Unfortunately, there are no statistics indicating proportions over several decades. The only numbers I could find refer to young noblemen, eight years of age and up, who were being educated or trained in one way or other in 1800.[133] According to Martiny's calculations, 60 percent were being educated at home; 13 percent were in training in the military; 5 percent were in the corps of pages at court, the corps of cadets, or a military academy;

10 percent were attending private schools or municipal Latin grammar schools; 4 percent were studying at a university; and 5 percent were in-service trainees in government or commerce.[134] Although these figures are problematic because they include so many age groups, and although they prove little with respect to the extent or quality of the education of Prussian noblemen, they do suggest a striking preference for a combination of domestic education and military training which contrasts sharply with the educational preference of the English aristocracy and gentry to be examined in the next chapter. It should be remembered that the argument advanced in this study does not depend on a claim that the Prussian aristocracy was badly educated, only that it was educated in a way which placed its members at a disadvantage once attendance at Latin grammar schools and universities became a prerequisite for entry into the higher civil service.

In the remainder of this section, I will deal briefly with the adaptation of the universities to the changing recruitment needs of the dynastic bureaucracy and with the social composition of student bodies, particularly in the faculties of law, which were gaining prominence after the reforms of the judicial and civil service. Was there a significant influx of nobles into universities in the second half of the eighteenth century?

University reform in the eighteenth century was guided largely by the desire to transform universities into useful instruments of statecraft. This was true of Halle as well as of Göttingen, the two leading German universities, founded in 1694 and 1737, respectively.[135] Cameralists here and there viewed university management in the light of mercantile policy, and from that point of view there was no essential difference between commercial state enterprises and universities. This attitude is neatly reflected in a new term which cameralists coined to refer to the university: "the academic mine."[136] The products to be mined there were above all useful, knowledgeable officials no longer bound by notions of territorial particularism and traditional rights, but inspired by reason of state and the new public law. Like other state enterprises, the academic mine was run on mercantile, cameral principles. These justified government supervision of and interference with education and called for attracting students from far and wide while keeping natives at the local institutions. If government interference undermined academic freedom, attracting foreigners implied a degree of tolerance for controversy. For by cameral reasoning, a lively intellectual climate might be justified as good business. Thus, it is not altogether strange that eighteenth-century Prussia should have given birth to one of the two universities that were considered "modern" and progressive in their time. Lest it be supposed, however, that either of them was a haven of academic freedom, one need only recall that Christian Wolfe, who had joined the new University of Halle in 1709, was run out of town "on pain of the halter" after the king was informed by Wolfe's enemies that the philosopher was teaching "fatalistic doctrines." Paulsen thinks that Göttingen was more liberal than that but hastens to add that its apparent liberalism was possible only because Münchhausen, who directed university affairs, was carefully selecting professors and rejecting men who might be expected to raise a controversy.[137] However that may be, Halle and Göttingen incorporated many modern subjects of learning, including mathematics, science, modern language, geography, history, political theory, and cameralistics.

It has been suggested that these new subjects and the reform of legal curricula were largely responsible for a new influx of nobles into the universities. Referring to Göttingen, Paulsen writes,

> From all parts of Germany, particularly the west and the south, the fashionable youth assembled here; above all, there came princes, counts, and barons of the Holy Roman Empire to study Germanic Law, the history of the Empire and the states .... Thus Göttingen became the university of elegant society. Persons of standing and everyone with an interest in general culture was inevitably attracted to the new university.[138]

In both universities it became standard practice to rank professors—indeed the disciplines themselves—according to the number of gentlemen they attracted. Chroniclers of the new universities enumerated how many nobles the university had enrolled. Halle boasted two princes, seventy-six counts, 103 *Freiherrn*, and 1,200 nobles among the 9,433 students matriculated in law during the first thirty years, that is, from 1694 to 1724.[139] Göttingen claimed eleven princes, 148 counts, and 14,828 "others" during the first half century, that is, from 1739 to 1787.[140] Unfortunately, these numbers do not indicate whether the magnitudes were in fact remarkable. The only other data we have, presented in Tables 1 and 2, come from a

Table 1. *Social Origins of Students at the University of Halle*

	1785–1787	1820–1822
Landowners, military officers, and rentiers	6%	6%
Government officials and lawyers with university training	17%	13%
Professors, clergymen, and other professionals	31%	33%
Government officials and teachers without university training	14%	17%
Tradesmen and artisans	25%	24%
Farmers and peasants	3%	7%
Commercial clerks, workers, and servants	3%	1%

Source: Johannes Conrad, "Die Statistik der Universität Halle," in *Festschriften zum zweihundertjährigen Jubiläum der vereinigten Friedrichsuniversitäten Halle-Wittenberg* (Halle: Universität, 1894), p.30.

systematic study of the social backgrounds of students at the University of Halle in 1785–1787 and in 1820–1822.

If, during the first thirty years after the University of Halle was founded, 14 percent of the students in law were in fact nobles, then it is quite possible that there was a modest increase of noblemen in the second half of the eighteenth century. One thing is certain, however. The University of Halle was much less socially exclusive than Oxford and Cambridge. Much the same, I am sure, might be said of Königsberg and Frankfurt/Oder, the other two Prussian universities. Göttingen might well have attracted more nobles, but given the fact that Prussian noblemen were not allowed to attend foreign univesities, Göttingen cannot have made an important contribution to the education of the Prussian aristocracy.

By and large, the evidence seems to suggest that Frederick the Great and his ministers had good reason to urge young noblemen to attend universities but also that their urging was not very successful. On the eve of reform, born gentlemen were clearly in the minority even in the study of law, which ranked highest on the social scale. The social-legal gulf between the status groups was still matched by a gulf between educational patterns. Gentlemen were still neglecting their studies because they were devoting themselves to military

Table 2. *Social Origins of Students at the University of Halle:
Faculty of Law*

	1785–1787	1820–1822
Landowners, military officers, and renticrs	14%	16%
Government officials and lawyers with university training	41%	33%
Professors, clergymen, and other professionals	13%	17%
Government officials and teachers without university training	11%	11%
Tradesmen and artisans	16%	18%
Farmers and peasants	1%	4%
Commercial clerks, workers, and servants	3%	1%

Source: Johannes Conrad, "Die Statistik der Universität Halle," in *Festschriften zum zweihundertjärigen Jubiläum der vereinigten Friedrichsuniversitäten* Halle-Wittenberg (Halle: Universität, 1894), p. 31.

service. If more nobles were attending universities than in Cocceji's time, the difference certainly was not spectacular. A reform that would close access to the higher civil service to all but graduates of Latin grammar schools and universities could not but give the middle class an advantage, at least until the nobility would change its educational preferences. In England, as we shall see in the next chapter, the social structure of education was rather different. There, unlike in Prussia, the reformers had every reason to expect that civil service reform would give gentlemen a considerable advantage.

3. The English Historical Background

The general pattern of the English development turns on aristocracy and Paliament rising above the crown and operating the levers of patronage for the benefit of family and faction. In the second section of the present chapter the analysis will be extended to an account of the social and political functions of patronage, the sole method of recruitment to offices under the crown until well into the nineteenth century, administrative and political reforms notwithstanding. The third section will underscore the English aristocracy's turn to higher education, thus highlighting the sharp contrast with the educational pattern deriving from the militarization of aristocracy under the rising Prussian crown. The final section will analyze the expansion of the English conception of gentility, which facilitated the incorporation of those professionals and upper-middle-class men who had received the education of gentlemen at public schools and at Oxford and Cambridge. As we shall see in the next chapter, a virtual mirror process took place in Prussia, where status boundaries were fixed in law. There a small group of reform-minded, educated nobles joined a sort of "counter aristocracy," composed largely of middle-class academics, who in fact claimed that personal education was the knighthood of modernity.

The Historical Pattern

The sixteenth and seventeenth centuries witnessed the rise of royal absolutism on the continent. Everywhere the effective power of the

91

provincial assemblies, checking the fiscal appetite of the prince, was reduced, and expansive dynastic administration was encroaching on the politics of notables in the provinces. Although the Tudor monarchs of the sixteenth century also enhanced the stature of the crown, they were not absolute rulers, and their successors in the seventeenth century lost their bid for absolute power. Thus, while the French *états*, the German *Stände*, and the Russian *zemskii sobor* were declining in political significance, the English Parliament, the peculiar institution of the aristocracy and gentry, was limiting the prerogatives of the crown.

The older concept of "Tudor despotism" has virtually disappeared from English historiography and has given way to appreciation of the restrictions on the power of the crown. Lacking a standing army and a professional administration, the crown had to rely on the cooperation and consent of the aristocracy and gentry in local administration and in Parliament. Although the new prerogative courts and legal procedures derived from Roman law might be a forceful instrument of royal supervision, they did not displace the justices of the peace and the supremacy of common law. The latter was monopolized by an organized status group of barristers drawn from the same ranks of society as the justices and the members of the House of Commons. At the national center, parliaments had become an established, if not yet regular, feature of political life. Parliaments had to be summoned for the purpose of passing important legislation and, especially, granting of extraordinary taxes. Although the crown had the initiative and Parliament was not entitled to impose policies which the king did not wish to follow, the political constraints of the Tudor system were not favorable for royal absolutism.

For one thing, the crown was not strong enough to unleash so fundamental a change as the Reformation on its own but had to secure the cooperation of Parliament, thus enhancing the members' prestige and sense of their own importance. For another, the crown did not have an administrative arm with which to undermine the structure of local government. The local commissioners of the crown, particularly the justices of the peace, were anything but professional civil servants. Appointed by the crown but drawn largely from the ranks of the landed gentry, they were amateurs who administered without a salary though not without profit (for the fees of office were theirs) and certainly not without regard to the interests of their status groups. Since the crown could not have counted on the willing cooperation of these country gentlemen in collecting a non-parliamentary tax, it might as well ask Parliament, representing the same class of people, for their cooperation in voting a legitimate subsidy.

Although constrained by Parliament and local government, the power of the Tudor monarchy increased. Parliament underwrote a significant augmentation of the crown's financial resources when it cooperated in the confiscation of monasteries. It thus improved the ability of the crown to live on its own and to keep Parliament at arm's length for extended periods of time. More importantly, by improving also the crown's ability to reward loyal service, Parliament did much to increase the power of the king in securing the cooperation of Parliament when subsidies were needed, primarily for war. Still, the Tudor monarchs did not establish a permanent system of dominance over the Commons. The crown might strengthen its influence and effective power through a system of patronage and skillful management; it might attract the country establishment jockeying for favors at court; but the cooperation between local government and Parliament, on the one hand, and the court, on the other, was dependent in the final analysis on the solvency of royal finance. When the royal system of finance began to totter owing to severe inflation, the diminution of the crown's capital, the increasing cost of warfare, and, not least, the extravagance of Elizabeth's successor, the relative harmony between the court and the country during the sixteenth century came to an end.[1]

The English rulers of the seventeenth century were unable to control Parliament for long. They tried it by every imaginable means. They managed elections, tampered with borough franchises so as to reduce electorates, engaged in election frauds, and governed without Parliament as long as funds would last. They spared no effort in building a court party in Parliament by means of the crown's patronage, that is, pensions, sinecures, places, and honors. They augmented their finances by reorganizing customs farming, by levying emergency taxes every year, by coerced credits and foreign loans, and even by selling honors to the highest bidder. If the vast increases in royal income, say of Charles I, did not enable the king to dispense with Parliament forever, the reason was that the crown was still unable to meet the cost of war without the consent of Parliament. Parliament, in turn, understood how to exploit the crown's financial dependence and used it as a leverage for expanding the prerogatives of the legislature.

In the end, the crown, not for lack of trying, failed to overcome the two great obstacles to royal absolutism, Parliament and local government. The Revolution of 1688, coming after decades of confrontation and civil war, once again asserted the claim of the aristocracy and gentry to local independence and participation in the central affairs of the state. After the execution of Charles I and the flight of James II, specter of royal absolutism was much diminished. The landed classes were as secure in their localities as ever, and the Bill of Rights and the new Coronation Oath provided for regular, frequent parliaments and elections free from the influence of the king.

Now that Parliament met every year and elections were held regularly, once every three years from 1695 on, the political power of a seat in Commons became more secure and financially rewarding. Political investments were no longer threatened by the prospect of a short Parliament and new elections, and men were more inclined to advance larger sums to get elected in the expectation of government patronage. At the same time, English society was deeply divided after decades of conflict over religious and constitutional issues. In every county and borough Whigs and Tories vied with one another for control over the electorate and access to the myriad of jobs, pensions, sinecures, and other freeholds which would fall to the victorious party.

And so the political stability of oligarchic, one-party rule, the hallmark of the eighteenth century, did not come directly with the victory of Parliament. Indeed, it has been suggested recently that the struggle between competing parties of the ruling class over the rewards of parliamentary representation fanned party strife and the instability of heated electoral contests for several decades after the Glorious Revolution. Yet the underlying causes of that rage of party in the early eighteenth century also contained the seeds of oligarchy and a stable, expanded system of political patronage, which eventually dissolved party strife.[2]

The story of the decline of party and the rise of oligarchy is complex and cannot be dealt with in detail. However, it is useful to single out briefly two aspects which will help to delineate the outlines of the structure of politics and patronage that was to prevail from the middle of the eighteenth century to the eve of the civil service reforms in Victorian England. The first aspect was an increase in election costs. Inflation and the development of trade increased the number of voters in counties and boroughs. Controlling this expanding electorate became an ever-more expensive business, feasible only for men of substantial wealth. Ultimately, election costs were rising simply because contending parties were bargaining up the price they were willing to pay for "parliamentary property." That price became extremely high, especially after the Septennial Act of 1716. Extending the tenure of elected office to seven years, the act significantly increased the promise of returns from patronage. In any case, the increasingly large advances required by a successful political entrepreneur tended to crowd out minor competitors for parliamentary seats and local preeminence and tended to reduce them to clients, whose residual "interest" in a borough or county might be traded for *quelque chose de par le roi*. Parliamentary patrons, in return for support of a ministry, might expect some patronage for themselves to compensate them for their election outlays as well as something for their clients. Plumb argues that the promise of returns was the most important factor in enhancing party strife in the early decades of the eighteenth century and that the rising cost of electioneering was the most important factor in the rise of oligarchy. Party strife was enhanced up to a point where electioneering became "a hobby which only rich men could afford," whereupon party feelings dissolved in an expanded and settled system of political patronage.[3]

The second aspect of the rise of oligarchy was the expansion and centralization of patronage. Central administration expanded in the decades around the turn of the seventeenth century, particularly in the Treasury, which was also imposing its control over all previously independent agencies concerned with revenue and taxation. Similarly, the army and the navy (the largest one in Europe at the beginning of the eighteenth century) expanded dramatically and developed a more complex and numerous administrative apparatus. The number of government servants, Plumb suggests, "grew faster between 1689 and 1715 than in any previous period of English history, and perhaps at a rate not equalled again until the nineteenth century."[4] This expansion of central administration opened up new opportunities for patronage. At the same time, the ties between parliamentary government and the patronage of the court became stronger, and the Treasury was emerging as a central agency, coordinating not only the financial system as a whole but also the dispensation of the government's patronage. By the middle of the eighteenth century, parliamentary cabinets managed the majorities in Parliament through the sinecures, pensions, and jobs at the disposal of the Treasury. In the province, wealthy county and borough patrons controlled their clients and electorates by a steady flow of favors coming from the center. This, in broad outline, was the structure of politics and patronage that prevailed to the eve of reform in Victorian England. In the next section some of the details of this structure will be filled in so as to highlight the social and political ramifications of patronage—the chief method for recruiting men to government office until the introduction of civil service examinations.

Patronage and the Unreformed Civil Service

The English patronage system, like the patronage system in the northeast German territories before the rise of royal absolutism, was much more than a system of political rewards. It was also a "welfare system" of the aristocracy or, as the East Prussian estates referred to the offices under the crown, the aristocracy's greatest benefice. In the present section, we shall deal with the most important characteristics of the English patronage system of the unreformed civil service and with the modifications that were made in the decades around the turn of the eighteenth century. Despite these reforms, however, patronage appointments remained the sole method of recruiting men to public office until the reforms of the mid-Victorian era.

We sometimes forget that the public dole is a venerable institution, not an invention of the modern welfare state. What is modern about it is not only that the lower classes have gained access to it but also that they are often stigmatized for making applications. Until well into the nineteenth century, office holding in England was part of a "social security system" for families of gentle rank. Finding themselves in a financial pinch, they might apply to the king or his minister for some place or other favor, and they might add, as did

Lord Harrington in 1757, that "extreme straightness of my Family circumstances is the only Consideration that could have emboldened me to make an application of this kind."[5] A favorable response was almost certainly motivated not only by charitable feelings but also by a concern with maintaining the respect for social rank.

In a society in which status distinctions implied socially sanctioned inequalities of living standards as well as political rights, care was taken lest aristocratic rank be debased by pecuniary want. The political class never doubted that they had a legitimate claim to be maintained by the state, be it by means of office, sinecure, pension, or other favor. Nor did the asking imply a moral stigma though it is true that pensions from the Secret Service Fund were sometimes refused for their "rather too private a nature," as one supplicant put it.[6] An office in church or state was considered a "public honor," which might be used not only to mend financial difficulties but also to confirm or even enhance one's social status. In his speech on "Economical Reforms," Burke never questioned the propriety of this aspect of patronage. Noting that public offices were "filled with the descendants of the Walpoles, of the Pelhams, of the Townshends— names to whom this country owes its liberties," he exclaimed, "May such fountains never be dried up."[7] At the beginning of the nineteenth century, William Cobbett, among the reformers and critics of patronage a great defender of tradition against the inroads of industry, still wrote approvingly that public office ought to serve the purpose of "upholding and cherishing those among the ancient nobility and gentry, who otherwise might fall into a state that would inevitably bring disgrace upon rank and would, thereby, leave us no aristocracy but that of wealth, ten thousand times more grinding and insolent than the lords of the worst feudal times."[8]

If the aristocracy had a legitimate claim to be maintained by the state, it took "interest" and "connexion" to land a job or receive some other favor. In fact, to get on in virtually every sphere of life, in the professions as well as in government, it took a patron to smooth the way and unlock the doors. Under such a system it was quite natural that family ties were perhaps the most important transmission belts of favor, for what better "connexion" could there be for a young man than a kinsman in high places? And so family "jobbery" must be regarded as another of the most important characteristics of the unreformed civil service.

Ministers were deluged with requests and applications. Among them there would always be notes from relatives, like Lord John Russell's second cousin, who wrote in 1849,

> You may ask now, as you might have asked when I had the pleasure of seeing you, what right have I to expect anything from your hands? None except that of distant relationship. A drowning man catches a straw but I look upon it as a very substantial straw, you being not only the greatest man in England but the most powerful man in the world (for I look upon one who wields the destinies of this vast empire as such) and when I reflect that your mother and my father were first cousins, I hope to come within the warmth of your rays. We now propose sending my son to Cambridge—an expense we are ill able to meet and hoped to have been spared by entering him at once into his profession for life, but he will be able to perfect his education and in the meantime I shall live in the hope that he may at some time, if not immediately, be placed by you in some suitable situation.[9]

Not only the ministers themselves but also members of their families found themselves deluged with requests when one of their kinsmen took office. Thus, Disraeli's sister complained, "I had to grant perpetual audiences yesterday to people who want something. First came my little postman to ask me to put him on the town district. . . . Then came . . . a letter from a lady who wants a place for her husband."[10]

Among those who might "bring disgrace upon rank" in general and some family in particular were not only the impecunious, of whom there were many, but also those who were poorly endowed in body and mind—those who could not succeed in education or secure an honorable occupation elsewhere. In their famous report "On the Organization of the Permanent Civil Service," Trevelyan and Northcote charged that

> it is for the unambitious, and the indolent or incapable, that . . . [the Civil Service] is chiefly desired. Those whose abilities do not warrant an expectation that they will succeed in the open professions, where they must encounter the competition of their contemporaries, and those whom indolence of temperament or physical infirmities unfit for active exertion, are placed in the Civil Service, where they may obtain an honorable livelihood with little labor, and with no risk. . . . It may be noticed in particular that the comparative lightness of the work, and the certainty of provision in case of retirement owing to bodily incapacity,

furnish strong inducements to the parents and friends of sickly youths to endeavor to obtain for them employment in the service of the government.[11]

To the editor of *The Times* Trevelyan put it even more bluntly.

> There can be no doubt that our high Aristocracy have been accustomed to employ the civil establishments as a means of providing for the Waifs and Strays of their families—as a sort of Foundling Hospital where those who had no energy to make their way in the open professions, or whom it was not convenient to purchase one in the Army, might receive a nominal office, but real Pension, for life, at the expense of the Public.[12]

Not unexpectedly, Trevelyan's unflattering assessment of his colleagues and clerks drew vigorous protests, but there are many applications which bear it out.[13] Trevelyan himself provided an amusing example, which also shows what other "family" members might be provided for in the civil service.

> The Dukes of Norfolk, for instance, have provided for their illegitimate children in this manner, generation after generation. There are still several of them in the Public Service, and one of them is the most notorious idler and jobber in it. Another, who shocked his fellow Clerks by continually falling down into epileptic fits, was put into the Treasury a few years ago, and nothing could exceed his astonishment at his being told by me that he was expected to work like his fellow Clerks.[14]

Beyond the family, but still within its purview, there were always old servants who had to be provided for. "Some little employment of fifty or sixty pounds a year" for a servant "who has served . . . upward of thirty years, with great integrity," was a common favor asked by a man whose "situation does not afford me the means of making any provisions for this old servant."[15] Disraeli landed a job for his father's dear old servant Tita, for

> it was dreadful to think that a man who had been in Byron's service, and soothed his last moments, who had been the faithful attendant and almost the companion and friend of my father, for so many years, who had actually died in his arms, should end his days in the usual refuge for domestic servants, by keeping a public-house, or a greengrocer's shop.[16]

So it was, but it never occurred to Disraeli that he might pay a pension from his own pocket for so worthy a man or that it was in any way disreputable to let the public roll pay for Tita who "was appointed chief messenger at the new India Office . . . without the liability of having to carry messages."[17]

Public offices were often made over to individuals for life or even to families in perpetuity and held in much the same way as landed property. If there were fewer of those in the nineteenth century than before, it was still true that gentlemen as a group regarded public office as something rather less public than we do now.

Civil servants had a special claim on the bounty of office, and, as we shall see, many of them put up a staunch fight when the Trevelyan-Northcote report was published. One of the reformers suggested to Gladstone, "The existing corps of civil servants do not like the new plan, because the introduction of well-educated, active men appointed on a different principle will force them to bestir themselves, and because they cannot hope to get their own ill-educated sons appointed under the new system."[18] Jobs for sons of dependents were a lucrative fringe benefit; and perhaps more than one civil servant was motivated principally by "the connexion which public [office] offers," particularly as a "means of pushing out five boys (and perhaps more hereafter) . . . ."[19] However that may be, the politicians agreed on "the great importance of giving every fair encouragement to those excellent officers who are at the head of great departments and upon whose zeal . . . so much depends."[20]

Important as the "charitable" function of patronage was, it was equaled if not exceeded in importance and scope by the political functions to which we must turn now. By the middle of the eighteenth century, party feelings had declined. The political oligarchy, unified on virtually all constitutional issues, formed a single "party." This party controlled the electorate. The purses of the wealthier families and clans had triumphed in an era of rising election costs. As a result, there were fewer contested elections than before. Questions of "influence," "interest," and "nomination" (a gradient from partial to total control over votes) were settled by and large. Over half of the counties and boroughs were practically owned by wealthy families of peers and country squires or by the government. And although the rest were occasionally disputed by rival families, disputes tended to foster compromise settlements and sharing of spoils owing to the exorbitant cost of electoral contests.[21]

Trading one's "interest" in a county or borough, marketing one's voice and loyalty in the House, or even leasing one's "nomination" to someone else were every bit as legitimate as collecting rents from tenants or drawing profits from trade. In the absence of party divisions and clashing principles capable of aligning votes through party discipline and loyalty against the threats of the mighty and the promises of the rich and influential, political transactions turned into quasi-commercial undertakings by individuals and families.

A young man of slender means was dependent on some patron to make his way in the world. If he had some "influence," which might be based on tradition and good will, he had something to trade. If, in addition, he had "interest"—that is, control through threats or bribes over a portion of the electorates—his prospects were considerably better. He could sell or lease it for cash or some office. If his family had the "nomination" of a borough—best of all—he might be returned to Parliament himself, which was an excellent base from which to acquire *quelque chose de par le roi*: some sinecure for himself to offset his outlays in maintaining his interest in the service of the present government; something for his brother so that he too might remain "well attach'd"; and perhaps some suitable employment for the gentleman "who lives near town and hath a considerable influence over many of the voters."[22] But then there were many who used their seat in Parliament not so much to seek profit. To some of the country gentlemen, "what mattered . . . was not so much membership of the House, as the primacy in their own 'country' attested by their being chosen to represent their county or some respectable borough."[23] To them the maintenance of an election base was an investment expected to pay off in the currency of local power and prestige.

The structure of politics of mid-eighteenth-century England has been brilliantly analyzed by Namier.[24] His work is full of vivid samples of letters that demonstrate the working of the system. Clearly there were two principal political functions of the patronage system. The first was to keep parliamentary majorities aligned with the government, and so cabinet ministers were under considerable pressure to respond favorably if they received a request of this kind.

> I flatter myself your grace will before the meeting of parliament honour me with your recommendation to some employment, as nobody has

been a more constant supporter of Government, and your Grace has promised me so frequently your assistance.[25]

A variation of this function was for the government to help some loyal M.P. to maintain his local interest from one election to the next by compensating him for his election expenses. This was the source of requests of the following kind.

> It is not in my power any longer to support or even maintain the interest I so dearly bought at the last general election at Lincoln (by the desire of Mr. Pelham, more than my own inclination) if your Grace will not think of me; and that the spending of £ 7000 and upward exclusive of my house being like a fair for two years should not have entitled me to some small favor before this, I own I think hard.[26]

The second basic function was to co-opt constituencies. This was done by the patron in the quasi-proprietary counties and boroughs but as a rule not without the help of some government patronage. In the Treasury or Admiralty boroughs, those controlled by the government as safe seats for its interest, the government moved into a fairly direct relationship with the electorate, which might consist of a few aldermen and some burgesses recruited by co-optation. A report from Orford in 1761 suggested that the majority of this corporation were gentlemen residing in and near London and having some employment under the government. Apparently they traveled to Orford regularly so as to discharge their election duties to their government employers.[27] The majority of boroughs was sufficiently small for inducements in cash or office to do the political trick.[28] Significantly, between 1742 and the First Reform Act no cabinet minister was defeated in general elections. Changes in governments occurred, but these resulted from conflicts within the government and from disputes between ministers and their parliamentary following.[29] Although the demand for patronage was beginning to outstrip the supply, the political results would seem to argue that the latter was adequate for parliamentary cabinet governments to maintain control over their electorates. In the fifty years preceding 1832 a number of reforms, aiming to separate politics and administration, cut into the patronage system, but, rather than abolishing it, merely skimmed off a layer of practices that had come to be thought of as corrupt.[30] Neither patronage nor many other practices which would be considered corrupt in another century were swept away. In fact, many of them got a new lease on life with the abolition of closed boroughs, the establishment of new voter registration societies, and the gradual breakdown of the one-party system.

A number of political measures in 1782 disfranchised some 50,000 revenue officers and disqualified government contractors from sitting in the Commons. They struck at the heart neither of political patronage nor of managed elections but were in line with the general reduction in the number of parliamentary placemen, that is the number of M.P.s holding administrative posts, court appointments, sinecures, and pensions.[31] On the administrative side, a series of commissions, investigating the existing state of public offices, recommended changes which were by and large completed by 1840. Of these, two are particularly relevant in this context.

One series of acts abolished many sinecures, that is, offices which had become totally nonfunctional and were merely a source of income without corresponding responsibilities. Similarly, it eliminated the widespread practice of discharging the duties of functional offices by deputy. The political obstacle that had to be overcome is clearly brought out by the cautious caveat of a commission recommending the abolition of sinecures.

> We do not mean to violate, in the slightest Degree, any Right vested in an officer by virtue of his office. The Principles which secure the Rights to private property are sacred, to be preserved inviolate; they are Land Marks to be considered as immovable: But the Public have their Rights also; Rights equally sacred, and as freely to be exercised. . . . If useless and expensive office cannot be suppressed . . . , be the Necessities of State ever so urgent, without intrenching upon the Right of the Possessor, and violate Public Faith, the Evil must be endured, until the Power of the Legislature can, without the Imputation of Injustice, be exerted for the Relief of the State.[32]

For a time, the experience of the French Revolution heightened preservative sentiments and the proprietary conception of public office. The old system with all its manifest abuses was clearly preferable to the Jacobin threat. Yet after an interval of some ten years the reforms moved gradually forward again, and by 1834, the Select Committee on Sinecure Offices reported only 100 remaining sinecures with combined emoluments of nearly a hundred thousand pounds per year.[33]

Another series of administrative measures eliminated the traditional emoluments of office, namely, fees of office, and replaced them with salaries and pensions. Similarly, they prohibited use of public funds for private profiteering. By 1832 civil servants in all departments were paid salaries and pensions though scales differed from office to office. If the first series of acts aimed at separating administration from politics, the second was a step in the direction of preventing the incumbent from appropriating his office. Both reforms, bureaucratic in the technical sense, challenged the proprietary concept of office holding but left untouched the principle of patronage in recruiting officials.

The abolition of sinecures, of deputizing official responsibility, and of appropriating fees and funds of office—all these new regulations were in line with a growing body of opinion that an office holder, recruited though he may be through patronage, should be at least minimally qualified to discharge the duties of office. Merit, if not yet *la carrière ouverte aux talents*, was beginning to encroach upon property rights and mere political and social considerations. Peel, who was particularly conscientious in these matters, wrote to the patronage secretary, the government's chief whip, when he became prime minister.

> So far as I can judge, I have nothing to dispose of except household offices, parliamentary offices and chance seats occasionally falling vacant at a Board of Revenue. Every other appointment within the range of my patronage either requires previous service in subordinate situations, as in the Revenue, or professional knowledge and habits if it be connected with the law. . . . Some civil employment is what every lady asks for, but the patronage of the executive government is in truth professional patronage.[34]

Patronage was not only declining owing to new regulations and the encroachment of merit upon political transactions. The number of patronage jobs that might be disposed of by an incoming government was limited generally by the fact that the English system had not developed into a system of party "spoils." During the eighteenth century, there were no sharp party lines but shifting personal and political coalitions which did not as a rule purge the appointees of a previous government. Besides, the strong, proprietary conception of office holding militated against the "in-and-out" conception of office, which was to become the rule in the United States. As the proprietary conception and practice of office holding was declining in England, patronage appointments were immediately tempered with the modern conception and practice of permanent tenure. Thus, one form of permanent tenure succeeded another without an intervening period of patronage in the manner of American party spoils. Indeed, it has been suggested that officials in the nineteenth century became even more immune to purges on political grounds than they had been before. In any case, while English officials in the first half of the nineteenth century would only accede to office on the highway of politics, their American cousins would also be evicted by a turn of political fortune.

Patronage was not only declining relative to the demand for it; it may also have become somewhat of a nuisance around the middle of the nineteenth century. While governments continued to be inundated by political requests and jobbing cousins, they had less to give than before and so must have frequently found themselves displeasing friends and supporters. Peel's new patronage secretary, Freemantle, was forced to write Gladstone in 1843,

> I hear that your application in favour of young Mr. Walker is not founded on strong political claims. It is more a case of kindness and charity—such as I should more readily consider than any others if I were at liberty to do so—but at the Treasury we must look first to the claims of our political supporters and our patronage is, as you know, quite inadequate to meet applications of members of the H. O. C., in favour of their constituents who naturally consider all of our patronage theirs. . . . Pray excuse me for my frankness in explaining to you how these things are viewed within the corrupt walls of a Secretary of the Treasury's room.[35]

Many politicians might well have begun to wonder about the usefulness of the patronage system when it spawned as much disappointment as gratitude. From the political point of view, in any case, patronage was on the decline if only because there were fewer sinecures and half-functional offices to give. From the point of view of administration, however, patronage was still the sole method of recruiting men to office, tempered though it may have been with considerations of merit. The very decline of favors at the disposal of governments may well have retarded the advance of merit by subjecting the remaining jobs to pressing political obligations that might otherwise have been discharged with a sinecure.

Although some of the early reforms were bureaucratic in the technical sense, it must not be supposed that the "Economical Reforms" of the late eighteenth century which Burke opened in 1780 were motivated primarily by a bureaucratic concern for efficiency and merit or even, as has been suggested, a businesslike concern with diminishing public expenditures.[36] Nor should it be supposed that the reforms resulted only from the pressure of a rising middle class. Rather they were triggered by a renewed struggle between the crown and the aristocracy and motivated by a desire to reduce the political influence of a king who attempted to use patronage in extending the royal prerogative. As Halévy put it, "Reform dated from the moment that George III showed his intention to exploit the old abuses for his own ends."[37] It may well be that the reform caught the imagination of the middle class and that it aligned commercial interests with the Whigs, but this struggle against some forms of patronage was still essentially a struggle within the landed ruling class. The effect was no doubt a greater measure of economy and perhaps even efficiency. But more important from the constitutional point of view was that government, in the words of Keir, "came less and less to be considered the personal concern of the sovereign, and more and more as the business of leaders of the dominant political party in Parliament and especially the Commons."[38]

Whatever the difficulties with patronage in the first half of the nineteenth century, the landed classes were still in control vis-à-vis the crown as well as the lower sorts of people. Many of the features of the unreformed political system continued. Some pocket boroughs with one or two votes, like famous Old Sarum, vanished. But others remained, and between them and large constituencies, like Manchester, most characteristics of the old system were still very much alive. As Gash sums up his study of politics in the age of Peel, "There was scarcely a feature of the old unreformed system that could not be found still in existence after 1832."[39] In the counties, the power of the landed gentry was strengthened on balance by the enfranchisement of the most dependent group of tenants and by an increase in the representation of counties as against boroughs. The latter were still varied, ranging from small nomination boroughs like Newark to very large ones like Liverpool, where it was impossible to bribe more than a small portion of the voters. The majority was still sufficiently small to be managed in traditional ways.

Parliaments elected after 1832 were much like parliaments before. Wealthy business men were still willing to leave politics to landed aristocrats so long as their interests were not neglected. The political oligarchy represented in Parliament was much the same as before though a slight shift toward new wealth packaged in traditional education at Oxford and Cambridge became noticeable.[40] Despite Wellington's alarming prophesy that no gentleman will want to sit in the House of Commons after the reforms, some 500 landed gentlemen, 200 of them heirs of peers and baronets, were returned in 1833.[41] The proportion of aristocrats was almost the same in 1865.[42] On the cabinet level the picture was much the same. "Of the fourteen new men in the thirteen cabinets of the period [between 1832 and 1866] only three can be regarded as middle-class politicians, representing the specific aspirations of their class. . . . The rest were career politicians, mainly lawyers."[43]

But then, the First Reform Act was never meant to change the guards or to change more than what was necessary to legitimate the existing order of things. In the words of one proponent,

> Any plan must be objectionable which, keeping the franchise very . . . exclusive, fails to give satisfaction to the middle and respectable ranks of society, and drives them to a union founded on dissatisfaction, with the lower orders. It is of the utmost importance to associate the middle with the higher orders of society in the love and support of the institutions and government of the country.[44]

This it did. It co-opted the middle class and by giving it the satisfaction of the franchise, though not much representation, cemented that spirit of deference which writers like Bagehot and Engels have regarded as the distinctive trait of the English bourgeoisie.[45] The economy was developing fast in the hands of that class and seems to have absorbed all of its talent and ambition whereas the social structure of politics remained much as it had been in the eighteenth century.[46] Similarly, until the second half of the nineteenth century, most of the administration remained, in the words of John Bright, a "gigantic outdoor relief department of the aristocracy of Great Britain."[47] New men with professional backgrounds and dispositions were brought in to support a system that was expanding in response to new administrative exigencies of the industrial revolution.[48] But then the new men were gentlemen because they had received the education of gentlemen at Oxford and Cambridge. If the First Reform Act had given satisfaction to the bourgeoisie, a much less conspicuous incorporation of professionals into the ranks of gentlemen had given satisfaction to that rising status group. It is to the social structure of English education and to this process of incorporation that we must turn now. Thus, in the next section we will sketch the social structure of education up to the eve of civil service reform in the nineteenth century; in the final section we will turn to the redefinition of gentility and social conditions other than education facilitating the incorporation of professional gentlemen.

The Social Structure of Education

The incorporation of professional men into the circle of gentility was facilitated by the unique social conditions of English education since the second half of the sixteenth century and the first half of the seventeenth century. Whereas the Prussian aristocracy, drawn into the dynastic officer corps and a military way of life, did not embrace the education of grammar schools and universities, the English aristocracy turned to serve the state in a nonmilitary capacity and in a crisis of its way of life began to educate its youth in a new manner.[49] That new education was rather more bookish than the traditional education of the aristocracy, oriented as it was to military knight service in the retinue of a local lord. It was oriented to government office, membership in Parliament, law, and the efflorescent culture of the court and London society. This educational reorientation was so extraordinary in scale and so much linked to grammar schools and universities that it dwarfed comparable developments on the continent associated with humanism and the domestication of the aristocracy. In the words of Stone, it represented "one of the really decisive movements in English history."[50] For our purpose, that movement was decisive in that it created the conditions under which professional men, rising to prominence with the expansion of society in general and the civil service in particular, could be incorporated into the circle of gentility, which was increasingly defined as encompassing all those who had received the status education of gentlemen at public schools and one of the two great universities.

The standard explanation of the educational reorientation in England around the turn of the sixteenth century points to the impact of Italian humanism with its new gentleman ideal. Yet, as Stone argues persuasively, there were tangible reasons why the English aristocracy was so receptive to these ideas. The landed status group began to embrace and expand education and institutions of higher learning because of a growing fear that the nobility was losing its hold on the important positions in the changing state. The changing conditions of warfare, the growing influence of the court, and the rise and expansion of central administrative and judicial institutions rendered the traditional noble education partially disfunctional. The replacement of the celibate clergy with educated laymen from the lesser gentry and even the lower orders threatened to monopolize the nonmilitary service by an upstart intelligentsia that would upset the traditional hierarchy among the ranks. The turn to state service and the turn to education were but two sides of a social adaptation by which the old ruling class managed to preserve its predominant position in state and society.

As social expedients often turn into valued ends legitimated by appeals to lofty principles, the demand for education soon outstripped the functional requirements of state service. Scarcely an intrinsic requirement of administrative office, classical education became the fashion of polite society, and the number of men seeking it turned out to exceed available posts. The effects were twofold. First, the educational boom, by creating ambitious discontent for want of suitable positions and blocked opportunities in church and state, also created an alienated intelligentsia whose arguments accentuated the moral and political rupture between the court and the country, which led to the civil war.[51] Hobbes may not have been too rash in supposing that the

chief leaders were ambitious ministers and ambitious gentlemen; the ministers envying the authority of the bishops whom they thought less learned; and the gentlemen envying the privy council, whom they thought less wise than themselves. For it is a hard matter for men, who do all think highly of their own wits, when they have also acquired the learning of the university, to be persuaded that they want any ability requisite for the government of the commonwealth.[52]

Second, and more important for our purpose here, the educational boom brought about a sort of "cultural revolution" among the aristocracy and gentry that outlived the educational depression of the second half of the seventeenth and first part of the eighteenth centuries. Book learning, whether pursued at school or with a private tutor at home, became compatible with gentility, as the humanist propagandists had argued earlier to a reluctant nobility. It was not yet an essential attribute of a gentleman, nor was education alone sufficient to make a gentleman; but wealth ripened by ancestry could now be enhanced further by the finishing touches of a school, a private tutor, or a university. This amalgamation of the older notion of gentility with classical education was one of the most remarkable characteristics of the English case. Gentlemen might live up to the humanist ideal to various degrees or not at all, but the ideal itself was not seriously questioned.

The influx of nobles into schools, universities, and Inns of Court was part and parcel of an educational expansion that affected also other social groups: merchants and artisans, tenants and even copyhold families in the villages.[53] Unfortunately there are no statistics on the social composition of student bodies in the growing number of Latin grammar schools at this time. Such qualitative data as are sprinkled through the literature suggest, however, that the clientele was rather mixed, excluding only the poor in town and country.[54]

The statistical picture of the universities and Inns of Court is a little less hazy. It has been calculated that of the Oxford matriculants in the period between 1575 and 1639, roughly 50 percent were sons of aristocrats and gentry, 41 percent sons of merchants, yeomen, professional men, artisans, and laborers, and about 9 percent sons of clergymen, including archbishops and curates. Other calculations for St. John's and Caius College, Cambridge, for the fourth decade of the seventeenth century convey the same general picture though the social composition of the two colleges evidently varied. The proportion of aristocrats and gentry ranged from about a third to over one-half. It appears that the Inns of Court were even more exclusive than the universities. In the 1630s four-fifths of the law students were drawn from the aristocracy and the gentry.[55]

The degree to which the landed status group was educated in the middle of the seventeenth century is suggested even better by the fact that roughly 40 percent of the landed gentry in the county of Yorkshire in 1642, 70 percent of the members of Parliament in 1640–1642, and about 80 percent of the J.P.s on the Somerset bench from 1625 to 1640 had received some form of higher education at a university or Inn of Court.[56] Foreign commentators of the time were no doubt correct that the English aristocracy of the seventeenth century was unusually well educated.

Striking though the high proportion of aristocrats and country gentlemen in higher education at this time undoubtedly is, it is significant also that about 15 to 30 percent of the university students were described as sons of artisans, shopkeepers, husbandmen, plebeian, and *"mediocris fortunae."*[57] Compared with Germany, this proportion was certainly quite small, but compared with eighteenth-century England, when this group was squeezed out even more, it was relatively high. Evidently, the early seventeenth century still provided a channel of upward mobility through education, particularly into the clergy, to sons of artisans and the like.

The degree of upward mobility through education should not be overrated, however. The social and economic position of the clergy at this time was at low ebb. As in Germany, the social status of the clergy declined sharply for some time after the Reformation. Church livings became less lucrative, and positions in the lower ranks of the country clergy became outright impoverished. According to Stone, "vicars and curates [in England] were existing on an income hardly different from that of unskilled laborers."[58] Obviously, there was no attraction in that for gentlemen, nor were such jobs an obvious boon to nongentlemen of whatever station in life. In the early seventeenth century, between two-thirds and three-quarters of the parish clergy and as many as two-thirds of the bishops were nongentry. As a consequence, Stone suggests, even "the highest ranks of the clergy were generally regarded as inferior in status to the highest ranks of the legal profession, despite the presence of the former in the House of Lords."[59]

The status of the professions in general and the church in particular were to rise again in the latter part of the seventeenth and throughout the eighteenth centuries. Country livings became more valuable again, and gentlemen once more found their way back to them. Conversely, in the words of Kitson Clark, more country clergy came to hold a position in the countryside and to mix on equal terms with the gentry. More of them became magistrates. Their learning often became more secular and more liberal, they were more often antiquarians than theologians, and if refinement of manners was to be the test, such refinement was perhaps often more likely to be found in the vicarage than in the hall.[60]

As the century wore on, it was increasingly assumed that a man of the Church of England was in fact a gentleman. This assumption, however, was not only an artifact of the changing conception of gentility. It also reflected a greater influx of gentlemen into the profession, as well as the profession's freer social intercourse with the country gentry.

Like other jobs and sinecures, church benefices in the eighteenth century were drawn into the welter of property, patronage, and politics. Some of them became appropriated by certain country families and passed as heritable property from one generation to the next. Others remained more open, but recruitment, as for other jobs in the establishment, depended on the patronage of the rich and influential or, better yet, on parliamentary influence. Clerical careers required also a greater investment now and thus became less accessible to all but families of considerable means. There was no longer any point for parents to choose a clerical career for their son, Thomson D. F. Edgeworth warned in 1870, unless "they are fully able not only to defray the considerable expenses of his education, but add to his income, perhaps for many years, what may be sufficient to render him at least independent whilst he continues to be a curate."[61] And then, as in the other professions, it took "connexion" to smooth the way.

The educational scene of post-Restoration England, too, changed its complexion. The flow of charitable bequests to education declined. Endowments of the existing schools became relatively smaller owing to inflation. Financially hard-pressed, many grammar schools ceased to exist or had to operate on a reduced scale. The conservatism pervading social and political thought and action also gripped the educational sphere. The socially unsettling effects of an uncontrolled educational expansion was not lost on the contemporaries, and educational preferences and policy shifted to bring about "the crystallization of that all too familiar English association of educational opportunity with social status."[62]

As the landed classes triumphed over the crown and social, political, and cultural life gravitated back into the country, the aristocracy and gentry lost some of their educational zeal. At any rate, education seems to have shifted somewhat from the schoolhouse to the libraries of the country houses. The demand for domestic education under a private tutor increased, and it seems that the association of young gentlemen with children from the lower orders was no longer thought to be appropriate.

Many aristocrats and country gentlemen in the eighteenth century were reluctant to send their sons to boarding school. Yet the fact that the merits of a public school education became a matter of public debate seems to indicate that public schools were emerging as formidable competitors to domestic education.[63] In the end, they won out, the more so the less accessible they became to ordinary people. Although there is little hard evidence to support the view that only younger sons were sent off to boarding school, whereas older sons received their education at home, Weinberg suggests that

> the eldest son of a great family still would probably not have gone to one of the schools [even in the early nineteenth century]. The rough atmosphere was reserved for the younger sons. The tutor, whether resident or from the village parsonage, might teach the landowner's son. Sometimes village parsons even founded very small boarding schools for this purpose.[64]

However that may be, it is interesting to note that in Hans's study of eighteenth-century elite who were also peers or gentry, he found only one-third were educated at home.[65]

If a young gentleman was sent off to school, he was likely to attend one of these few grammar schools which became ever more socially exclusive and which eventually catered to none but the highest status groups in society. During the seventeenth and eighteenth centuries a preparatory education for universities and Inns of Court might be obtained from a private tutor as well as from a number of schools. The main types were endowed grammar schools, private schools, and dissenting academies.[66] The main burden of preparing students for the universities, however, fell on the grammar schools. Originally established to give a free education to townspeople and inhabitants of the surrounding countryside, they concentrated on teaching Latin grammar (hence grammar school) and a few of the classical authors. During the seventeenth and eighteenth centuries they were constantly criticized for their "gerund grinding" and their disregard of modern subjects that might be useful to students destined to occupations in trade, commerce, and manufacturing. They certainly did not provide a suitable education for the middle class. Nonconformists were understandably hesitant to send their sons to institutions controlled by the Anglican clergy. They and businessmen established private schools and academies that catered to middle-class needs.

Some of the financially hard-pressed schools taught little more than elementary subjects; others muddled through on the standard Latin fare; but still others introduced modern subjects for a fee and accepted boarders on tuition. Wherever the statutes of the foundation did not forbid such practices or where they could be stretched, it was possible to increase staffs, raise salaries, and improve the social status of the school in this manner. This process of converting some of the old grammar schools into fee-charging and boarding-type schools continued until the middle of the nineteenth century so that the Taunton Commission, reporting in 1868, considered the old designation "free grammar school" entirely misplaced.[67] But exactly what proportion of grammar schools was affected by this trend, or more generally how many grammar schools of one sort or another existed at any time during the eighteenth century, is not known. To make matters worse, the literature is full of conflicting assessments, from which one can conclude only that the bulk of grammar schools did not teach modern subjects, did not prepare students for the university, and, because of the narrow classical curriculum, did not provide the middle class with an occupationally suitable education.

Although a number of grammar schools grew wealthy, the majority suffered financial decline. The value of their properties on the outskirts of London and other towns multiplied with the expansion of urban areas. They took in boarders and raised tuition, and they increasingly replaced local day students with boarders of higher social status, who also monopolized scholarships originally set aside for poor townspeople. At the same time, the governing boards of these institutions, known as "public schools" by the beginning of the nineteenth century, changed from local to national notables. Another distinguishing feature of the great public schools, particularly the famous "seven," was their distinct form of communal living and code of behavior, which became exemplary for all grammar schools aspiring to public school rank.[68]

Table 3. *Social Composition of Student Bodies in English Public Schools, 1801–1850*

	Harrow	Rugby	Eton	Harrow Rugby Eton	Seven public schools: Estimate
Titled aristocracy	19%	5%	20%	16%	13%
Gentry	35%	53%	27%	36%	40%
Military	5%	5%	2%	3%	4%
Clergy	10%	18%	3%	9%	12%
Professions	5%	2%	5%	4%	4%
Middle class	1%	3%	1%	1%	2%
Lower orders	0%	0%	0%	0%	0%
Other	26%	14%	43%	31%	26%
Total N	3,326	4,077	6,625	14,028	24,397

Source: T. W. Bamford, "Public Schools and Social Class, 1801–1850,"*British Journal of Sociology,* 12 (1961): 225.

For our purpose, the most important feature of the seven great public schools that were linked as a group in the first half of the nineteenth century was their exclusive social composition. As shown in Table 3, one-half to nearly three-quarters of their students were drawn from the titled aristocracy and landed gentry.[69] Unfortunately we cannot be more precise. Although data on the social composition are available for Harrow, Rugby, and Eton from 1801 to 1850, the social background of a fair number of students is unknown. Twenty-six percent at Harrow, 14 percent at Rugby, and as many as 43 percent at Eton are unclassifiable for the entire period. If we assume that these "other" students were randomly distributed over the other occupational and status categories, then the social composition as shown in Table 4 would obtain.[70] However, this assumption is not altogether convincing. It is likely that students from the highest-status groups would have been recognized by the compilers of the school registers and that the bulk of the unclassifiable "others" therefore belonged to lower-status groups. For this reason, Bamford has examined the "others" for Rugby and reports that they were not local boys but "must have come from a distance and been boarders." Their parents "must have been reasonably rich and, on

Table 4. *Hypothetical Social Composition of Student Bodies in English Public Schools, 1801–1850*

	Harrow	Rugby	Eton	Harrow Rugby Eton	Seven public schools: Estimate
Titled aristocracy	26%	7%	35%	23%	18%
Gentry	48%	61%	48%	53%	54%
Military	6%	6%	3%	5%	5%
Clergy	12%	20%	6%	13%	16%
Professions	7%	2%	8%	6%	5%
Middle class	1%	3%	1%	2%	2%
Lower orders	0%	0%	0%	0%	0%
Total N	2,462	3,488	3,801	9,749	18,061
Others N	864	589	2,826	4,279	6,336
Total N	3,326	4,077	6,627	14,028	24,397

Source: T. W. Bamford, "Public Schools and Social Class, 1801–1850," *British Journal of Sociology,* 12 (1961): 225. Here the unclassifiable "others" have been excluded and the proportions are calculated relative to totals excluding the "others."

economic grounds alone, the number of lower- and middle-class children must have been small indeed." He goes on to say that below the landed gentry

> existed a large "border zone" of independent people who accepted gentry standards and way of life. This way of life may be defined as non-manual, non-professional, moneyed, leisured, having links with the land in the "estate" sense and living on income, preferably from property. They were educated either at home or with other gentry, and kept an establishment with servants. A few occupied their time as leaders of the community in local or national government, in the services and to a much lesser extent the clergy, in charity and "good works." In addition to the landed gentry proper local newspapers and other publications of the period reveal members of the community who were acceptable to the landed gentry, even at their most exclusive functions. Some of these lived on property too small to be included officially as "landed" (about 1,000 acres), others were not associated with the land at all while yet others came within the category of "gentlemen and ladies living on incomes." The number of these people was considerable and it is estimated

that some 66,000 boys of such parents had their twelfth birthday in the half century under review. In adopting the gentry mode of life it is probable that many parents conformed to the educational feature of this class and sent boys to Public Schools.[71]

If we accept Bamford's suggestion that most of the unclassifiable "others" must have belonged to a "border zone" of near-gentry status, and if we assume that this group, whose gentility was a matter of controversy at the beginning of the nineteenth century, included also individuals benefiting from new industrial wealth, then the proportion of "old" aristocrats and landed gentry must have been roughly as indicated in Table 3. If we assume that half of the 26 percent "others" in the seven exclusive public schools were members of the commercial, industrial middle class whose parents were pushing into the ranks of gentlemen, then the non-professional "middle class" would still have been a relatively small contingent of no more than 15 percent.

There can be no doubt that the seven great public schools were most exclusive educational institutions. In this aspect they were similar to the German nobiliary academies, but unlike these academies, which failed in the eighteenth century, the English public schools showed no signs of becoming less socially exclusive in the first half of the nineteenth century. The distribution of the status groups remained fairly constant over the fifty-year period. There was only one noteworthy shift at Harrow, where the clergy advanced somewhat at the expense of the titled aristocracy and landed gentry. Bamford sums up the public school clientele in these words: "The boys came from aristocratic, gentry or near-gentry homes, with minor additions from the clergy, and even less from the armed forces and other professional status groups. Indeed, all but the gentry-titled-clergy, and those who adopted their way of life can be ignored."[72] Nor can there be any doubt that the aristocracy and gentry as a whole was well educated in the first half of the nineteenth century. According to Bamford's calculations, more than half of the sons of titled aristocrats and "rather less" than half of the sons of landed gentlemen attended one of the eight top public schools between 1801 and 1850.[73]

In the early nineteenth century, a few day schools with excellent reputations ranked just below the seven great public schools. They were sometimes referred to as public schools even though they lacked the two qualifications which clearly distinguished the elite schools: boarding and social exclusiveness. Among these were such schools as St. Paul's and Merchant Taylor's in London, Manchester Grammar, Reading and King Edward VI in Birmingham. Only for St. Paul's do we have a good set of statistics for the first half of the nineteenth century (see Tables 5 and 6).[74] In the first two decades of the nineteenth century, a little over half the students were drawn from the lower and middle classes. However, there is a noteworthy shift in the third, fourth, and fifth decades. By the middle of the nineteenth century, the proportion of lower- and middle-class students had declined to about 15 percent whereas the proportion of boys from the professional-clergy group had increased to about 63 percent. Clearly this school was being transformed into a training ground for the rising professional status group. Unfortunately, there are no data on the other day schools of the type of St. Paul's. Although Merchant Taylor's is said to have been similar in social composition, we do not know whether this shift in favor of the professional groups can be generalized to all the schools of this type.

The Redefinition of Gentility

During the first half of the nineteenth century the simple test which would restrict gentility to members of the peerage and those listed in, say, Burke's *Landed Gentry* or Walford's *County Families*, became clearly old-fashioned.[75] Ever since the eighteenth century, the older test had been gradually augmented by the test of cultivation and education so that a gentleman was increasingly expected to have received the education of a gentleman at one of the public schools and at either Oxford or Cambridge. This shift in the conception of gentility created considerable confusion and uncertainty concerning gentle rank. Did the new test imply that the education of a gentleman was a sufficient condition of gentle rank? Were liberally educated professionals to be considered gentlemen by virtue of their education and profession and irrespective of their social origin?

This confusion was exacerbated by the growing importance of the professions with the rise of industry and the expansion of commerce. Urbanization and the rise of living standards heightened the

Table 5. *Social Composition of Student Bodies at St. Paul's, 1801–1850*

	Lower order	Middle class	Professions	Clergy	Military	Gentry	Titled aristocracy	Others	Total N
1801–1810	16%	35%	13%	4%	0%	10%	0%	21%	384
1811–1820	15%	33%	28%	5%	2%	10%	0%	6%	358
1821–1830	10%	32%	27%	15%	4%	7%	0%	4%	279
1831–1840	10%	20%	38%	17%	3%	8%	0%	3%	267
1841–1850	7%	17%	40%	23%	1%	6%	0%	4%	246
1801–1850	12%	29%	28%	12%	2%	9%	0%	9%	1,534
N	191	438	426	177	32	131	5	134	1,534

Source: T. W. Bamford, "Public Schools and Social Class, 1801–1850," *British Journal of Sociology*, 12 (1961): 225.

Table 6. *Hypothetical Social Composition of Student Bodies at St. Paul's, 1801–1850*

	Lower order	Middle class	Professions	Clergy	Military	Gentry	Titled aristocracy	Sub-total N	Others N	Total N
1801–1810	19%	40%	15%	4%	0%	11%	0%	302	82	384
1811–1820	16%	35%	29%	6%	2%	11%	1%	336	22	358
1821–1830	11%	33%	28%	15%	4%	7%	1%	269	10	279
1831–1840	10%	21%	39%	18%	3%	8%	0%	259	9	267
1841–1850	8%	18%	42%	24%	1%	6%	0%	235	11	246
1801–1850	14%	31%	30%	13%	2%	9%	0%	1,400	134	1,534

Source: T. W. Bamford, "Public Schools and Social Class, 1801–1850," *British Journal of Sociology,* 12 (1961): 225.

demand for professional services and literary products. This not only increased the sheer number of professionals and literary men and decreased their dependence on landed wealth; it also created the conditions under which the lower branches of the professions, like apothecaries, attorneys, and solicitors, as well as new occupations like civil engineers, architects, pharmacists, and others, were professionalizing and raising themselves to a social status above trade by means of improved education and associations charged with examining and licensing practitioners.

The reform of the ancient universities was part of this general development. As Rothblatt argued, that reform was a strategic move by dons to maintain and strengthen the traditional link between the universities and the expanding professions as well as a means for raising university teaching to the status of a liberal profession.[76] Though participating in the general rise of professional status, the lower branches and the newly professionalized occupations were still far from achieving the respectability of "gentleman practitioners."[77] The latter's professionalism was not based on expert training in apprenticeship but on gentlemanly education in the classics, which lifted a man above mere professional competence. Public school and university education, shared by men destined for Parliament and the Church as well as the judicial bench, took precedence to the more technical training acquired elsewhere. So long as the newer professionals could not boast the liberal education of gentlemen, they had to be content with a position below the divide separating gentlemen from the lower orders, including the commercial middle class.

By the middle of the nineteenth century it was generally accepted that liberally educated professionals were entitled to the status of gentlemen. Only "rather old or very stupid people," in the words of Kitson Clark, would think otherwise.[78] This redefinition of gentility was not merely a concession to the increasingly important social and political role of these men in the expanding society of Victorian England but a consequence of the fact that the liberal professions were associated historically with men whose status as gentlemen was secure even by traditional standards.

Under the English system of primogeniture a steady stream of younger sons of aristocrats and squires were separating from landed families to draw their livelihood not from the land but from military service, the law, clerical livings, government jobs, and even commercial occupations. Younger sons and nephews of landed gentlemen were entering the liberal professions precisely because these occupations had attained a reputation as honorable pursuits and were thus more likely to uphold the gentility of a man without independent income than any other job, except military service. If his parents did not purchase him a commission in the army, a young Englishman in need of a living might be sent up to Oxford or Cambridge, provided he had the aptitude and his parents were able to provide him with income until he was established through the patronage of "friends" or kinsmen in a professional career.

This continued movement of younger sons and relatives of gentlemen into the universities and the professions created a social group of town dwellers whose gentility was beyond doubt by any standard or whose more or less remote connections with landed families cast an aura of gentility on their style of life. The presence of such men, in turn, was convenient to those whose status was less secure and whose claims to gentle rank depended more on their association with and education as gentlemen. The majority of professionals in the first half of the nineteenth century were probably recruited from professional families, whose connections with the land were more or less tenuous. In addition, there were always some recruits from wealthy commercial families, who had given their sons the education of a gentleman and who might have been gradually turning themselves into country families. Nevertheless, the fact that church benefices in particular and the professions in general were regarded as "a fund for the provision of the younger sons of our gentry and nobles" was significant for the social rank of the entire university-trained intelligentsia.[79] For, in the words of Edgeworth, young men of "good families and fortunes" might be expected "by their manners and rank, [to] raise the whole profession in the esteem and respect of the public."[80]

If the connection of the professions with "good families and fortunes" enhanced the status of clergymen and barristers, the universities provided the link between the landed and professional status groups. The fact that they were the capstone of the education of a gentleman as well as institutions for the liberal education of professionals constituted one of the really significant differences between Prussia and England. The English landed aristocracy and gentry, unlike the Prussian, had embraced education early and, despite the decline of the universities in the eighteenth century, had not lost their identification with higher education, as the meager statistics of the social composition of Cambridge student bodies highlight. In the first half of the nineteenth century, Cambridge students were drawn almost exclusively from the landed classes and the professional status groups. The aristocracy and gentry furnished 31 percent, the Anglican clergy 32 percent, and other professionals 21 percent. Only 6 percent were sons of businessmen.[81] Clearly the new men of the industrial order had not yet penetrated the universities, nor was there room for artisans, who were furnishing such significant contingents to student bodies of German universities.

The English universities were rather different from the universities at Halle, Leipzig, or Frankfurt/Oder. By German standards, the cost of an education at Oxford and Cambridge was exorbitant. They proved to be a severe burden to gentlemen of modest means, like Thomas Malthus' father. Paying £ 100 to educate his son at Jesus College in 1784, he complained that the continuously rising costs of higher education would soon force the clergy to send their sons to Leipzig, where they might receive a higher education for a quarter of the cost.[82] Thirty years later, most students spent between £ 180 and £ 210 per year.

Such scholarships as were set aside for poor students were awarded almost without exception to sons of gentlemen in straitened circumstances. In the words of Rothblatt,

> In the nineteenth and early twentieth centuries dons were usually satisfied that scholars and exhibitioners could legitimately claim financial need, being sons of widows, younger sons of gentlemen of limited means or professional men in reduced circumstances. The definition of needy was sometimes very generous. It was implicitly conceded that a professional man and his son had to live in a certain style which it would be unfortunate to alter.[83]

Finally, the most expensive period of the nineteenth century was precisely those forty-odd years before the reform of the civil service.[84] The gentlemen who reformed the civil service and those who would immediately benefit from the reform thus belonged to the most expensively educated generations in English history.

Professional men had distinct interests, even if their conception of history and their vision of the good society did not generally give recognition to the fact that they, who wrote about these things, were an interest group in their own right.[85] Their vision of the good society was thoroughly informed by functional considerations, professional expertise, and selection by merit rather than family. Trained expertise, talent, and achievement were the only proper claims to and justifications of power, and there was nothing so likely to disclose talent and achievement as an examination administered by other experts. Fanatics for examinations, the Benthamites among them, campaigned tirelessly for that unfailing method for raising efficiency and disengaging sectional interests from social and political institutions.

Their motives, however, were not as disengaged as their apotheosis of disinterested service might have suggested. They were partisans not so much on behalf of the middle class whose ideology they fashioned but on behalf of their own interest as a group in professionalizing various occupations, from university teaching to government service, which meant opening up new career opportunities to men who had received the education of gentlemen. This was a particularly vital objective in a society in which everyone still seems to have taken for granted that the son of a professional would ordinarily follow in the footsteps of his father as did the son of a tradesman or a farmer. Thus, a growing professional status group also meant a growing demand for the education of a gentleman, and a growing student body at public schools and universities also meant an increasing demand for positions suitable for "ingenious gentlemen." As we shall see in Chapter 5, the opening of new professions to men of liberal education was foremost on the minds of those dons and headmasters who formed the nucleus of what Annan called the "intellectual aristocracy." That writer is undoubtedly correct.

> If they can be said to have had a Bill of Rights it was the Trevelyan-Northcote report of 1853 on reform of the civil service and their Glorious Revolution was achieved in 1870–1871 when entry into the public service by privilege . . . [was] finally abolished. Then it was ordained that men of good intellect should prosper through open competitive examination; and that the examination, as Macaulay had recommended for the Indian civil service, should be designed for those who had taken

high honours at the university. No formal obstacle then remained to prevent the man of brains from becoming a gentleman.[86]

Lest the cult of the expert and examinations be overrated, it must be remembered that the Benthamite belief in the social utility of education and the efficacy of examinations was tempered, if not obliterated, by the gentleman ideal, which gave precedence to the broadly and comprehensively educated amateur as against the narrowly trained expert. The reformers of the civil service left no doubt that they wanted for the higher civil service men who had received the expensive general education of a gentleman whereas the lower, subordinate positions might be filled with men who had received a less expensive and more practical education. As Burn puts it, the gentleman

> was a safeguard against the ruthless and rootless expert, the Edwin Chadwick ... [and] the method by which he was appointed, was a safeguard, too, against the sudden introduction of an administrative system based on abstract political principles and staffed exclusively by those who had these opinions.[87]

Above all, the new employment conditions, which made the administrative world safe for gentlemen, were meant to maintain, if not to restore, the high social status of the civil service. Even the "ruthless and rootless" Chadwick argued the preservation line, when he testified that "however high the present social position of the service, I should say that the proposed measures might be supported as being needed, and as calculated to check its downward social tendency, produced by the present system of patronage."[88] We will return to this argument and others of this kind in Chapter 5, where the reforms will be examined in detail. Here I wish to suggest merely that the abolition of patronage, though certainly in the interest of the professional status group anxious to open careers to talent, was scarcely a victory of the middle class but of gentlemen against persons of lower condition. The aristocracy was on the defensive, compelled to bring in liberally educated gentlemen to raise the efficiency of the service, but these gentlemen were neither narrow experts nor democrats but men who wished to keep the administrative machinery within that circle of gentlemen to which they and almost everyone else in society thought they belonged on the eve of the civil service reforms.

4. The Prussian Civil Service Reform

The civil service reform of 1770 had introduced a system of examinations administered by a civil service commission. In this respect, it might well have been discussed in the present chapter rather than with the background of the civil service reform. In another respect, however, it really was a "reform before the reform," for it did not introduce higher education as a requirement of access to the higher civil service. Although the career sequence of university education and in-service training became quite common during the generation preceding Prussia's defeat in 1806, the requirement of higher education was formally introduced only in the context of the Stein-Hardenberg reforms. These reforms, including the abolition of serfdom and other status prerogatives and liabilities, the reorganization of the army and the civil service, Humboldt's reorganization of schools and universities, and the introduction of municipal self-government— these reforms were so broad and so far reaching that they dwarfed the reforms of employment conditions in the civil service. As a result, the latter are scarcely even mentioned in the texts on constitutional history, even those specializing on the Stein-Hardenberg era. Aside from the regulations themselves, there is little documentary evidence bearing directly on the reforms of employment conditions, hence also little direct evidence of the intentions of the reformers. Yet the little which does exist, combined with the evidence of the reforms as a whole, suggests that the Prussian reform of employment conditions, like the English, was motivated by "technical-functional" pressures as well as by "political" considerations of making the bureaucracy safe for men educated like the reformers. That these men would be largely middle-class types was not lost on the reformers, whose general program was to free economic and educational as well as administrative institutions from the constraints of "caste," as they referred to the monopolized status order of the Frederickian era.

In the first section of this chapter, I will examine some of the reform documents which bear on the civil service reform and which also convey a sense of the reformers' orientation and intentions. In the next two sections I will turn to the broader economic, social, and cultural changes that were related to the Stein-Hardenberg reforms in general and the reform of employment conditions in particular. In the final section, I will examine the reform of employment conditions in the light of the reform of education, which, I will argue, was part and parcel of the Prussian civil service reform.

Stein-Hardenberg Reform Memoranda

When Prussia was defeated at the hands of Napoleon, its territory and population reduced to half its former size, the reformers and the leading intellectuals regarded the crisis as an inevitable consequence of delayed reform and fundamental reform now as an absolute necessity for revival of the ailing state. "A great world plan of a wise providence," explained Minister Freiherr von Hardenberg, "lies behind the upheavals of recent years. Its hidden purpose is to sweep away the outmoded remnants of the past, everything lacking in vitality and energy, and to revive Prussia's progress to perfection." Continuing in the style of the enlightenment and with a touch of German idealism, he depicts the task confronting Prussia's reformers in the crisis of 1806, "to grasp the spirit of the times, and by means of government to realize that world plan without impetus of violent upheavals."[1]

This was a common formula of the reform: change is inevitable, but one might hope to avoid bloodshed and terror; in order to accomplish the necessary changes something of the popular élan of the French Revolution had to be evoked but in a way so as not to unleash the violence of a revolution from below. Hardenberg thought it an illusion to think that revolution may be prevented simply by strengthening outmoded institutions or by enforcing traditional ideas. Such measures generally accomplish exactly the reverse, and any state which does not heed the obvious lessons of history to this effect will decline or else be forced to change. For all these reasons, the principle of the Prussian reform, he thought, must be a "revolution in the good sense, directly realizing the purpose of perfection of mankind by means of a wise government rather than violent impetus from within or without . . . democratic principles in a monarchic government: that appears to me the proper form of the *Zeitgeist*."²

To proceed in harmony with the *Zeitgeist* and the providential world plan meant, above all else, the abolition of traditional status monopolies. If at any other time one might have had scruples to propose so drastic a change of the Prussian constitution, such scruples are out of place in the present, desperate state of affairs. At this point, the Prussian phoenix might rise from the ashes of Jena and Auerstedt only through "the greatest possible freedom and equality."³ Not that anomic liberty and equality of the French Revolution, mind you, but the freedom and equality "according to the wise laws of a monarchic state."⁴ In short, if the state wishes to avoid a revolution from below, it will have to see that "the natural freedom and equality of the citizens [is limited] no more than required by their stage of cultural development and their own welfare."⁵

The first concrete recommendation following from these general principles of Hardenberg's reform plan reveals the meaning of "democratic principles in a monarchic government" and also just how much freedom and equality the reformers thought appropriate in the conditions of Prussia at the time.

> Every position in the state, without exception, shall be open not to this or that caste only, but to deserving, talented, and able men of all status groups. Every position shall be the object of general competition, and no man, however lowly, shall have his ambition stifled by the thought that he will not be able to achieve a goal for which he has eagerly and actively prepared himself.⁶

Only after this declaration, which spoke directly to the aspirations of the middle-class intelligentsia, follow the recommendations to abolish the nobility's exclusive right to own landed estates, to abolish the nobility's tax privileges, to abolish serfdom, and so on. In short, "democratic principles in a monarchic government" meant above all "equality of opportunity," and Hardenberg did not hesitate to admit that the bourgeoisie would be the chief beneficiary if access to offices and landed estates were to be opened to all the world.

It must not be supposed that the reformers were motivated only by high ideals, their invocation of the *Zeitgeist* and much German historiography notwithstanding. Their problems were tangible indeed. The Prussian state was in shambles, reduced to half its former size in population and territory, and burdened with war tributes beyond the capacity of its economy, shackled in addition by mercantile constraints. Former students at Göttingen or Königsberg, the reform bureaucrats were familiar with the most advanced doctrines of their time. Many of them had been students of Kant and Krause, who, even more famous than Kant at the time, had introduced a generation to the teachings of Adam Smith.[7] Naturally, the writings of the reformers are spiced with references and allusions to the teachings of these intellectual mentors. That in turn has lent itself to unwarranted interpretations that the reformers were true liberals both in the sense of "political liberals" and "economic liberals."[8] Yet their memoranda convey an altogether different picture. The reformers borrowed selectively, and they were masters in adapting liberal doctrines to their ideology of enlightened bureaucratic absolutism which lacked such liberal ingredients as representative government, separation of powers, or even economic laissez faire.

If they were no liberals, they were no conservatives either. Unlike the ideologists of the *Ständestaat* and the apologists of aristocratic privilege, they saw social change in the light of rational reform. On that score they certainly agreed with the philosopher of the categorical imperative, as well as with his vision of a society composed of formally free and equal citizens rather than dependent subjects. But then, Prussian careerists like Stein, Hardenberg, or Altenstein scarcely needed Kant or Fichte to teach them that society might be altered by the state.[9] That much was common coin among Prussian kings and bureaucrats although if it suited their purpose, they might invoke the *Zeitgeist* in support of reforms that proposed neither constitutional monarchy nor free trade. The few who were constitutionalists and free-trade liberals agreed wholeheartedly that administrative reform had top priority. Most of the reformers were in fact interested in stimulating a quasi-revolutionary vitality but just as interested in harnessing it within a reformed administrative system. They might promise men of property and education some participation in the affairs of state, but they were busily devising ways of co-opting elected representatives into the bureaucratic fold. In short, theirs was a plan not only for stimulating initiative and concern for the commonweal but also for discouraging unwanted political opposition and economic independence.

The reformers were fond of pointing out the hiatus between the *Zeitgeist* and the backward Prussian conditions. Chief councillor Altenstein suggested that the greatest European intellects, the representatives of the *Zeitgeist,* "had recognized . . . the necessity and importance to abolish all those systems in which man is not recognized as such, but as an object of other men."[10] Still, Prussia remained stubbornly in the clutches of tradition.

> There remain sharply divided castes or status groups—a condition that became worse in recent years. There remains a nobility with many essential privileges, especially exclusive possession of all that bestows unearned honor, prestige, etc.; a bourgeoisie with municipal rights, guilds, and monopolies that are seemingly beneficial but are actually paralyzing the nation's energy; and a very large part of the nation altogether unable to acquire property and in condition of personal slavery.[11]

Altenstein stressed the divisiveness of Prussia's system and suggested that modernization required greater unity among the parts of the system. The castes or status groups, rigidly isolated from one another by the Prussian code, struggled against one another and against the encroachments of the state. There was no nation, not even provinces, only local estates, each with its own particular interests. There was no institution in which the parts might participate in the interest of the whole, no center of gravity and common purpose. The bureaucracy, staffed by salaried officials so as to counteract the evil of independent estates, took sole care of the central affairs of state. As a result, there emerged general indifference toward administration, and no one felt responsible except if hired and paid by the state. Worse even than that, administrative reforms which might have enhanced the welfare of the whole were resisted, blocked by privileged groups anxious to maintain their prerogatives. This sorry state of affairs, Altenstein concluded, not only caused the defeat of Prussia at the hands of a state grown powerful through constitutional change but will continue to keep Prussia down unless reforms invigorate her to an even greater strength than that of France. "Everything must be removed that might paralyze the most effective expansion of power and hinder the realization of mankind's highest goals. This principle may also be characterized briefly as the necessity of the state to undertake an internal revolution without incurring the painful tremors of a revolution developing on its own."[12]

Altenstein discusses in great detail the abolition of status privileges, monopolies, and liabilities that would transform the old-status order into a class society of formally free and equal citizens under a monarchic state. Then he considers how that new civil society, no longer merely an aggregate of competing estates and status groups, might be tied to the administration so as to place the state in control of the nation's energies. The old assemblies of the estates, once the intermediaries between the state and the individual, will not do because affairs have grown too cumbersome for them and they too troublesome for the bureaucracy. Imbued with the spirit of caste, they are incapable of promoting the common interest. Besides, the members of these assemblies do not have the necessary education to give advice and assistance to the intricate bureaucracy or even grasp its spirit. Were one to inform them of everything, the machinery of government would become too cumbersome. Hence, if we wish "to give the nation more participation in administration and to save the bureaucracy from the demise that sooner or later must follow, if it remains exclusively in the hands of salaried officials—there remains no other choice than a kind of national representation."[13]

What kind of national representation did the reform bureaucrats have in mind? Hardenberg told the king that he was in full agreement with "the idea of national representation as conceived by Herr von Altenstein." But he was quick to preface his summary of that plan with an assurance that it would do no harm to the monarchic constitution. "The concept of a dangerous national assembly is not applicable." The plan was merely to draw a few elected officials into the bureaucracy. This "amalgamation of the representatives with particular administrative offices . . . will bring benefits without liabilities. The national representation will get no constitutional body of its own, nor will it establish separate offices."[14] Elected representatives would simply be a new kind of official, serving without pay, and associated with administrative offices all the way from the municipalities and rural localities on the bottom to the ministerial offices on the top. They would be elected not according to their social status but at large. Unlike the deputations of the estate assemblies, they would not be accountable to their electorates. The bureaucracy would determine their qualification in point of education and experience. Their number would be quite small, perhaps two in each district and three at the ministerial level. Altenstein summed up the purpose of the scheme in these words.

> (1) The administrative offices wherein they are given seat and voice would benefit from their advice . . . ; they would be informed about the ideas of the administration and, if necessary, could speak out with or apart from salaried officials. (2) They will inform the people they represent about the ideas of the administration; they will guide the disposition of the people when necessary and facilitate the realization of those ideas; at the same time, they will supervise the affairs of the communities according to the better insights they will have attained.[15]

A bureaucrat's dream, more public relations than politics, designed "to fasten the nation to the administration so as to get all of its energies under control,"[16] this reform scheme was also the immediate goal of Stein. Unlike Hardenberg and Altenstein, Minister vom Stein was inclined to give the ancient estates, properly reformed, a new lease on life. Scion of an old family of imperial knights, oriented to the English experience, and outspoken critic of red tape, Stein was "earnestly and fervently convinced of the superiority of properly constituted estates."[17] Unlike Altenstein, he saw them as "a powerful means of strengthening the government through knowledge and the prestige of all educated classes."[18] He too wanted "to divert [these classes] from idle sensual pleasure or empty metaphysical chimeras or pursuit of merely selfish purposes, and to maintain a well-formed organ of public opinion . . . ."[19] If he envisioned a political future that would combine German traditions with modern English political ideas and practices of self-government, and if his thinking was less rationalistic and less oriented to the political ideas of Kant and Fichte than was the thinking of Hardenberg, Altenstein, Schoen, and Stegemann, his Nassau memorandum was no less a document of administrative reform, containing little more than the memoranda of Hardenberg and Altenstein.[20] Its hallmark, too, was "participation in administration," and it was motivated by the same considerations. Like the others, he was concerned to ration "representatives" carefully so as to safeguard the predominance of the administration. "We must not establish the dominance of a few landlords . . . in the place of the bureaucracy; rather the goal is participation in the administration of provincial affairs by all owners of significant property of whatever kind so that all may be tied to the state with equal responsibilities and prerogatives."[21] At the local level he hoped to maximize participation and even self-government by elected owners; at the provincial level he was willing to allow a few representatives of the estates; on the ministerial level, finally, he expected a close working relationship between deputations of practical men of business and academic experts, on the one hand, and regular salaried bureaucrats, on the other. The professional bureaucratic staff was to be leavened with elected notables serving without pay. Stein was quick to point out savings of some 150,000 thaler in salaries alone if estate deputies be incorporated in the twenty-three provincial Boards of War and Domains.[22]

A similar reform of the municipal magistracies would yield another 200,000 thaler. But more important than this financial gain would be "revitalization of the public spirit; utilization of dormant or improperly governed energies and scattered knowledge; harmony between the spirit and the needs of the nation, on the one hand, and those of the officers of state, on the other; and the revitalization of feelings for fatherland, independence, and national honor."[23] Finally, Stein was particularly anxious to open the doors to the stuffy board rooms and chancellories of the bureaucracy. He hated red tape and, as he put it, the military and mechanistic grind of bureaucratic life. He felt that deputies from other walks of life might help in forging a new administrative style. "The incorporation of people from the whirl of practical life will crush the formalist rubbish and official mechanism in the boards and replace it with a lively, progressive, creative spirit and a wealth of opinions and feelings taken from the fullness of life."[24]

The reformers were obviously interested primarily in reform of administration. All else, "national representation" included, was at best an adjunct of bureaucratic reform. Gneisenau, one of the partisans of constitutional monarchy, put it neatly at the end of Stein's short-lived ministry. "The organization of the administration is very simple, and I have no objections except that so little thought has been given to a constitution."[25] In the remainder of this section we will briefly summarize some of the basic principles of the administrative reform, that is, the *reorganization* of the administration, which forms the immediate context of the reform of employment conditions.[26]

At the top of the hierarchy, the reformers were campaigning to abolish the royal cabinet and to establish the heads of the major administrative departments according to the principle of ministerial responsibility. While parliamentary "cabinet government" of the English variety was the stronghold of a ruling landed oligarchy, Prussia's royal "cabinet government" was the instrument of absolute monarchic rule. Except for the name, the two forms of "cabinet" government had nothing in common. In fact, the Prussian cabinet was no "cabinet" at all but a "bureau" of the king's personal staff of advisors and secretaries. That cabinet had taken an increasingly active part in formulating policy and keeping the king isolated from his top officials in the bureaucracy. Not responsible for the execution of cabinet orders, the cabinet increasingly came in conflict with top bureaucrats, who could not report directly to the king. Whereas Frederick II had dominated the cabinet as he had dominated the bureaucracy, Frederick William II allowed the cabinet to dominate him. Meanwhile, the reform bureaucrats, risen to the top and intent on emancipating the administration from royal tutelage, found themselves opposed by low-ranking privy councillors who had managed to interpose themselves between the bureaucratic elite and the king.

Stein bitterly assailed the character and ability of some of the royal councillors and warned that "the displeasure of the inhabitants of the state concerning the present administration of public affairs, the decline in the prestige of the monarchy in the public opinion, and the necessity of change in the current state of things is the necessary consequence of an inadequate institution and a faulty choice of personnel."[27] Therefore, the immediate goal was to reinstitute the direct relationship between the king and the highest officials and to form a true cabinet of responsible ministers. Without this change the principals of the reform party could not hope to concentrate the necessary power in their hands.

The second principle was to organize the central and provincial administration on strictly functional lines.[28] From the top to the bottom, the administrative hierarchy was to be reshuffled according to the principle of a strict division of functions between major departments. At the center this meant abolishing the so-called provincial ministers and integrating all business into the four or five functional ministries. At the provincial level, this meant introducing the new office of *Oberpräsident,* who, unlike the old provincial ministers, would reside in the provinces, link the center to the periphery, and direct the work of the functionally divided *Regierungen.* The latter were to take the place of the old Boards of War and Domains.[29] Many provincial functions, which had been placed outside of the old boards, for example in judicial or special offices, were now placed directly in the care of the *Regierungen.* Although this provincial streamlining was also to be guided by the principle of strict functional division, the reformers retained the older principle of collective decision making largely, it seems, because of their plans concerning the national participation of notables in administration. That plan, incidentally, never materialized. Many reformers, like Minister von Schroetter, had been skeptical about the scheme from the very beginning.

> How many well-to-do *Particuliers* are there who will leave their estates out of sheer patriotism and devote themselves to public business, and how many will have the necessary qualification to do it with benefit. As to the poorer part of the nation, where one might find most of the subjects combining talent with good will, these people will not be able to serve because of their lack of subsistence.[30]

The most revolutionary plans of the reformers concerned the reorganization of local administration in the country.[31] Here administrative and judicial functions were still attached to ownership of manorial estates, and the executive officer of the rural district, the *Landrat,* was still nominated by his peers. Although not as independent as the English J.P., he nevertheless represented the interest of the owners of manorial estates, and so effective administrative authority often did not reach below that office. Emancipation of serfs and free trade in landed estates, the reformers agreed, would have to entail some modification in the old structure of patrimonial government, but there was also agreement that a sudden abolition of all patrimonial political and judicial rights was out of the question. Indeed, neither the earlier plan of Stein, Schroetter, and board president von Vincke nor the more moderate ideas of Hardenberg on the subject could be realized. The complete reorganization of local administration planned between 1806 and 1812 was completely defeated by landed interests which were vigorously protesting any significant encroachment on their power. Only the reform of municipal administration, one of the major achievements of Stein, could be realized in the area of local government. But then, in the municipalities the aim was not so much to wrest jurisdiction from traditional bearers as to revive old corporate organs of self-government.[32]

The overall purpose of these plans, whether they succeeded or not, was summed up in the announcement of 16 December 1808. "The purpose of the new constitution is to give to the administration the greatest possible unity, power and vitality."[33] Only a streamlined and modernized administration could hope to modernize the old society in its present crisis.

As in England, the reformers argued that the old administrative reforms were no longer adequate to contemporary needs, quite apart from the present crisis. The volume of business had expanded; administration had become more complex and differentiated with the extension of Prussia's borders; the size of the bureaucracy had increased; and special offices and overlapping jurisdictions had grown like vines on the trunk and branches of the bureaucracy. Large and cumbersome, the bureaucracy was acting at cross-purposes and was constantly embroiled in jurisdictional disputes. Moreover, the reformers were unhappy about the personnel of the old administration. Now that the need for better qualified and educated officials was beginning to be recognized widely, there were too many insufficiently qualified officials from a past when regulations had often been disregarded. Altenstein recognized that Prussia's officials, if compared with those of other states, were quite competent and professional and that the old conditions might well have prevailed a little longer had it not been for that "impetus from without" which magnified outmoded conditions and revealed them more glaringly than before. Wrote Altenstein,

> As soon as the more fortunate condition changed and the state suffered one of the greatest trials which ever a state has met, all the miserable consequences showed up clearly and so strongly that almost no one dared to interpret the matter differently. It was no longer possible to prop up the collapsing edifice. One of the most significant consequences of that faulty operation is still manifesting itself now as a lack of officials suitable for higher purposes.[34]

The reformers agreed that the necessary structural changes and the new, progressive administrative style they envisioned might be realized only by way of a new personnel policy. Thus the first order of business was to "remove entirely the harmful persons."[35] Altenstein surmised that "some ministers will leave on their own if they cannot hope to be named to chief posts [in the reformed administration]. Secret cabinet councillors, chief fiscal councillors, and diplomatic councillors might be retired or transferred, and many of them would be satisfied with suitable subordinate positions. The whole thing can therefore be managed without large expense and undue commotion."[36] Stein agreed that it is "necessary to change persons if one wishes to change procedures."[37] Besides, "the new administration may gain confidence only if the old members are removed, since they have sunk deeply in the public opinion, some of them being branded severely with contempt."[38] The removal of these remnants of the past would give the reform party access to the key positions, and the next stop would be a reform of employment conditions, unchanged since 1770, which would require university training and provide a new staff educated and thinking like the reformers, thus redressing "the lack of officials suitable for higher purposes."

The Crisis of the Aristocracy

In this section and the next we will turn to some of the broader economic, social, and cultural changes that were leading up to the Stein-Hardenberg reform in general and the reform of employment conditions in particular. Like the English reform of the civil service, to be discussed in the next chapter, the Prussian reform was not merely a response to internal administrative stresses and strains stemming from growing size and functional complexity of the bureaucracy. Nor was it only a result of Napoleon's "impetus from without" although the defeat of the Prussian army dealt a blow to the prestige of the aristocratic officer corps, and the financial crisis precipitated by the conquest was a powerful cause of the infusion of "liberal" principles into the bureaucratic-mercantile state. The Prussian reform, like the English, resulted also from a shift in class and status relations. In the Prussian case, this shift may be described as a decline of the aristocracy and a rise of the professional-bureaucratic middle class.

To the extent that a reform may be analyzed in terms of a declining and a rising group, it may be viewed in a dual perspective. From one point of view, the reform has the appearance of a victory of the rising group's strategic interests. From the other, it looks rather more like a concession of the declining group interested in maintaining power in altered circumstances. According to the conceptual frame of reference sketched earlier, these two perspectives are not so much antagonistic as complementary, and a full analysis must address itself to questions raised by either way of looking at the problem. This is indeed the underlying texture of these chapters. But if both the Prussian and the English cases may be seen in both perspectives, what is the basis for viewing the Prussian case more in the light of a contest of the rising professional middle class?

In England, I argued in the last chapter, the incorporation of liberally educated middle-class professionals into the circle of gentility was essentially completed on the eve of reform. Although the reform may well be regarded as a last milestone of the rising "intellectual aristocracy" on the road to social recognition, the abolition of patronage and the introduction of educational tests were already thought of as devises for *keeping the lower orders from gaining access* to the bureaucracy. And for good reason, as we shall see in the next chapter. Whatever significance the reform may have had with respect to the changing relationship between gentlemen of birth and gentlemen of education, the reform as a device for keeping gentlemen of either kind at the helm of the civil service and the lower orders at bay does not meet with anything comparable in the Prussian case. On the eve of reform, educated Prussian burghers, though pleased to regard themselves as aristocrats of culture, were still struggling to improve their social standing vis-à-vis the aristocracy—much more so than middle-class members of the English liberal professions, to whom only the most old-fashioned aristocratic opinion would deny the status of gentlemen. In Prussia, by contrast, only the most progressive aristocratic opinion would concede to them the status of gentlemen. To put it differently, around the turn of the eighteenth century, the aspiring Prussian "aristocracy of culture" was rather more concerned with improving its social position vis-à-vis the aristocracy than with consolidating its position vis-à-vis the lower ranks. Half a century later, the story would be different; the ideology of cultivation or the notion of an aristocracy of education would get a chance to exhibit its conservative potential; but on the eve of reform it was still the ideology of an aspiring group struggling for social recognition and for *la carrière ouverte aux talents*.[39]

During the last decades of the eighteenth century, the privileges of the aristocracy in state and society were vigorously debated in pamphlets, books, and the nascent periodical literature.[40] The debate which turned largely on the question of qualification for high office, pitted the claims of ability against those of heredity, and of cultivation against those of breeding.[41] It signaled a decline of aristocracy in the esteem of middle-class intellectuals and, concomitantly, a growing opinion claiming that education and cultivation were the true marks of a gentleman. Fichte even went so far as to reverse traditional social attitudes when he wrote approvingly about the new social consciousness of burghers. "The nobleman who is nothing but that will be tolerated in the circles of the respectable burgher estate, the scholars, the merchants, and the artists only by making an effort to display extraordinary humility."[42] Just how many aspiring "aristocrats of culture" would have followed him in reversing traditional patterns of superiority and humility is uncertain, but most would have agreed that nobility devoid of cultivation and education was entitled to no place of honor in an enlightened and, some would say, revolutionary age.

It was a crisis of the aristocracy. Several aspects of this crisis have been dealt with already and need only be summarized at this point. Bureaucratization during the eighteenth century had fundamentally altered traditional authority relationships. Where upstart burghers might be placed above nobles of old lineage in the official hierarchy, and where time-honored notions concerning precedence and nearness to the throne were undermined by the exigencies of bureaucratic life, traditional legitimating principles and self-conceptions were hollowed out. The relative moral consensus of an earlier time was giving way to conflicting claims to right, expressed as they were by a growing literature, on the one hand, extolling aristocratic virtue and ideolizing quasi-medieval pretentions and, on the other, claiming rights for men of talent and education. Moreover, the precarious position into which the rising bureaucratic order was placing aristocrats was scarcely improved by their status group's decided preference for military careers and, bound up with this preference, its negative attitude toward higher education. Legacies of the thoroughgoing militarization of Prussia, these sentiments precluded easy adaptation to the new order, strengthened ultraconservatism, and thus fueled the arguments of middle-class ideologists.

In the remainder of this section, I will turn to other social changes that were undermining the old order and were deepening the crisis of the aristocracy so as to enhance the chances for a reform that would give official recognition to the civil service and its functions as the old Prussian code had not. First, in the closing decades of the eighteenth century a number of conditions conspired to undermine the aristocracy's economic power base and to thrust increasing numbers of relatively impecunious gentlemen on government offices for support. Second, a sharp increase in ennoblements contributed to further sap the prestige of the aristocracy, much as the "inflation of honors" had done in seventeenth-century England. Third, the crisis of the aristocracy culminated in 1806 when the officer corps, its most prominent and, one might say, exemplary part met a humiliating defeat at the hands of Napoleon, thus destroying whatever credibility the claims of aristocrats concerning their inbred military prowess might still have had.

The crux of the economic problems of the aristocracy was the old system of neofeudal land tenure, especially those property relations which were meant to ensure noble status to each family member by giving him a share in the family patrimony. If the law entitled each son and daughter to a share of the land or a dowry, there was also a strong corporate desire to maintain the integrity of the family estate and keep it from being subdivided generation after generation as it was done customarily in Russia. However, the two principles conflicted. Equal inheritance and maintenance of an estate were possible in most cases only by mortgaging the estate so as to cover cash settlements, allowances, dowries, and the like. And so the desire to maintain the noble status and financial independence of individuals resulted in the progressive indebtedness of the status group as a whole. According to one estimate for 1799, the nobility of the Mark Brandenburg was indebted to the bourgeoisie in an amount roughly equivalent to half the value of their estates.[43] To this must be added debts incurred to family members, for many inheritance claims were in fact settled by promissory notes. In any case, this heavy indebtedness rendered the Prussian nobility especially vulnerable to agrarian recessions and crises.

It was not always easy to sell or even mortgage a troubled estate. For one thing, the land market was restricted to gentlemen and was therefore chronically depressed. For another, transactions such as these required the consent of the entire kinship group, consisting of all male descendants of the ancestor who had brought the fief into the family. Meant to strengthen family unity and prevent irresponsible management, this practice was helpful only so long as credits or sales could be forestalled by prudent management. Once economic conditions deteriorated so that mortgaging and selling were the only viable options, dissension among the agnates, expressed as it was in constant litigation, forced many estates into bankruptcy. At best, it diminished their ability to modernize by adopting newer methods of production, which were to raise agricultural incomes, and thus improve land values, toward the end of the eighteenth century.

Frederick II, as we have seen earlier, was concerned lest the aristocracy get separated from the land and thus precipitate the decay of the dynastic military-bureaucratic system. Yet until the reforms of 1807, few aristocratic families followed his recommendation to modify the old property relations through so-called *Fideikommisse,* according to which an estate was heritable only by a single heir and according to which allowances to other family members were reduced to economical proportions. Until then, the old property relations and the legal prohibition to sell manorial estates to all but aristocrats forced many estates to the brink of ruin.[44] As we have seen too, between 1770 and 1788 the state propped up the nobility by instituting rural credit associations on the basis of joint liability of all owners in a district. Part of a deliberate conservative policy, the king wished to slow down the rising number of bankruptcies and sales during the hard times following the Seven Years' War. These threatened not only to increase the number of landless and impoverished nobles but also to break up the patriarchal relations between lord and peasant which were such an important sociological ingredient of the Prussian system. The Prussian officer corps was not to become a mere professional elite. It was to retain its role as rural ruling class, and the authority in the barracks and on the manor was to remain in the same hands. The Prussian legal code of 1794 which underscored the significance of the manorial-military structure was designed to forestall the emergence of a nominal aristocracy.

Nevertheless, the social reality had outgrown legal restrictions and stipulations. Though the sale of manorial lands was still officially prohibited, some 10 percent of all manorial estates were owned by burghers around the turn of the century.[45] As a group, these owners were in the forefront of that rationalization of agriculture which improved agricultural revenues in the closing decades of the century.[46] Moreover, since royal domains could be leased only by commoners and lessors of aristocratic manors were generally burghers, too, there were (roughly) 2,000 bourgeois owners and lessors as against 4,000 noble owners and operators of manorial estates.[47] The fact that more than a third of Prussia's landed wealth, including royal domains, were operated and exploited by commoners, shows clearly how the neat legal division of society into hereditary estates of landed aristocracy and municipal bourgeoisie was already considerably blurred. To round out the picture of the Prussian aristocracy's alienation from the land, we might add that there were roughly four times as many noble families as there were noble agricultural estates, that a quarter of the aristocratic owners were absentee owners, and that almost three-quarters of the landed aristocracy had resided in the city for extended periods of time.[48]

There is little "hard" evidence on the extent to which the landless aristocracy was impoverished, but literary assessments and other circumstantial evidence around the turn of the century suggest that the problem was considerable. "This great number of poor, propertyless nobles in Prussia," wrote Stein in 1810, "is most burdensome to the state. They are uneducated, in need of help, arrogant, and they force themselves into every sort of position."[49]

Frederick II had attempted to check the proliferation of poor, landless nobles with the old patrimonial device of requiring and sparingly granting permission to his officers to get married. A man with little financial support from his family or little revenue from his estate was not likely to get the royal consent. In fact, the king rarely granted permission to any young officer and often enough refused even high-ranking, older men, particularly if the bride-to-be was poor and nonnoble. Frederick was not only convinced that married men made poor combat officers but also extremely reluctant (perhaps unable) to expand the pension roll for widows and orphans.[50]

Like Frederick William III, he might have wished to check the rapidly expanding corps of cadets, which, it has been suggested, grew as fast as it did largely because of the growing number of impecunious and uneducated gentlemen.[51] However that may be, his strict policy of marriage consent facilitated the downward mobility of families in straitened circumstances. The majority of the officer corps might have remained unmarried, but that did not prevent gentlemen from keeping mistresses and siring illegitimate children who did not have to be recognized by either "society" or state. While the fathers were thus kept within the circle of nobility to serve as gentlemen in arms, their illegitimate children were born without their rank.

Still, the state found it necessary to augment its welfare rolls and pension chests for widows and daughters of former officers. In the year of the French Revolution it entitled all officers who had served twenty years to draw a pension, however small. And it looked after a particularly embarrassing and pressing problem which the king described in these words.

> It has come to the attention of His Majesty, that there are many invalid soldiers in the country leading a most wretched life for want of support, some even begging their subsistence, thereby causing a most pressing burden to the state and especially to the country, and that a similarly sorry destiny has overtaken even well-deserved officers.[52]

If the structural conditions for the rise of a landless, dependent nobility had been counteracted somewhat by Frederick's policy of marriage consent, they were set free when his successor adopted a most permissive policy. Frederick William II (1786–1797) went even so far as to recognize and ennoble many of the illegitimate children sired during the reign of his predecessor. This royal largesse caused not only an additional financial burden on budgets and welfare funds but also many personal financial problems which endangered military careers so that "very many officers," heavily indebted, were leading wretched lives and were, according to one document, "seeking ways and means to insinuate themselves into the civil service without being invalid."[53] Indeed, in the last decade the influx of poor and uneducated nobles into the lower ranks of the bureaucracy enhanced that differentiation between the higher and the subaltern service, which has been mentioned already. Frederick William III (1797–1840) once more reverted to a stricter policy. From now on illegitimate children were to be recognized only in exceptional circumstances and only if parents were able to provide for their education "in order that . . . [these children] do not increase the number of eligible candidates for cadet schools."[54]

The deteriorating condition of the aristocracy, or at least a significant proportion of it, would have been sufficient, perhaps, to lower its esteem in the eyes of many burghers whose official rank raised them above most aristocrats or whose credits propped up estates of an exclusive social group to which they had no access. To make matters worse, the crown fueled the crisis of the aristocracy by an "inflation of honors," that is, a steep increase in ennoblements. In this respect, too, Frederick II had been frugal whereas his successors, especially Frederick William II, evinced uncommon largesse. It is true that Frederick II had conferred twice as many titles as his predecessor, but Frederick William II conferred five times and Frederick William III two and a half times as many as Frederick II.[55] Much as in England in the early seventeenth century, such an inflation of honors could not but sap the prestige of aristocratic rank, particularly at a time when democratic social ideas from France and German neo-humanism were reverberating among the intelligentsia and when educated middle-class bureaucrats were smarting under the competition of preferred, but less tutored nobles, whose arrogant consciousness of rank clashed with bourgeois claims based on merit and ability.

Finally, the officer corps, the finest jewel in the Prussian crown, was no longer what it had been because it had not changed very much since Frederick's time. Its general officers were old men, locked into past ways of doing and thinking and complacent about the strength of Prussian arms.[56] Meanwhile, the French army had made advances in tactics, organization, and technology, and its "national" troops were fired by that élan and vitality which the Prussian reform party so much admired yet found altogether lacking in the Prussian ranks. There is no need here to pursue the military reasons for Prussia's defeat at the hands of Napoleon except to point out that the reformers were convinced that two of the main reasons were Frederick's rigid exclusion of bourgeois officers and the officer corps' deplorable level of education. "The melancholy belief that one must belong to a special class in order to defend the fatherland," wrote General Grolman, "has done much to plunge it into the present abyss, and only the opposite principle can pull it out again."[57] Stein could not agree more. "What can we expect from the inhabitants of these sandy steppes—these artful, heartless, wooden, half-educated men—who are really capable only of becoming corporals or book-keepers?"[58] Once sentiments such as these held sway among the enlightened bureaucracy and the Prussian intelligentsia, the crisis of the aristocracy was complete.

The Rising Middle Class

When the rising middle class is considered in the Prussian case around the turn of the eighteenth century, it must be emphasized immediately that the major portion of the bourgeoisie was scarcely "moving" at all but remained exactly where it had been throughout the century: in the clutches of tradition. Artisans were producing in traditional ways and for local markets regulated by monopolistic guilds. Like retailers and petty merchants, they were still more concerned with regulating competition than with promoting free trade. Although free production and free trade was beginning to undermine traditional monopolies, and although merchant capital was beginning to flow into putting-out ventures that were helping to transform handicraft into factory production, especially in textiles, these developments did not yet affect a large sector of the Prussian bourgeoisie. Moreover, most of Prussia's relatively large-scale pro-duction—textiles, luxuries, and military equipment—and, conse-quently, much merchant and finance capital were entwined in a web of monopolies and privileges spun by the state.

Hence, the rising middle class refers largely to the academic in-telligentsia within and on the fringes of the dynastic state and, perhaps, to a small stratum of merchants and financiers. Both groups had made significant inroads into previously aristocratic strongholds, one competing with the aristocracy in the offices under the crown and the other advancing in the sphere of landed property. Even before the reforms, far-sighted observers argued that the neat com-partmentalization of the status groups in the Prussian code was out of date and that it would be only a matter of time before these developments would have to be recognized in law.[59]

A generation or more behind England in industrial development, Prussia was importing a liberal ideology which found little resonance outside the universities—in the circles of the intelligentsia and the university-trained officials. It is true that public opinion inside and outside official quarters was beginning to turn against the excessive traditionalism of municipal guilds, but it is no exaggeration to say that the doctrines of Adam Smith, taught in the new economic seminars at the universities, appealed largely to students and intellectuals oriented to bureaucratic careers and to reform officials beginning to think that the state's tax base might be expanded better by enlarging the scope for free trade and entrepreneurial activity than by the heavy hand of mercantilist policy. Gerth has stated the idea succinctly.

> Since the middle of the eighteenth century, we perceive a continually growing readiness of the German intelligentsia to accept bourgeois liberal thought from France and England. While the emergence of these ideas was in these countries linked to the practical interests of the commercial bourgeoisie, and while broad strata of the intelligentsia there were related to these interests, this connection was almost entirely missing in Germany. Here the development of the commercial bourgeoisie was initially significant only indirectly as a base of recruitment from which individuals might move up into the intelligentsia, not directly as the engine of the development of political ideas.[60]

Like the doctrine of free trade, political ideas about representative government were equally beyond the major portion of the Prussian bourgeoisie. "A change in the organization of the state in our fatherland," wrote Hippel, the novelist and friend of Kant, in his constitutional brief of 1808, "is not desired by many, indeed only by the so-called middle class: the political neologists among the academics, officials, middling merchants and bourgeois owners of landed estates. Those alone wish equality of rights. . . ."[61] Those were also the groups who were lodged betwixt and between the major status groups—travelers between two worlds who shared in some respects the privileges of the aristocracy yet were distinctly second in rank to the nobility in others. Moreover, of these groups who were receptive to ideas concerning representative government, only the officials were organized. They furnished that small group of high military and civil officials who attempted to call a national convention as early as 1808.[62] With popular resonance altogether absent, the revolution in France stimulated discussion only among the intelligentsia; and in these circles, the abolition of the feudal privileges of the nobility and, more generally, the freeing of Prussian subjects from hereditary burdens and disabilities were considerably more important than political representation because *la carrière ouverte aux talents* would in fact give the politically conscious segment of the middle class access to the controlling positions of the state. In the remainder of this section, I will suggest that deteriorating career opportunities, stemming in part from the noble reaction at the close of the eighteenth century and in part from an oversupply of educated talent relative to the demand for it, not only strengthened the intelligentsia's receptivity to liberal ideas but also explains why these liberal ideas were bent so much in the direction of equality of opportunity. Huber has expressed the idea succinctly.

> Prussian absolutism, unable to integrate the new forces of the bourgeoisie, provoked the opposition of bourgeois society, which first turned away from it only in order to suffuse it later. In the beginning this opposition was pitched on the level of a philosophical critique. But the opposition party moved by the ideas of Kant and at the same time by the liberal, democratic, and national concepts of the French Revolution, pressed for the renewal and transformation of the state itself.[63]

One might almost say that the Prussian official bourgeoisie was fighting the French Revolution in the context of bureaucracy by leveling status distinctions between themselves and the hereditary nobility and by seizing a greater share of administrative power.

The sons of artisans and petty merchants who followed in their fathers' footsteps entered a world in which practice still followed traditional norms and in which a man's social position was relatively secure, economic fluctuations notwithstanding. But the young men who were sent in increasing numbers to the university in anticipation of lucrative and prestigious positions in the government or the church faced uncertain futures. Part of the problem was simply an increase in the number of students in excess of new opportunities in the bureaucracy or the church. Although statistics are hard to come by, some evidence may be found in the periodicals of the time, which began the incessant complaints that are quite familiar to the historian of the nineteenth century. "The number of young people envisioning careers in the civil service," wrote one observer in 1788,

> is so considerable that all the administrative boards are overflowing. Given the number of posts that might open up even in case of high mortality there remains no hope whatever that all of these young men—

look at the majority of them—can be accommodated in a manner so
as to compensate them for the numerous sacrifices they have incurred
during their training.[64]

Another writer sought ways and means of reducing the "mass of
students from the lower orders who have no natural calling for
scholarship but push into the learned status groups." He was frankly
concerned lest the influx of students from poor as well as newly
affluent merchant homes, whom he thought equally uncultured,
lower the prestige of the learned status group.[65]

The prince in one of Justus Möser's "patriotic phantasies," written
in 1775, thought that parents would do better to let their children
learn a craft.

> To hell with this desperate studying; all of my subjects want to let their
> children study [at the university], and if this continues, they will soon
> have to plow the fields with pens. Listen, my dear chancellor, draft an
> edict that no one shall study without my permission; Rectors and Masters
> shall accept no one without a written pass signed by me, and I will not
> issue one except upon the most thorough investigation whether the boy
> has enough genius and property for his studies.

The prince's chancellor, obviously representing Möser's opinion,
thought that in the realm of education laissez faire was in the best
interest of the state.

> As Your Highness commands, but Your Very Highness complained to
> me yesterday that among all your officers there is none to whom you
> might entrust the command of your troops in the next campaign. If
> among four hundred officers, who represent the heart of your realm,
> there is none to whom you can entrust a major task, how can Your
> Highness demand that the few who will receive permission to study
> shall turn out to be the very people needed by the state? Oh, a hundred
> and maybe a thousand must learn to strum before you get a single
> virtuoso, and among ten thousand legal scholars you may find no Mevius,
> no Struve.[66]

Möser's satire seems to have captured something of the outlines of
an issue that was debated not only at the end of the eighteenth
century but again and again at various times during the next century.
In 1836, after a brief respite, the problem was again debated, and
the editor of *Minerva*, worried about the political effects, warned,
"The matter deserves utmost attention; for if this evil is not controlled,

then the number of politically discontented among the middle class, which is now at the base of the life of the state, must necessarily increase in mounting progression."[67] At the turn of the century the middle class might not as yet have been at the base of the state, but the career difficulties of educated youth then as a generation later were a powerful lever of discontent and receptivity to liberal ideas.

The overproduction of educated talent, to borrow a phrase from a later period, increased the waiting periods between graduation and installment to office and greatly increased the need for temporary employment of private tutors in the homes of noble and well-to-do bourgeois households. Although this type of interim employment, which might last a long time for many a young scholar, was more characteristic of candidates in theology or philosophy than for aspirants to the bench and civil office, the institution of private tutor was so typical a phase in the careers of leading German intellectuals that we must give it some attention here. Kant, Herder, Fichte, Hegel, Schleiermacher, Hölderlin, to mention only a few illustrious names of the period, had been private tutors and had experienced its tensions and formative influences on their lives.

Tutoring gave the unemployed intelligentsia without independent means the wherewithal for subsistence as well as an opportunity to meet influential patrons that might launch them on a career in the government, the church, or a school. The last aspect was not insignificant at a time when patronage was still the dominant method of appointment, however tempered it may have been with educational qualifications and demonstrated ability.

Tutoring, contemporaries and historians agree, had important psychocultural consequences. Some point to the remarkable refinement in manners which a noble household would cause the bourgeois tutor to assume; others think that the private tutor did the nobility much good by stimulating interest in and respect for book learning. More important, perhaps, are the formative influences which this stage of life may have had on the changing consciousness of the bourgeois intelligentsia in the era of the French Revolution. While some men, like Fichte and Hölderlin, wrote fondly and glowingly about the elegance and refinement ordinarily out of reach to petty bourgeois scholars, others were wont to recall the sense of inferiority and the many humiliations of a role that cast them halfway between servant and companion. This is what Dilthey had in mind when he wrote, "The years as private tutor, what misery of the future clergyman and educator in those days. The young generation of those days experienced them as oppressive, the more so as it grew up under the impression of the French Revolution."[68] Those who went through this attractive and yet oppressive stage must have experienced rather more painfully what Freiherr von Knigge felt during his keen sociological observations.

> My very soul is affected when in many a noble house I see the tutor sitting quietly and humbly at the table of his gracious employer, not daring to engage in any conversation or to place himself in any way on equal terms with the rest of the company, even when the children in his charge are given precedence by parents, friends, and servants—precedence to him who should be regarded as the most important benefactor of the entire family if he discharges his duties properly.[69]

Benefactor or beneficiary, the tutor was in a tension-ridden social position, which was eminently conducive to the ambivalent attitudes toward the nobility which we find throughout this period—attitudes that might oscillate between deferential imitation and defiant self-assertion. If, as Dilthey suggests, the situation of the tutor was experienced as oppressive the more so as he grew up under the impression of the French Revolution, his attitude toward his betters changed from deference to defiance the more he came under the spell of *Bildung*—that revolutionary, liberating yardstick for judging human worth, which may have been, at least in part, a creative response to the situation of the bourgeois intellectual as tutor in a noble household and which was to become a new bond between educated men regardless of social status.[70]

The career difficulties of middle-class university men were due not only to an increase in the number of aspirants for bureaucratic employment but also to changes in the sphere of employment. Some jobs in the civil service were no longer suitable entry points for graduates of gymnasia and universities. Minor posts as scribes, copyists, registration clerks, and ordinary secretaries fell beneath the station of young men with a higher education. As noted earlier, up to and including the reign of Frederick II this had not been the ordinary state of affairs. Neither under Frederick William I nor under Frederick II—indeed, nowhere else in Europe including England—was there a sharp distinction between lower and higher civil service posts. Well educated men might start as copy clerks and secretaries and might be promoted from these ranks to even the highest ministerial posts if they were found capable or otherwise suitable to patrons higher up.

Two principal conditions seem to have altered this state of affairs in Prussia. On the one hand, the last decades of the century sharply increased the reserve army of military invalids and pensioners. On the other, the abolition of Frederick II's monopoly of tobacco trade created a pool of redundant officials.[71] All of these "pensioners," as they were called, had to be provided for, and the deteriorating financial conditions under Frederick William II seemed to have given special prominence to public offices as the most economical way to provide relief. In any case, toward the end of the eighteenth century, the lower civil service became more than ever a social security and welfare roll for former soldiers, invalids, and redundant clerks. A cabinet order in 1799 reminded all ministers to fill as soon as possible all petty positions (cashiers, bookkeepers, expeditors, registration clerks) with pensioners and invalids. None but pensioners and invalids were henceforth to be considered for such posts, and any exceptions required royal consent. Indeed, Frederick William II went even further. Whereas his predecessors had employed unpaid in-service trainees fresh from school or university on tasks not altogether different from those of petty officials, he was determined to reduce the number of aspirants for higher office in the lower jobs so as to make room for invalids and pensioners. These, incidentally, seem to have included increasing numbers of uneducated and impoverished noblemen.[72]

The upshot of that tendency was not only a change in the quality of office life but also a noticeable change in the prestige of what in fact if not yet in law became a lower rung of Prussian officialdom. As Naudé put it, "Intelligent, young, ambitious officials with good backgrounds but nevertheless willing to serve from the bottom up, were successively replaced by dutiful, hard-working, and honest if lethargic officials without education and breeding, and without drive or ability to work themselves up to higher positions."[73] Contemporary commentators well into the nineteenth century seemed to have good reason to note that the vast majority of Prussia's petty officials, including even country schoolmasters, were former drill sergeants

and the like. Imbued with Prussian obedience and a penchant for
red tape, these men epitomized the sort of official practice which
Stein and the other reformers detested and repeatedly and con-
temptuously characterized as mechanical, "formalist rubbish."[74]

Thus, a large segment of the civil service became increasingly
unattractive to educated burghers in the closing decades of the
eighteenth century. In addition, they appear to have received increasing
competition from nobles in what gradually became the higher civil
service. Of course, there had always been positions, such as district
councillor (*Landrat*), to which none but noblemen could reasonably
aspire; and of course everyone knew the Great Frederick's preference
for nobles, everything else being equal. Although the middle class
advanced in the Frederickian bureaucracy, it was a well-known fact
of life that the higher the position, the stiffer the competition from
nobles was likely to become. There is reason to believe that noble
competition increased around the turn of the century—not only in
the higher ranks but also at the lower levels of a judicial and civil
career.

In both branches of the bureaucracy, university graduates generally
entered at this time as in-service trainees (*Auskultatoren*). This position
they held for about two years. Then they advanced to the second
stage of in-service training (the position of *Referendar*) via an examination. At the end of some four or five years in this position,
a candidate passed through the great state examination and thence
to the position of *Assessor* until a councillorship opened up. This,
in any case, was the sequence in the judicial service, which was ever
more closely approximated in the civil service.

Between 1786 and 1806, the proportion of nobles among judicial
Auskultatoren, *Referendare*, and *Assessoren* was 9, 12, and 12
percent, respectively.[75] Surprisingly low, these proportions do not
appear to have changed significantly during the fifteen-year period.
As we move to the rank of judicial councillor, however, we find
that 35 percent in the judiciary were nobles in 1801.[76] Unfortunately
there is no indication whether that proportion increased in the
fifteen or twenty years before the battle of Jena, but the marked
increase of nobles in the rank of councillor suggests the bias against
which nonnobles had to advance—and, moreover, that this bias
was not limited to the officer corps.

Between 1786 and 1806, the proportion of nobles among *Referendare* at the Boards of War and Domains was a surprising 35 percent whereas at the same period only 26 percent of the councillors nominated to the boards were nobles.[77] Here it would seem that the bias worked the other way around. Yet if we consider all councillors, including tax councillors as well as *Landräte*, the proportion of nobles is considerably higher. Indeed, we find that the proportion of nobles among all councillors increased from 38 percent in the period 1770–1786 to 45 percent in the period 1786–1806, thus lending some statistical support to the familiar theme of noble reaction in the period of the French Revolution.[78]

While middle-class careerists were thus confronted with many obstacles, the fusion of the hereditary nobility and the educated, official middle class into a privileged upper rank of society was to some extent already on its way and rendered the remaining inequalities between the status groups all the more frustrating and increasingly out of date. Like the nobility, the educated officialdom (including also clergymen, academics, and high school teachers) was exempt from patrimonial and local municipal courts and assigned instead to the privileged jurisdiction of the state's higher courts. In this way, the Prussian code recognized that education and the honor of government office conferred at least some of the privileges which were birthrights of the nobility.

This was not the only respect in which the law recognized the rising middle class and its partial fusion with the nobility. During the eighteenth century, for example, Prussian noblemen were also legally barred from marrying women of the lower orders. In the first half of the eighteenth century, the law specifically named those occupational groups which were thought unsuitable sources of marriage partners. Since the law gave rise to much litigation, the lawgivers felt it might be easier to define the higher orders than the lower and so, not unexpectedly, applied the criterion of education (*Bildung*) as the bridge between the nobility and the upper middle class. Increasingly, the marriageable upper ranks of society were thought to include all "educated classes."[79] This social-legal development was in fact progressing in exactly the direction which Fichte had in mind when he suggested that the natural order of things recognized only two status groups: "one which forms only the body for mechanical work and another which primarily educates the mind.

Between these status groups there is a true *mésalliance*. Within them, there is none."[80]

Beyond the law, education became in fact a new social bond that united enlightened and educated noblemen and commoners into a status group set apart increasingly from the mere nobility and its old-style concept of rank, on the one hand, and the mere commercial middle class with its excessive deference to aristocratic rank, on the other. Those of the nobility who thus joined the bourgeois intelligentsia and its ideology of education (*Bildung*) also broke away from the outmoded notion of a separate noble education. "Acting as individuals," writes Rosenberg,

> they sought to affirm their social superiority without putting primary emphasis on the privileges of birth and on titled position. Instead they aimed at the preservation of leadership status by new means, by developing the faculties inherent in themselves and by excelling as upholders of intellectual culture and, in professional and public life, as superior performers.[81]

Thus, indeed, was the outlook of a younger generation of gentleman bureaucrats coming up the ranks in the closing decades of the eighteenth century. It was a generation alive, like the young Humboldt, the future Minister of Culture, to the claims of individual and corporate freedoms against those of arbitrary state power. They were generally aligned against the despotism and rigidity of the bureaucratic-military apparatus which, in their view, not only trampled on the rights of men but also stifled individual and social initiative. They weren't liberals and democrats, but they wished to infuse the bureaucracy with the élan of that new order of things which was coming into being outside Prussia and which was exciting the imagination of the young intelligentsia in and out of government. It is from the ranks of younger officials thinking in these terms that the reform party within the bureaucracy developed even before the defeats at Jena and Auerstedt. If the aristocrats among them were perhaps inclined to view their politics as a renewal of the aristocracy by adapting it to the new conditions of life, their middle-class colleagues were striving for equality of opportunity, administrative power, and elimination of those obstacles which still barred their full inclusion into the upper social rank.

Civil Service Reform and Reform of Education

The reform party that swept to power after Prussia's collapse was a coalition of officials around the major reformers, not a political party in the normal sense of the word. Their "program," deriving from many sources, converged in the conviction that Prussia needed an orderly "revolution" from above, directed by the most educated, enlightened portion of Prussian society: the status group of professional bureaucrats, in which, according to Hegel's definition, "the consciousness of right and the developed intelligence of the mass of the people is found."[82] Most of the reformers, who would certainly have agreed with Hegel, were officials in the financial administration and had typically studied law and cameralistics before entering the bureaucracy as in-service trainees at a Board of War and Domains.[83] Relatively few of them were officials in the judiciary or the diplomatic service. Huber goes so far as to suggest that "the reform movement was a party of administrative lawyers whereas the restoration movement was a party of judicial lawyers."[84] However that may be, the reformers wished to free military, administrative, and economic institutions from the constraints of the old monopolized status order, to open careers to talent, and to extend to men of education a monopoly of the higher civil service. One by one they issued decrees revising the old status order as it had been defined in the General Code of 1794.

These revisions, to be sure, did not abolish privileged corporate groups, such as the corporate group of officials (*Beamtenstand*), which had been recognized by the code and like the aristocracy exempted from many civic obligations. The reform legislation only abolished certain monopolies of hereditary status groups, opened up careers, occupations, and property to competition and free trade, and so restratified the society according to education, property, and official standing. The reformers incorporated new professional groups into the privileged *Beamtenstand* when they raised such groups as teachers of reformed schools to civil service status. The overall impact of the reform on the stratification of Prussian society was characterized succinctly by a contemporary.

> The stratification of the population along the lines of the old estates was not completely eliminated, but the divisions became less pronounced and the difference between officials and non-officials more accentuated

than those between nobles and non-nobles. The civil service absorbed members of all these traditional estates and amalgamated them into a new estate dominating the others.[85]

The reform of employment conditions in the civil service, though a relatively inconspicuous part of the entire reform scheme, was quite significant in that restratification because it closed the higher civil service to all but men of higher education. The regulations of employment conditions that were issued during Stein's ministry have been described as a continuation of the old pattern of the eighteenth century.[86] This is not altogether correct. Although they continued the old practice of requiring a different preparation for careers in the judicial and civil service, they broke the pattern of the preceding decades in that they required a university education as a condition for entry into in-service training. Stein explicitly decided to keep apart the two career trajectories, holding that identical forms of education and training would be ill-suited for judges if too cameralistic, detrimental to administrators if too much oriented to the law, and injurious to both if a combination of the two.[87] But his business instructions of 1808 demanded "thorough university studies in political-administrative science (*Staatswissenschaft*) and related subjects such as technology, statistics, experimental physics, chemistry, botany, and economics."[88] As before, one year of practical experience in commerce or agriculture was required, but it was no longer specifically restricted to service on a domain.

The regulations of the Hardenberg period, while confirming the requirement of university training, broke with the traditional ways and laid the foundation of the nineteenth-century pattern of educating and training civil servants in the classics and the law.[89] "In order to be acceptable as *Referendar*," the new regulations of 1817 prescribed, "the candidate must have had a good education in ancient and modern languages, history, and mathematics." In addition, he was to have attended a university and have acquired knowledge in political-administrative science and related subjects, as well as "thorough knowledge of the law."[90] Finally, he had to prove some prior experience in agriculture or other major trade "and so far as it is possible have worked as trainee (*Auskultator*) in a judicial office."[91]

The emphasis on practical orientation, especially to the business of the domains administration, was now clearly on the decline as was, more generally, the orientation to cameralistics. The reformers, many of them lawyers with a classical education, were more interested in the intellectual culture of candidates for the higher civil service than in acquaintance with the minutiae of running an estate. They were oriented rather more to the "new economics" of Adam Smith than to the teachings of the cameralists. And as exponents of the *Rechtsstaat*, they were much less inclined to regard the formalism of the law with the contempt of Frederick William I or Frederick II. Although cameralism was declining in favor of the law, it must not be supposed, however, that it was about to be replaced by legal training altogether. Even the regulations of 1846, although requiring two years of in-service training at a court as prerequisite for in-service training in the civil service, still asked for a test showing that the candidate had "some familiarity with the political-administrative sciences, the principles of political economy, policy and finance . . . and at least a general acquaintance with the cameralistic auxiliary subjects, agronomics in particular."[92] Put otherwise, in 1817, employment conditions were switched on that dual track of legal *and* cameral studies leading to legal *and* cameral in-service training, which was to prevail throughout the first half of the nineteenth century. Thereafter, the emphasis on the legal side was to crowd out cameralism.

Friedrich suggests that the leaning toward law was in part conditioned by the prestige of jurists who had eclipsed the cameralist administrators in social status. He thinks that the changing relative status position of the two branches would sooner or later "produce a movement for the recapture of some of the lost territory." In his opinion, "one way of going about that was to approximate the training of administrative to that of judicial officials."[93] There is much to be said for this view. Yet the struggle between the two branches of government was not merely a matter of recapturing lost prestige. The legal reform and codification under Carmer and Svarez, Ministers of Justice, in the closing decades of the eighteenth century, had given the judiciary a sort of constitutional supremacy, a monopoly in the making and interpreting of laws—a supremacy which Altenstein interpreted as a "dangerous preponderance over the whole" of the state.[94] Guardian of the General Code of 1794, hence of the traditional status order, hence of the privileged hereditary estate, as the reformers saw it, the judiciary in league with landed interests was the principal opponent of administrative reform. For the reformers it was a struggle of the administration, oriented to the interests and the welfare of the whole, against the judiciary, oriented to the interests and the welfare of the dominant estate. One of the reformers even spoke of a "judicial murder of the general good."[95] Hardenberg wasted no time to check the ascendancy of the judiciary, to subordinate it to the executive, and to assert for the administrative branch a monopoly of the law-giving function. If the emerging emphasis on legal training may in fact be explained in terms of a competition between the two branches of the Prussian service, it would seem that the struggle for constitutional supremacy must have been at least as significant as the contest for prestige.

Interesting as the shift to legal training is, the important reform of employment conditions was the fact that since 1808 candidates for the higher civil service had to have attended a university. The reform of 1817, in addition, specified a classical secondary education, thus pointing to the reform of education, which was in fact an integral part of the reform of employment conditions. Thinking as they did in idealist terms, the reformers regarded the reform of education as a major building block in the reconstruction of the state, not merely an adjunct to the reform of employment conditions. Although we are chiefly interested in employment conditions in this study, a brief aside on the broader significance of education in the reformers' view may be in order.

The reformers envisioned no less than a new specie of "culture state" (*Kulturstaat*). That state would embody the most progressive, most enlightened cultural values and would through its "philosopher bureaucrats" educate the nation for higher purposes.[96] There is a faint echo of this conception of the state in the many versions of that royal pronouncement that held that the state would have to regain in the realm of the spirit what it had lost in the realm of military power.[97] In order to raise the nation from its present calamity, the state would have to guarantee certain freedoms in intellectual life, just as it would have to in economic life. More importantly, the state would have to create the conditions for intellect and culture to suffuse the very state itself, spiritualize it, and so raise it above particular interests and the pragmatism of power politics. Education, in brief, was the means by which the culture state and through it an enlightened nation would come into being. Hegel was to give philosophic expression to this ideology of an official intelligentsia whose claim to right and recognition rested on its education and culture and which promoted its own status characteristics as the very essence of the state. Moreover, when Hegel conceptualized the bureaucracy as a universal status group of enlightened officials governing according to the dictates of reason, above the pulling and hauling of civil society, he shed some light on how the reformers conceived of their own role and of the bureaucratic *Kulturstaat* they were aiming at. Where intellectual life and statecraft were thought to be so intimately bound up with one another that some of the reformers thought of the *Kulturstaat* as primarily an *Erziehungsstaat* or tutelary state whose function it would be to awaken the dormant spiritual powers of the nation, the first order of business was naturally to assert the state's sovereignty in matters of education. In fact, one might sum up the reform of education as a "nationalization" of education within Prussia.

The first aspect of this nationalization was the centralization of authority in the sphere of education and the imposition of a master plan of educational institutions. Rational coordination and a linked sequence of levels leading up to university study were the watchwords. Although the General Code of 1794 had in fact recognized the sovereignty of the state in educational matters and had specified, in the words of the lawgiver, "that schools and universities are institutions of the state," the actual domination of the state in this area was not very great, and the "system" was in fact a labyrinth of different, partially overlapping schools, sponsored by the church, private individuals, municipal corporations, provincial estates, as well as the state.[98] For the most part, the state's sovereignty was no more than a matter of ultimate authority, eminently compatible as that was with heterogenous principles of administrative practice, training of teachers, methods of instruction, and so forth. Hence, the school system which the reformers inherited from the eighteenth century was an open field for rationalization and transformation into a bureaucratic department of state.

The second aspect of nationalization followed from the first. The only way in which the secular and national aims of the state might be finally realized was to bring the teachers under its direct control. This meant professionalizing them and raising them to civil service status. Professionalization, moreover, involved standardization of training and employment conditions, including a whole set of new civil service examinations.

The third aspect of nationalization, finally, concerned the examination of students. From the educational point of view these examinations were meant to standardize performance and to facilitate the transition of students from one level or one type of school to another. From the point of view of this study, however, these examinations were also parts of the new system of civil service examinations. For a "leaving" examination at one level of education might serve as entrance condition not only at the next level of education but also as a condition of entry into the civil service. State educational examinations and the corresponding certificates in fact did double duty as educational and civil service entitlements. If this aspect was not yet completely apparent at the outset of the reform, it certainly became prominent in the aftermath as the divisions of the educational system into elementary, secondary, and higher educational institutions turned out to correspond rather neatly to the tripartite division of the service into lower, intermediate, and higher-service grades. As in England fifty years later, the divisions of the civil service and the divisions in education were two mutually dependent developments.

Following Humboldt's master plan, the new system of education was divided into elementary schools, gymnasia, and universities. Since the elementary school reform is not important for our purpose, I will only describe briefly the salient features of the reformed institutions of secondary and higher education with special emphasis on the system of state examinations linking those institutions to one another and to the state bureaucracy.

Around the turn of the century, a secondary education was offered in a variety of schools, especially Latin grammar schools (*Gelehrtenschulen*), non-Latin burgher schools (*Bürgerschulen*), military academies, and private schools. Humboldt's predecessors, subscribing to the modernist tendency that stressed contemporary languages, natural science, and subjects useful in commerce and government, were planning to eliminate the old Latin grammar schools, and most observers around the turn of the eighteenth century would probably have predicted that this "French" tendency would sooner or later dominate the educational scene.[99] Humboldt, a declared opponent of the modern approach, built his new system around neohumanist, idealist principles, stressing Greek, Latin, German, and mathematics. An opponent of educational pluralism and specialization, he promoted the classical gymnasium as the "universal" type, alone entitled to prepare students for the universities. Ostensibly opposed also to any kind of status education—as if classical gymnasia were altogether free from status connotations—Humboldt campaigned also to change the old nobiliary academy at Liegnitz and even to abolish cadet schools. With respect to the former, he held that education "would have to be a learned one, as good as that in a gymnasium, and encompassing thorough study of Latin and Greek."[100] As to the latter, the reform of secondary education would make the cadet school superfluous.

> For if the class of schools offering a general education necessary for all persons and citizens is properly established, then the general needs of all status groups are met and the cadet schools will no longer be able to accomplish anything that regular schools, resting on a higher standpoint, may not be able to accomplish even better.[101]

The old municipal schools, finally, were reduced to preparatory schools for gymnasia and, somewhat inconsistently with the plan, to schools serving the occupational needs of commercial strata. Many of them were eventually turned into so-called *Real-gymnasien,* which specialized in mathematics, natural science, and modern languages but which were not authorized to grant certificates entitling students to matriculate at the university.[102]

This reorganization of secondary schooling was accomplished in part through the introduction of state examinations in the subjects defining a classical gymnasium. Although the leaving examinations, the so-called *Abitur* or certificate of maturity, was introduced as early as 1788, it was revised and extended in 1812 and again in 1834. From 1812 to 1834 a student might enter the university on the strength of a certificate of maturity but was entitled, if he lacked one, to take an entrance examination administered by the university. This alternative route to the university was blocked in 1834. Henceforth, the classical gymnasium had a monopoly not only as a preparatory school for the university but also as the training ground for future higher civil servants. Thus, when the employment regulations of 1817 required a classical secondary education plus university study in law, they reflected the institutional linkage between classical gymnasia and universities which the reformers were forging at the time but which was not completed until 1834.

The employment regulations of 1817 also formalized the distinction between the higher civil service (*höherer Staatsdienst*) and the subaltern "bureau service" (*Bürodienst*). Since this subaltern service was still filled largely with military pensioners, whose educational attainments were very low, the culture gap between the two service ranks had widened with the reform of the higher civil service. In order to bridge this gap a new regulation in 1827 established the so-called higher bureau service (*höheren Bürodienst*), that is, a higher subaltern rank, recruited from graduates of classical gymnasia. It was an essential aspect of this scheme that candidates, also referred to as "civil supernumeraries" (*Civilsupernumerare*), would be recruited from the same secondary schools as candidates for the higher civil service. They were to have received the same status education as their superiors in the higher civil service, and it was hoped that the higher subaltern service would thus gain some of the prestige enjoyed by the higher civil service.[103] However, the provincial chiefs evidently were somewhat less than dutiful in screening candidates for the higher bureau service and in fact admitted for some time men who did not have the proper educational credentials.[104]

As to the reform of higher education, the defeat of Prussia at the hands of Napoleon might well have given a boost to the plan of Humboldt's predecessors to abolish the old universities and introduce the "better" French system of specialized academies for the training of doctors, teachers, clergymen, civil servants, and so forth. Yet once again Humboldt's principle of "universality" won out over von Massow's educational pluralism. This principle not only entailed that the different branches of learning be gathered together into a single institution thought of as an "organic whole" but also that this institution would unite teaching and research, thus bridging the stark division of the French system into research academies and teaching academies. Finally, the reformed university would be a good deal more than merely the top of an educational ladder to professional employment under the government; it would also be the summit "in which everything that happens to the moral culture of the nation comes together."[105]

The second principle of the university reform was the principle of academic freedom in research and teaching, including also corporate self-government of the university. It must not be supposed, however, that the state left the university to its own devices. Humboldt himself reserved the hiring of faculty members to the state, arguing that that would serve academic freedom by counteracting the growth of guildlike traditionalism among university professors. Another means of meddling in curricular affairs, and one more important for the purpose of this study, was the system of state examinations, which was extended during the reform era. As Ringer has pointed out,

> Every regulation that was introduced to confer a privilege or to set standards for a state examination inevitably had a certain effect upon the curriculum and the organization of German higher education. This was true to some extent even for the universities, where the standing of a given discipline in the pattern of course offerings could be changed by altered requirements for a government test.[106]

Beginning with the state examination of university students destined to become secondary school teachers, the Prussian reform bureaucrats, much like the British university reformers, were well aware of the utility of civil service examinations for affecting performance in teaching and changing the curriculum. Whereas civil service examinations in England remained outside the province of the university, however, the civil service examinations in Prussia, that is, the *first* state examination in the career of a higher civil servant, became so much a part of univesity life that it displaced academic examinations just as civil service certificates displaced to a large extent the traditional academic degrees.[107]

As the reform of the civil service and of education, linked by the new state examinations, was evolving into a comprehensive, interlocking system of education, training, and selection of candidates to office, it created that official elite whose education and cultivation was to become one of the strongest social barriers in German society.[108] During the reform era, however, the emergence of education and cultivation as a profoundly conservative ideology of an established elite was barely on the horizon. The new "aristocracy of experts who purport[ed] to be the true representatives of the general interest," in the words of one Rhenish official, was still something of a counterelite pitting its ideology of cultivation against the claims of mere nobility.[109] The aristocracy of birth was still handicapped by its lack of the kind of education required by the new personnel policies, and university-trained officials were still capturing positions previously held by nobles. As the nobility would turn in larger numbers to the education previously thought of as the education of burghers and as middle-class officials increasingly accepted aristocratic valuations, the distinction between aristocracy and bourgeoisie in the bureaucracy would diminish in the face of education and cultivation. "In Germany," Paulsen would write in the latter part of the century,

> the academically educated constitute a kind of intellectual and spiritual aristocracy. . . . They form something like an official nobility, as indeed they all participate in the government and administration of the state. . . . Together, they make up a homogeneous segment of society; they simply recognize each other as social equals on the basis of their academic cultivation. . . . Conversely, anyone in Germany who has no academic education lacks something which wealth and high birth cannot fully replace. The merchant, the banker, the rich manufacturer, or even the great landowner, no matter how well he stands in other respects, will occasionally be harmed by his lack of academic training. As a consequence, the acquisition of a university education has become a sort of social necessity with us, or at least the acquisition of the *Abitur*, the potential right of academic citizenship.[110]

Such indeed were the long-run consequences of the reform of state employment conditions and the reform of education.

In the short run, the reform brought a drastic increase in the proportion of middle-class bureaucrats in the higher civil service. Between 1806 and 1829, the proportion of burghers in the central, ministerial bureaucracy increased from 36 to 60 percent; at the same time, the proportion of the *old Prussian* nobility declined from 40 to 20 percent.[111] In the *Regierungen*, three-quarters of all positions were held by burghers around 1820, and half of all presidencies, previously virtual preserves of aristocrats, were occupied by the middle class.[112] After the reforms had run their course and as the fusion of the two status groups was already on its way, aristocrats found their way back to the offices under the crown, though by now the new examination system was screening out all but university-trained men. Thus, in 1847 and 1862, men of old lineage held 64 and 60 percent, respectively, of the leading positions in the central ministerial bureaucracy.[113] Moreover, from 1820 to 1845 the proportion of nobles on provincial boards increased from 25 to 33 percent.[114] Although the proportion of aristocrats in the lower ranks, such as councillors and chief councillors, seems to have been lower than in the higher ranks, the resurgence of the aristocracy in the governing positions was not lost on liberal bourgeois critics, nor was the fact that aristocrats were once again rising faster than their bourgeois colleagues up and down the hierarchy.[115]

Meanwhile, the reformed secondary schools and universities were graduating more students than ever before and, indeed, more students from families of subaltern officials, merchants, artisans, peasants, and other nonacademic groups. Between 1816 and 1846, the number of students in gymnasia and the number of university students rose 73 and 40 percent, respectively.[116] Between 1820–1822 and 1832–1836, the total number of students from families of subaltern officials, merchants, artisans, peasants, clerks, workers, and servants, increased 80 percent at the University of Halle whereas the total number of students increased only 38 percent.[117] What is more, during these years the *higher* civil service does not seem to have expanded at all; in fact, the higher provincial administration was reduced in the twenties from 600 to 500 men so as to save costs.[118] Despite the increase in population and the increase in the number of students, the higher civil service did not increase beyond those figures until after 1848.[119]

Beyond the civil service, most of the other professions, too, were lagging behind population growth and the growth of graduating classes. Only secondary teachers seem to have kept pace.[120] And so by the 1830s, another wave of anxious comment on the excess of candidates over available positions in state and society was sweeping the press.[121]

There was good reason for anxiety. The number of students studying law almost doubled between 1820 and 1830 as the result of the new civil service regulations, and the ranks of in-service trainees in the judiciary and the civil service bulged, to 3,000 in the judicial service alone.[122] With opportunities in the professions slight, commerce depressed, in-service training in the civil and judicial service clogged, and more than a thousand examined *Assessoren* waiting for openings of tenured positions, the government warned parents in 1839 to stop sending students to the universities or at least to encourage only those "who possess superior ability and those who are prepared to support themselves for ten additional years after completion of university study."[123] Still, the number of *Assessoren* on waiting lists for permanent positions kept increasing, 25 percent in the judiciary during the 1840s, and when the revolution of 1848 began there were 2,000 of them waiting for promotion.[124] In the civil administration, too, training periods as well as waiting periods increased. According to Gillis' calculations, "those who had entered the service during the 1830s took an average of 6.6 years to pass through the training period; in the 1840s the time was 7.4 years. . . . In the 1830s the young *Assessor* could expect to wait 6.6 years for appointment; by the 1850s, the duration of the waiting period had stretched to 10.4 years."[125]

The bureaucracy was heading for a crisis. Aspirants to high office, more of them now from relatively humble social backgrounds, were again experiencing severe career difficulties. The reform had run its course; the aristocracy was preserved and was moving back to positions captured by the middle class during the reform era; and bourgeois officials were increasingly defending their privileged position against an expanding younger generation of university-trained men who wanted in. The relatively small bureaucratic elite was losing the authority which it had gained during the reform era. As it was turning its ideology of cultivation into a quas-aristocratic justification of its good fortune, a growing number of equally educated but dispossessed and frustrated men were deriving from their own academic status political rights challenging the "aristocracy of experts" in the absolutist bureaucracy.[126] Whereas in an earlier crisis preceding the reform era, the frustrations of burghers did not evoke much political unrest, now they spawned agitation for political rather than administrative reform.

5. The English Civil Service Reform

The English civil service reform, unlike the Prussian, appears to be at first glance a relatively self-contained social change abolishing the patronage system and instituting civil service examinations. It was not obviously a part of a larger reform movement, and raising the efficiency of the old system seems to have been a prominent concern. Still, the reform was not an isolated event or series of events but a process tied to many other transformations in English society. These linkages, which are pointed up in various specialized monographs on education, the professions, politics, and the empire, will be explored in this study and gathered together into a comprehensive analysis.

As before, we will begin with a look at the dominant reform document, the Trevelyan-Northcote report on the organization of the civil service. This will be followed by a section analyzing the internal, technical-functional stresses and strains, that is, the pressures for reform within an expanding yet outmoded civil service. The third section deals with political parliamentary pressures on the civil service to achieve greater economies and raise the aptitude of officials. The next section links the civil service reform, especially the aspect of qualifying examinations, to public school and university reform. In the fifth section the relationship between civil service reform and the rise of qualifying examinations and licensing associations in the professions is explored. The next section calls attention to the reforms of the Indian civil service, where the group of reformers were associated just prior to the civil service reform

167

and where Macaulay's conception of the liberally educated gentleman administrator was institutionalized. The seventh section will focus on the intentions of the reformers as evidenced by internal memoranda that were written in response to two attacks on the reform scheme. The eighth summarizes the main lines of opposition after the report was presented to Parliament. The final section will describe the system of limited competition, which was all the reformers could get owing to opposition and which was not replaced with open competition until 1870. I will conclude this section with a hypothesis bearing on the still unresolved question why Prime Minister Gladstone's first Liberal government abolished patronage and introduced open competition in 1870.

The Trevelyan-Northcote Report

The reform of the English civil service was touched off by the famous Trevelyan-Northcote report "On the Organization of the Civil Service."[1] This report is a short, twenty-three-page pamphlet summarizing the findings of a commission charged with investigating the employment conditions of the home civil service. Unlike other reports of this kind, no transcript of hearings was appended, only a lengthy letter by the Reverend B. Jowett, fellow and tutor of Balliol College, Oxford. An enthusiastic supporter of the reform, Jowett offered detailed recommendations on the education and examination of future candidates for the civil service. Before analyzing the reasons behind the work of the inquiry commission and the debate which the report touched off, it is necessary briefly to summarize Trevelyan and Northcote's main argument.

After some preliminary remarks on the expansion of public business and the increasing need for an efficient civil service, the report launched a bitter attack on the patronage system. One should think, Trevelyan argued, "that so important a profession would attract to its ranks the ablest and the most ambitious youths of the country," yet the existing conditions are exactly reverse. Civil offices are a haven for the "unambitious," the "indolent," the "incapable," and "those whose abilities do not warrant an expectation that they will succeed in the open professions." The majority of civil servants enter as junior clerks, and since their initial duties are not very important routine matters and their performance not very conse-quential to the functioning of the departments, the typical chief is "naturally led to regard the selection as a matter of small moment, and will generally bestow the office upon the son or dependent of someone having personal or political claims upon him, or perhaps the son of some meritorious public servant, without instituting any very minute inquiry into the merits of the young man himself." The higher-staff positions, however, are frequently filled with outsiders. In part, this results from the fact that chiefs frequently cannot find clerks capable of filling obviously important posts and hence bring in "someone of high standing in the open professions, or someone distinguished in other walks of life." In part, this pattern of recruitment results from the patronage system, that is, the tendency to bring in outsiders of "slender abilities" but considerable political influence. In any case, the mass of clerks, who advance by seniority, are either incapable because of inadequate selection procedures or discouraged and unmotivated because strangers with the right connections are frequently brought in over the heads of capable clerks. Add to this the fact that there exists no servicewide system of promotion but that a man is locked into his department, and the effect is to "ex-tinguish the spirit of emulation and competition" and to "encourage the growth of narrow views and departmental prejudices."

How can the staffing be improved so as to provide the service with a steady supply of good men? The reformers rejected the idea of recruitment from other professions. They thought it best to train young men in the service. The lower the age at the point of entry, the better. For "the superior docility of young men renders it much easier to make valuable public servants of them than of those more advanced in life . . . ." Besides, it would be much easier "to secure the services of fit persons on much more economical terms." Finally, it would reduce the evils of patronage, for "the temptation of jobbing, and the danger of decidedly improper appointments being made, is also considerably less in the case of the selection of young men than in that of persons more advanced in life."

The general principle of the reform was clearly stated.

> We advocate . . . that the public service should be carried on by the
> admission into its lower ranks of a carefully selected body of young

men, who should be employed from the first upon work suited to their capacities and their education, and should be made constantly to feel that their promotion and future prospects depend entirely on the industry and ability with which they discharge their duties, that with age, abilities and reasonable application they may look forward confidently to a certain provision for their lives, that with superior powers they may rationally hope to attain to the highest prizes in the Service, while if they prove decidedly incompetent, or incurably indolent, they must expect to be removed from it.

The chief instrument for realizing this principle would be a *central* system of examination. It will not do to leave the testing to the several departments. In the larger offices, the chiefs are far too busy to concern themselves with such matters. More importantly,

a large proportion of the persons appointed to a public department usually consists of young men in whose success the heads of office or the principal clerks take a lively personal interest, owing to relationship or some other motive connected with their public or private position; and an independent opinion is hardly to be expected from an examiner who is acting under the orders of the one, and is in habits of daily intercourse with the other.

The fairness and consistency of an examination depends on it being designed and administered by a central board of examiners. The examinations of this board would be strictly competitive and open to all who have passed a preliminary inquiry into their age, health, and "moral fitness." The reformers allowed that "where character and bodily activity are chiefly required, more, comparatively, will depend upon the testimony of those to whom the candidate is well known; but the selection from among the candidates who have satisfied these preliminary inquiries should still be made by a competing examination." The reformers repeatedly argued that only an open, entirely competitive examination would "attract the proper class of candidates," select "the fittest persons," and avoid "the evils of patronage."

An integral part of the reform of recruitment would be a relatively strict division of the service into "intellectual and mechanical labour." Thus, incoming men would be divided into two broad classes of clerks. The superior class, recruited from men between the ages of nineteen and twenty-five, would be groomed eventually to occupy staff positions, including the highest posts in the service. By contrast, the lower class, recruited from men between the ages of seventeen and twenty-one, would remain in positions of routine work, such as copying, keeping accounts, and collecting taxes. Presumably, both of these divisions would be internally stratified into a number of service grades. Trevelyan and Northcote did not strictly rule out the possibility that a clerk in the "mechanical" rank might be promoted to the "intellectual" rank if he showed ability, nor did they distinguish sharply between the intellectual and mechanical grades. Rather, the maintenance of this distinction would "depend more upon the discretion and management of the chiefs of offices and those immediately below them than upon any general regulations that could be made by a central authority." They referred to the precedent for such a division in the form of "supplementary clerks," who had for some time been employed in several offices at a uniform salary and who were frequently transferred from one office to another as the need for their services arose. Trevelyan and Northcote expected that the "mechanical" division would retain this aspect of mobility. This and the superior standard of examination they proposed for the higher class would clearly distinguish the two service divisions.

This brings us to the standard of education and examination envisioned by the reformers. "We are of the opinion," they wrote, "that this examination should be in all cases a competing literary examination." For the superior situations, the aim would be to "secure the services of the most promising young men of the day, by a competing examination on a level with the highest description of education in the country." They added, "In this class of situations there is no limit to the demands which may ultimately be made upon the abilities of those who, entering them simply as junior clerks, gradually rise to the highest posts in them." They recognize that "it would be impossible to impose upon each candidate for a clerkship, as a positive test of his fitness for the appointment, the necessity of passing an examination equal to that of first-class men at the universities," but they argued that "if, on the occurrence of a vacancy, it is found that a number of candidates present themselves, of whom some are capable of passing such an examination, there can be no reason why the public should not have the benefit of such men's services, in preference to those of persons of inferior merit."

The precise content of the examinations, that is, the specific subjects to be tested, was left to the envisioned Board of Examiners. However, Trevelyan and Northcote emphasized the "advantage of making the subjects as numerous as may be found practicable, so as to secure the greatest and most varied amount of talent" for the service. The aim of the test would be to single out men of broad, comprehensive education and to reject men of narrow training. "Men whose services would be highly valuable to the country might easily be beaten by some who were their inferiors, if the examination were confined to a few subjects to which the latter had devoted their exclusive attention; but if an extensive range were given, the superiority of the best would become evident." They suggested such subjects such as history, jurisprudence, political economy, modern languages, political and physical geography in addition to "the staple of classics and mathematics." And they added, significantly, that the adoption of such qualifications for superior clerks would "probably do more to quicken the progress of our universities, for instance, than any legislative measures that could be adopted."

Although the emphasis of the report was on competitive examination as an antidote to patronage and as the only certain means of raising the efficiency of the service, the scant references to education suggest that the authors had in mind public schools and universities as the proper education for the "intellectual" ranks of the civil service. Nevertheless, neither Trevelyan and Northcote nor Jowett in his appended letter gave the impression that the higher ranks would be restricted to those who had attended such institutions. Indeed, Jowett explicitly took a broader view. "The system of our public schools, or our two English as well as of the Scotch and Irish universities, as well as the case of those who had not been to a university or public school, should be fairly considered in the arrangement of the plan."

As to the subjects of the proposed examination for the higher service, Jowett, too, did not restrict them to the subjects taught at the public schools and universities.

> The knowledge of Latin and Greek is, perhaps upon the whole, the best test of regular previous education. Mathematics are the predominant study of one of our universities [Cambridge]. Moral philosophy is a principal subject at Oxford, no less than at Edinburgh and Glasgow.

An increasing class of persons receive a foreign or an English education, in contradistinction to what may be termed a classical education. Some of the candidates again may be entered at Inns of Court. Lastly, it may be remarked that there are subjects, such as physical science and civil engineering, which, notwithstanding their immense growth in the last few years, have scarcely yet found their way down into education, and in reference to which the proposed examination may be made to operate fully.

Unlike Trevelyan and Northcote, Jowett also gave some idea of what a "literary examination" for the "mechanical" ranks would look like. It should consist, he thought, of reading aloud to the examiner, writing from dictation, arithmetic, some geography, writing a letter, making an abstract, an oral test on subjects "calculated to test general intelligence, and, perhaps a paper on questions about common things." Anticipating sceptics, he wrote, "A smile may be raised at the idea of subjecting excisemen and tidewaiters to a competing literary examination, as there might have been thirty years ago at subjecting village school masters to a similar test." But then he invited his readers to remember that there is really no other means for "getting rid of the evils of patronage" and for rendering "the lowest public servant fitter for his position."

Jowett certainly shared the Benthamite enthusiasm for examinations and for raising the efficiency of the public service. As an educator, however, he was particularly interested in "a subordinate aspect" of the reform scheme. Echoing Trevelyan and Northcote's sentiments, he felt that the scheme, which linked the higher civil service to education in a broad range of higher subjects, "must exercise a great influence on the higher education of the country." Similarly, the examinations for the lower-service grade "will exercise the happiest influence on the education of the lower classes throughout England, acting by the surest of all motives—the desire that a man has of bettering himself in life." And again in the final sentence of his letter, he reiterated the same idea. "The effect of [the scheme] in giving a stimulus to the education of the lower classes can hardly be over-estimated."

Internal Pressures for Reform

The Trevelyan-Northcote report was the result not of a single inquiry but of a series of inquiries into departmental affairs. These had started in the late forties and continued until 1854. Their purpose was summarized by Gladstone in the Treasury Minute that commissioned Trevelyan and Northcote to appraise the service as a whole. They were charged with considering the possibility, among others, of abolishing or consolidating redundant offices, eliminating obsolete work processes, establishing a distinction between mechanical and intellectual labor, and "generally [of] so revising and readjusting the public establishments as to place them on the footing best calculated for the efficient discharge of their important functions . . . ."[2] It was anticipated "that the public service will be conducted in a more efficient manner," as well as "by a smaller number of persons than is the case at present."[3] The key terms of the reform, thus, were efficiency and economy.

This flurry of official inquiry was spawned by expansion in size, function, and expenditure of public administration, which had been nudged by the developing industrial society and its problems.[4] Factory inspection and educational grants in aid as early as 1833 and the creation of police forces in 1829 and 1835 were some of the beginnings. The Poor Law Amendment Act of 1834, the several Factory Acts, and the Public Health Act of 1848 greatly expanded the inspectorate of the central government. The Post Office, too, grew particularly after the introduction of the penny post in 1840, as did virtually all the older departments. The volume of paper and the number of men who copied and expedited them increased everywhere. Though they are not very reliable, the following numbers give some clue to the comparative size of the civil service in the first half of the nineteenth century.[5]

1797	11,267	1841	16,750
1815	24,598	1851	39,147
1821	27,000	1861	31,943
1832	21,305	1871	53,874

Most civil servants were concentrated in the revenue departments, the Post Office, the Inland Revenue, the Customs and Excise, including the dockyards, and an increasing number of them in the new social service departments. Of the roughly 40,000 people in 1854, a third were secretaries, undersecretaries, commissioners, inspectors, collectors, comptrollers, and clerks. More than half were employed in "mechanical" work as postmen, sorters, weighers, stampers, tide-waiters, and so forth. The rest were messengers, office keepers, and servants.[6]

The accumulation of new administrative functions created a host of problems in the old system and evoked a number of pressures for reform, two of which are particularly germane for our purpose: pressure on the traditional organization of the civil service and pressure on the traditional style of management. The related pressure toward Treasury control over the entire service has been treated elsewhere and need not be dealt with here.[7]

The old organization in need of modernization was the system of administrative boards. Prior to the nineteenth century, expansion of administration meant addition of new administrative boards rather than new departments with monocratic heads. Boards used to be devices for keeping ministers from becoming too powerful vis-à-vis the crown. Although they declined in favor of monocratic ministries, once administration became primarily responsible to Parliament, many of the old boards were still very much alive when Trevelyan and Northcote made their inquiries. The reformers argued that the board system was now clearly out of date. A haven for patronage appointees, it "lacked in the promptness, vigor and unity of action required for the successful performance of executive functions."[8] The only way of achieving responsible and efficient government was to centralize authority in responsible ministers throughout the civil service. Indeed, Trevelyan suggested that centralization of authority would somehow solve the problem of patronage.

> If the administration of each of our great departments depend upon a single individual, with one or more superior officers to advice him, and to take his place during his absence, it would be impossible to appoint incapable persons to these situations, and each successive government would, for its own sake, look out for the ablest person who could be found to be appointed to its vacancies.[9]

Trevelyan was probably correct that the majority of board members, appointed through political patronage, were not fond of work and preferred to take their ease. But he could scarcely have believed himself that simply changing the boards into monocratic departments would be sufficient to prevent successive governments from appointing incapable individuals. He was only too well aware that the patronage system, combined with the increase of public business, was creating serious management problems in those departments which were in fact operating under a single head. The basic problem was simply that there were not enough capable officials to whom work and authority could be delegated. To be sure, some men who were qualified and able to exercise authority were brought in, mostly on the top, but the quality of the staff in general was such that ministers or department heads often preferred to run their departments with the help of a private secretary and perhaps an able chief clerk.

When Palmerston was running the Foreign Office in the thirties, he told the House, he was in the habit of reading "every report, every letter, and every dispatch received . . . down to the least important letter of the lowest vice consul."[10] He also answered every one of them. Not every minister was as diligent as he, but he exemplifies the old management style, which concentrated preparation and formulation of policy in the ministers and no more than a handful of senior members of the permanent staff and which relegated the vast majority of clerks to mechanical work scarcely distinct from that of copying clerks. As the public business expanded, even Palmerston, for whom it had been a matter of pride to take care of all the business of the day, was falling behind—"swamped by business," which "has accumulated by the regular overflowing of almost every day."[11] And whereas earlier in his career he had been loath to delegate power for fear of raising a "bureaucracy" of the continental style, by 1854 he informed the House of Commons that it was

> impossible to overrate the advantage to the public service of having in each department of the government a permanent secretary, not belonging to any political party, not swayed by passion and feeling, but a man who, being the depository of the lore and knowledge belonging to the particular department was able . . . to give the newcomer into that office information as to past events, as to the principles regulating the department, as to the knowledge of individuals, and as to the details of transactions, without which it was impossible for any man, let him be ever so able and ever so expert, to perform his duties with satisfaction to himself and advantage to the public.[12]

He was voicing the same sentiments which led Trevelyan to write,

It may be safely asserted that, as matters now stand, the government of the country could not be carried on without the aid of an efficient body of permanent officers, occupying a position duly subordinate to that of the ministers who are directly responsible to the crown and to Parliament, yet possessing sufficient independence, character, ability, and experience to be able to advise, assist, and, to some extent, influence, those who are from time to time set over them.[13]

Already in the report of his inquiry into the Treasury of May 21, 1849, Trevelyan was deeply troubled by the "great defect" of the Treasury—namely, that no provision was made for relieving and supporting executive officers, who have "always more on their hands than they can get through in the time in which it ought to be done." Generalizing this experience, he continued.

It is a serious imperfection in the system of public office that any individual should be necessary to its efficiency; and the most experienced officers of a department ought not to be so completely engrossed in disposing of the current business, as to have neither the time nor strength to attend to the general objects connected with their respective duties, which are often of more importance to the public interest than the everyday transactions of official routine. Lastly, it may be observed, without entering upon personal considerations, that any class of officers should not be habitually overwrought and should know what it is to have a few weeks' vacation without being followed by such a quantity of business as to prevent them from enjoying any real relaxation.[14]

Complaints were coming not only from the Treasury but from every quarter of the service. Lord Grey was "sensible that the load of business and responsibility which now presses upon me is beyond what I have the strength to bear, and that . . . many things are not attended to as they ought to be, and much business is very imperfectly performed."[15] Unlike Palmerston, Grey had always been willing to delegate authority when he had a good staff, but in the particular circumstance at hand he was troubled by the poor quality of his "advisors." He was sorry that he could not get rid of the poor officials and replace them with a handful of good men. "If we had in the office five or six men such as Elliot or Taylor and the necessary copyists, the work would be infinitely better done and somewhat more cheaply than at present."[16] George Arbuthnot, who thought of himself as the senior civil servant, argued, "Official habits have become inadequate to the urgency and volume of modern business."[17]

Complaints such as these were given extra poignancy when three of Trevelyan's senior colleagues at the Treasury—Brookbanks, Arbuthnot, and Crafer—broke down, one of them dying in office, apparently under the strain of work. Indeed, Crafer's death, Trevelyan observed, "has created a great sensation here, as it well might."[18] The more Trevelyan inquired into the organization and management style of public offices, the more he became convinced of the need for an efficient body of higher civil servants between the executive top and the great mass of "mechanical" workers. He advised Gladstone in 1853, "As I acquire greater experience of the public service, I become more deeply conscious of the insufficiency of the time and strength of the best and most efficient officers properly to discharge even the most indispensable functions of government."[19]

Political Pressures for Reform

The pressure for reform was, of course, not merely a matter of strain internal to the public service. The very social and economic changes that were stimulating expansion of central administration were also evoking social and political discontent and antiaristocratic feelings. These surfaced in the agitations of Chartism, the movement for repeal of the Corn Laws, and again during the Crimean affair. The First Reform Bill had not delivered what it seemed to promise. The traditional oligarchy was still in command, and the middle classes were still playing second fiddle in politics. The Anti-Corn Law League, playing on widespread resentment against the continued dominance of the traditional elite over the new forces in English society, turned the campaign against the Corn Laws into a generalized attack on aristocratic monopolies.

Those who shared John Bright's expectation that the repeal of the Corn Laws signaled the coming of a period of fundamental reforms were bitterly disappointed. There was no new reform bill, and many anticipated reforms were shelved or were left incomplete, not to be taken up again until 1867. The forces which had combined around the repeal of the Corn Laws broke up after 1846, and aside from the last major assertion of Chartism in 1848, English society seemed to settle down in that posture of "equipoise" and "deference" which has become the hallmark of recent opinion on the mid-Victorian state of affairs.[20]

Though the acute social tensions may have passed, effective pressure for electoral reform may have evaporated, and Chartism may have turned into practical trade unionism, antiaristocratic sentiment was not altogether disappearing. True, most people would still concede to gentlemen certain innate virtues considered indispensable to leadership in Parliament, the army, and the higher civil service. But the stark contrast between an aristocracy of born leaders and a middle class of money grubbers became as old-fashioned as the denial of gentility to the liberal professions. Increasingly, a new image of aristocratic bunglers and freeloaders of the public purse—the "Tide Barnacles"—became popular with the aid of striking literary portrayals of these abuses.[21] Still, such antiaristocratic sentiments did not generally attack privilege as such, only privilege unaccompanied by merit and demonstrated orientation to the public good.

If men were still content to have gentlemen in office, they increasingly claimed a right to expect public servants to be fit for office. On that claim, certainly, there was a clear convergence of opinion. Radicals could agree with Tories or Peelites on principles of utility and efficiency in selecting civil servants and reordering the old "circumlocution office" into the semblance of a modern bureaucracy. And if radicals envisaged a new order with new men at the helm of the state, the others were concerned simply to modernize and refurbish the old house without so much as a change of managers.

Impatience with official bungling and waste came into its own during the campaign for economy in government spending that coincided partially with the inquiries into public offices between 1848 and 1853. The first act featured incessant retrenchment demands in Commons, particularly after 1846, when agitation was resumed following a respite during Peel's ministry. Protectionists and radicals alike fished in the troubled waters of the civil service budget, denouncing overpayments, extravagance and waste. One protectionist member felt, "As the legislature has cut down the price of everything in the country [by adopting free trade], it was unjust to retain the present scale of salaries to officers of the state."[22] Cobden did not think the service as a whole overpaid, only that "the higher functionaries in the civil departments were paid more than they need be."[23] Hence, he recommended a 10 percent cut of the salaries of higher civil servants. Hughes is probably correct that "these retrenchment demands in Commons forced the government to appoint commissions of inquiry into various departments."[24] Before that happened, however, Edward Romilly, chairman of the Board of Audit, responded to those pressures with a pamphlet "Promotion in the Civil Service."

> Notwithstanding the constant interference of the House of Commons in matters relating to the civil service, the reform of that service remains just where it was. Their single panacea for all the evils they supposed to exist in it is, was, and ever will be *retrenchment,* the abolition and consolidation of offices. The mode of making the service *efficient* seems never to have entered their minds and the reform of the civil service is still left for the civil service itself to accomplish. . . . A general impression seems to prevail that in order to meet a deficient revenue our civil establishments ought to be reduced and as in the present state of European politics the army and navy are considered sacred, the civil service is to be made the scapegoat, and consolidations and reductions of officers are in every one's mouth. But is it certain that the public officers are paid too much? May not the real evil be that they do too little? If it should turn out on inquiry that the civil service is not on the best footing and that its officers are not as efficient as they ought to be, will matters be mended by merely reducing their numbers? The truth is we are beginning at the wrong end. Our establishments should first be made efficient and then they may be reduced or rather they will reduce themselves.[25]

Here was sounded a keynote that was to appear again and again in the writings of the reformers: reduction of expense through increase in efficiency.

Before historians turned their attention to administrative expansion and regulation during what used to be regarded as an unspoiled era of laissez faire and before they emphasized the "collectivist" implications of Bentham's utilitarianism, the parliamentary pressure for economy in the civil service was largely seen in the light of classical liberal objections to rising government interference and cost.[26] However, it is quite clear now that the reforms were also pressed by the champions of government regulation and expert administration, as well as those who were inclined to agree with Chadwick that government need not be inefficient or wasteful in itself; given the proper reforms, it might even surpass private business management in economy and efficiency.[27] The attitude of the partisans for government control and efficiency was perfectly expressed in the title of a collection of Bentham's essays, *Official Aptitude Maximized, Expense Minimized.*[28] It so precisely depicts the attitude of the civil service reformers that Bentham's maxim might have been written on their banner.

The recent debate on the meaning of the reforms of the middle decades of the nineteenth century—on poor laws, factory inspection, public health, education, and administration—is largely beside the point when it turns into a controversy over whether the major actors were Benthamites or not.[29] It is even less interesting when opinions clash on the question whether the reforms may be explained as a sort of embodiment of a Benthamite spirit or whether they were merely a response to situational conditions and problems to be solved. Explanations have to deal with both. Where economic and political problems are solved in an arena of social conflict, solutions invariably contain legitimations in theoretical and moral terms. Nor need the legitimators always be aware of the precise philosophical locus of the ideas they espouse. Whether or not utilitarianism was the general intellectual framework of the reformers, there can be little question that "utility" had become a watchword of the professional intelligentsia; so had merit as opposed to patronage and wanton disregard of functional considerations. Indeed, Benthamism in this sense was at the heart of the professional ethos. It crossed party lines, demanding more or less objective study of problems and functionally adequate solutions. That the latter were also compatible with social and political interests goes without saying, but the propagandists and reformers of whatever persuasion shared a large fund of professional commitment to utilitarian principles, far more generalized than the Benthamite label would suggest.[30]

Perkin seems to me to ask the correct question and to suggest a persuasive answer.

The important question is not so much *who* Bentham influenced as why they were influenced by him, and the answer is that Bentham spoke to their professional condition. Despite his rentier's income and his apparent championship of the entrepreneurial ideal, Bentham was, above all in his chosen field of government, the apotheosis of the professional ideal. He stood for expert, efficient administration in the interest of the greatest happiness of the greatest number. Whether Benthamite or purely professional, the great social and administrative reforms were part of the *professionalization* of government which was the greatest political achievement of nineteenth-century Britain.[31]

There were also other men in government who felt that the time had come to reform the administration. In the turbulent months of 1848, Disraeli had already expressed his opinion on that score, and four years later he still felt that administrative reform might draw middle-class voters into the conservative fold. Administrative reform, he thought, was "the only question which really interests the country." He suggested to Lord Derby that a commitment to reform "would not only secure the session, but as many sessions as you wish."[32] Three years later, during the Crimean disclosures of mismanagement, he was even more convinced that "reform was the subject of the age, so far as English politics are concerned." And once more he suggested that it would provide "an opportunity for putting the party in a commanding position."[33] It is interesting in this context to consider Trevelyan's testimony before the Playfair Commission. "The revolutionary period of 1848," he recalled, "gave us a shake, and created a disposition to put our house in order, and one of the consequences was a remarkable series of investigations into public offices, which lasted for five years, culminating in the organization report."[34]

In the years after 1848, the patronage system became as outstanding a symbol of aristocratic dominance as Old Sarum or the Corn Laws had been earlier. But there was not the same outcry against it, excepting the flurry of agitation attendant upon the Crimean disaster. The Liverpool Financial Reform Association was only warming up to hurl the claim of practical business management into the parliamentary issue of civil service reform.[35] But that point of view was not clearly articulated until the Crimean War, that is, until *after* the publication of the Trevelyan-Northcote report.[36]

And so the question arises whether the "disposition to put our house in order" materialized as a strategy for removing a troublesome grievance and in such a way as to maintain or even strengthen the aristocratic grip on the system. The question cannot be answered unequivocally as yet, for there is little in the writings of the reformers up to the publication of the Trevelyan-Northcote report that would suggest motivation other than "efficiency and economy." True, the emphasis on "literary examinations" and the division of ranks into strictly "mechanical" and "intellectual" spheres might raise suspicion, as it apparently did to G. C. Lewis, editor of the *Edinburgh Review*. Trevelyan recalled Lewis' telling him "that the self-denial of the government in abandoning its patronage—for which it has always been suspected and blamed—surprises and staggers people." Trevelyan, writing to Gladstone, added, "This has always been the stumbling block of distrust between the government and the people of this country generation after generation, causing the government always to be suspected of interested motives."[37] In any case, it was only after the severe attacks upon their proposal that the reformers articulated a preservative defense. Until then, they indeed projected a disinterested image: the image of professional administrators, embued with a utilitarian ethos, confronted with a cumbersome administration, charged with expanding government services, and prodded by political pressure to economize.

Civil Service Reform and Reform of Education

In England, as in Prussia, there was a connection between civil service reform and reform in the sphere of education, even though the latter was not an integral part of the former. The reform of public schools and the reform of the examination system of the universities was not as in Prussia geared to the civil service, but the reformers in education and government agreed that competition and examinations were indispensable for raising performance, whether it be in teaching, the liberal professions, or in public administration. Besides, reform-minded educationists were eager to see the principle of competition and examinations established in the civil service, and some of them, Jowett at the head, became active partisans for civil service reform so as to advance their own cause of university reform.

During the 1840s and 1850s, the existing public schools were reformed and a whole series of new ones were established, some of them modeled after headmaster Thomas Arnold's reformed Rugby. Arnold's reform ultimately came from a vision of a revival of the church—a church that would suffuse the body politic and mend the cracks in the social fabric that had opened up in nearly every walk of life. His educational ideal was to strengthen the leadership of the elite, create a manly spirit, moral strength, and a public service orientation that would legitimate the preeminence of a ruling class challenged by religious and political dissent. As Bamford characterizes Arnold's aims,

> The church had to be broadened and its outmoded tenets, like the Thirty-Nine Articles, revised or removed so that a common front could be made with dissent. The church would then become a natural binding force between prince and pauper. As for the upper classes, they had to accept their responsibilities as leaders. They were the most educated and cultured section of society; they must set the example. It was to this end that he worked his school at Rugby, hoping that the boys, drawn largely from upper-class homes, would respond to his challenge. In the interest of the nation, it was his duty to place the ideal of service constantly before them.[38]

In this ideal of service may be detected a certain kinship with the "utilitarian" ethos of the professional status groups. Like the Benthamite enthusiasts, Arnold, too, espoused competition on the athletic field and in the classroom as the surest way to achieve excellence.[39]

It has been supposed that Arnold's reforms at Rugby reflected the interests of the rising industrial middle class. This is difficult to maintain, however, in view of the social composition of the student body, examined earlier. Until the middle of the century, at least, it remained firmly upper class and professional, and the classical curriculum was not modified in favor of science and modern studies. Arnold's education for his "christian gentlemen" meant what it promised: education for gentlemen, though his gentleman ideal, whatever religious meaning it might have had, overlapped generously with the ethos of the professional status groups. It gave the threatened aristocracy and gentry a new service orientation. It is, perhaps, a little too fanciful to claim that Arnold's Rugby "was the most successful incarnation of Bentham's 'Chrestomatic school' ";[40] but it is true that it incorporated many aspects of the "utilitarian" ethos. And if Arnold and his followers did not exactly embrace "the new entrepreneurial ideal and morality," they taught the sons of the upper classes that conception of a gentleman which was no longer antagonistic to the new "aristocracy of talent." There is much truth in Ariès' perceptive analysis that the new, nineteenth-century gentleman was a social type "which a threatened aristocracy would create, thanks to the public schools, to defend itself against the progress of democracy."[41]

Benthamites and dissenters had challenged the public schools with their own educational theories and institutions, and they had also established University College, London, as a sort of counter-institution to the ancient universities, restricted as they were to members of the established church and, because of high tuition, to the wealthy social classes. While Oxford and Cambridge offered only classical and mathematical studies, the new institution of higher learning was opened to the modern subjects of the dawning industrial age, particularly the subjects of the newer professions. From the beginning, the University of London was set up as an examining board devoted to "the comprehensive principle of testing acquired knowledge by strict examination, with reasonable evidence of antecedent continuous study."[42]

Until the beginning of the nineteenth century, the ancient universities did not have an effective examination system. The old disputations had become a farce. The university had ceased to teach medicine and law, and medical degrees, though still granted, were not based on tests of knowledge.[43] Much the same may be said of undergraduate and other higher degrees.[44] "To render a system of examinations effectual," wrote the Oxford commissioners of 1852, "it is indispensable that there should be danger of rejection for inferior candidates, honourable distinctions and substantial rewards for the able and diligent, with examiners of high character, acting under immediate responsibility to public opinion. In the scheme of Laud all these things were wanting."[45]

At the beginning of the nineteenth century, a new examination system began to be built, based on the mathematical tripos of the eighteenth century. Also, a new distinction between honors and pass degrees was established. Oxford started with triposes in mathematics and classics whereas Cambridge did not add the classical tripos until 1824. These examinations were meant to raise the standard of education, which had fallen severely in the eighteenth century. They were meant to prod students to exert themselves in education rather than recreation, and they certainly kept those students busy who competed for honors, which held out tangible prizes besides honorable distinctions.[46] Of course, only a minority, though perhaps an increasing one, competed for honors in the first half of the nineteenth century. Most undergraduates took pass degrees, amenable as they were to three years of idle leisure and recreation. Why should these privileged students exert themselves? "Many of the poll men," in the words of Rothblatt, "were secure of the future and saw no reason to abandon three years of leisure and recreation for the rigors of a highly competitive examination. Sons of noblemen and gentry, as well as sons of other wealthy families, frequently adopted this attitude—even those of considerable intellectual ability."[47] It was only the ambitious or those dependent entirely upon their achievements in later life to whom academic distinctions were important. The large number of poll men, though a constant embarrassment to reform-minded dons, subsidized the smaller number of honor students, whose instruction and examination was the chief object of the educational reforms of the universities.

The university had become little more than a degree-awarding institution, and the colleges were so many corporate islands co-opting members. Fellowships were mostly tied to particular localities or other conditions. In Oxford, only twenty-two out of 542 fellowships were open without restriction, and, in any case, they were awarded chiefly so as to reward undergraduate diligence rather than proven ability for teaching and research. If the university was no longer a forum of teaching, the colleges, too, had declined in the nineteenth century as real centers of instruction and preparation for examination. In the second quarter of the nineteenth century, college teaching was declining in Cambridge, and private coaches, many of them former lecturers and fellows, became the main teachers at the universities. But, as Rothblatt points out, "coaching was not simply a substitute for the teaching which the colleges neglected and which the university was unable to perform. It was the only practical school of education in Cambridge, the only place where a prospective university teacher could prove his worth in a competitive situation."[48] This freelance coaching became a constant reminder of the need of a reform which would break that embarrassing educational monopoly of a group of teachers who were not even members of the university.

Although the eventual reforms—Rothblatt's revolution of the dons—did not realize the recommendation of many members of the Royal Commission and select committees of the fifties and sixties that the colleges simply adopt the new coaching methods, the latter nevertheless became a more or less explicit standard of the eventual reforms. But that restructuring of college life and the introduction of intercollegiate teaching belong to the second half of the nineteenth century. When Trevelyan collaborated with Jowett on civil service reform and examination, conservative college heads were still vigorously resisting change.

There were some noteworthy changes in the area of examination before Lord John Russell acceded in 1850 to long-standing demands that the government inquire into the state of the universities. In 1843, Cambridge introduced a voluntary examination in theology, which most of the bishops came to demand as a prerequisite for ordination. In 1848, possibly in anticipation of impending government action, Cambridge instituted triposes in moral sciences and natural sciences, and these were the forerunners of the triposes in law and history which were to be established in 1868. When the commissioners reported in 1852, they acknowledged that "examinations have become the chief instrument not only for testing the proficiency of the students but also for stimulating and directing the studies of the place. . . . The general effect of this change has been exceedingly beneficial. Industry has been greatly increased."[49]

This comment is especially interesting, because it locates precisely one of the presumed functions of examinations, namely, the function of an opening wedge for institutional change. Introduce an examination in a particular subject, and the institution will improve teaching in this area. The commissioners recommended that the universities improve their professional teaching in law and medicine, and they were particularly eager to encourage and improve the study of mathematics and science. To this end, they urged the extension of the honor system and triposes.[50]

It is not surprising that reform-minded men of education to whom Trevelyan circulated his and Northcote's report for comment were all enthusiastic. Here was another examination, which could not but improve the cause of university reform. Jowett's opinion in this regard has already been mentioned. W. H. Thompson, Regius Professor of Greek at Cambridge, was sure "that the plan would contribute materially to the well-being, efficiency, and good management of the universities, by increasing the number of students, diminishing the relative proportion of the idle and dissolute, and adding to the social importance of these bodies in the eyes of the public . . . . A great stimulus," he added, "would also be given to studies which the universities do not possess the power of adequately encouraging, or to which at any rate they find it difficult to attract the attention of earnest students."[51] Dr. Jeune, master of Pembroke, wrote, "A vast power of the higher education of the country lies dormant in our hands: Parliament is, I believe, about to enable us to apply it vigorously." Addressing the reformers, he continued, "Supposing your project carried, you will in point of fact have established an imperial university, which will mould every college and school in the land."[52] Dr. Jelf, principal of King's College, London, even proposed to establish a civil service department "whether or not Parliament was to carry the project."[53] This enthusiasm in the quarter of academic politics proved to be a bit embarrassing to the reformers on the political-administrative side of the fence particularly when opponents like Lord Robert Cecil, the future Lord Salisbury, dismissed the reform proposals as "neither more or less from the beginning to end [than] a schoolmaster's scheme."[54]

That, certainly, was an overstatement. But it contained a kernel of truth. The leading advocates of administrative reform, Gladstone, Macaulay, Trevelyan, Northcote, and Lowe were part of an inter-institutional clique who facilitated each other's reform plans and supplied each other with information, arguments, and third-party influence. They were very much influenced by the ongoing reforms in the universities. Gladstone was guiding through Commons the bill which appointed an executive committee to carry out the recommendations of the University Commission of 1850, and it was also he who directed the University Reform Bill, introduced into the House of Commons in 1854. Among other things, this bill opened fellowships to merit proven by competitive examinations.[55] While drafting the bill, Gladstone had maintained close contact with Jowett, who was preparing an alternate version. Although the interests of the educationists and administrative reformers varied, they agreed on the efficacy of examinations, and they helped each other in many ways in the struggle for reform.[56]

Examinations in the Professions

It was not only in and around the universities that tests of qualification were widely discussed and accepted as a means of raising standards of performance. The first half of the nineteenth century witnessed struggles of the lower against the higher branches of the legal and medical professions over the issue of certification to practice and over the establishment of associations for registering and licensing practitioners. It is to these struggles that we must turn now because in the literature on the rise of the professions, the emergence of qualifying associations is often treated in conjunction with civil service reforms.[57]

There is an unquestionable linkage between the two. There were men in government, among them Disraeli, who spoke of the need to professionalize the service, and it certainly makes sense to suppose that the reformers were anxious to obtain, in Chadwick's phrase, "securities for special fitness" that had worked in other professional spheres.[58] Certainly, as Carr-Saunders and Wilson put it, "Gladstone, a double-first, and Macaulay, winner of an open fellowship by competitive examination at Cambridge, did not need to be convinced of the merit of the examination system."[59] Nor could they have been ignorant of the fact that the method was also applied in the legal and medical professions.

The story of these professional men in nineteenth-century England has been told elegantly in Reader's recent book.[60] There is no need to reproduce it in detail here. Reader's central thesis is that the initiative to establish a modern professional qualifying association arose not in the higher-status groups of the professions, the physicians and barristers, but among the lower branches still rooted in trade yet striving to improve their status. They were very much interested in establishing a clear distinction between themselves and quacks and malpractitioners, thus to make a case for their incorporation into the higher-status groups of the professions. In short, these associations arose not in the sphere of gentleman practitioners but among the middling sorts of people who were pushing upward on the social scale within their professions.

The first to score a victory were the general practitioners in medicine with the passing of the Apothecaries Act in 1855. It gave the Society of Apothecaries the right to determine the education required for entry into the profession, to examine candidates, and to grant as well as revoke licenses, which alone entitled the practitioner to the designation "apothecary." This act became a model for all nineteenth-century professional organizations.

It showed that other professions besides the ancient three might be self-governing and that the ancient three had no prescriptive right to overriding control of their "lower branches." It gave satisfactory force to the notion of formal professional education under the control of a professional body and tested by strict examination. Licensing was not made a function of the state, but was backed with the state's authority.[61]

The tests of knowledge introduced by the apothecaries were quite serious by the standards of the time. This could scarcely be said of the physicians' qualifications. After some twenty years, the latter had to admit that the apothecary system had done much good; yet they were still determined to stand aloof and prevent the forging of a single unified medical association. That, precisely, continued to be the aim of general practitioners—apothecaries and surgeons—who argued that since there was but one body of basic medical knowledge, there ought to be but one association. The pros and cons were aired in front of the Select Committee on Medical Education of 1834, and from 1840 onward bill after bill was presented to Parliament only to fail for various reasons, not least because of the obstructionism of the Royal College of Physicians. The seventeenth bill finally passed in 1858. It established the Medical Act of 1858 and created the position of Registered Medical Practitioner. In the meantime, twenty-one regional licensing bodies had emerged, all of which were recognized by the act. The most important gain of the act was the recognition of a common professional education. This qualification, tested by examinations, was to be certified by one of the recognized associations, certification conferring the right to practice anywhere in the kingdom. Thus, the general practitioners were well on the way to a unified profession. Yet it was to take another twenty unsuccessful bills between 1870 and 1881 before the outlines of a single professional association emerged following the Royal Commission of 1882 and the Medical Act of 1886.

The legal profession followed the same general course, as did such newer professions as civil and mechanical engineering. There is no need to recount their stories here. By mid-century it was fairly clear that professionalization meant the establishment of a licensing association, definition of a body of testable knowledge, and an act of Parliament to recognize the monopoly of duly qualified and tested members.

The sociological significance of these early struggles to professionalize, as Reader points out, was that they were strategies of advancement by lower professional orders barely emancipated from trade (apothecaries, surgeons, attorneys, solicitors) against the dominance of a liberally educated professional elite (physicians, barristers). It was a struggle against the closure of the elite and its association and against its claim to right—which was based less on intrinsic professional merit, which in many cases was inferior—but on the social status of men educated in public schools and universities. This raises the question whether professionalization in the civil service was an analogous process. Was there anything like a lower branch of civil servants challenging the monopoly of an elite by means of qualifying examinations?

Given the facts already discussed, it should be clear that a civil service examination based on public school and university curricula could have benefited only aristocrats and liberally educated upper-middle-class men who had received the education of gentlemen. While other middle-class civil servants might have welcomed the abolition of patronage and the introduction of promotion by merit, they surely could not reasonably have anticipated Jowett's examination scheme to work in their favor. Indeed, they had everything to lose and nothing to gain from a scheme that placed so much emphasis on "literary education." Hence we need to consider only whether the civil service reforms might be thought of as a strategy of liberally educated, upper-middle-class professionals challenging an aristocratic monopoly and whether, in this manner, the ubiquitous "rise of the middle-class" theme might be sustained. What merit is there in Reader's position, which is echoed in many treatments of the subject?

> Despite the torrent of reform which had been sweeping through the land for twenty years or so, the ancient ruling classes were still where they always had been: at the centre of affairs, and still very much inclined to regard official patronage as a natural and legitimate means of supporting their relations, pleasing their supporters, blackmailing their opponents, and discharging their obligations to their dependents.
>
> This was not an attitude likely to recommend itself to the kind of people who were fighting their way up the social scale in the manner described in previous chapters, and who were looking for wider opportunities of employment for themselves and their sons. If the gentry

wanted to hang on to political power, that in itself the middle classes did not very much object to, but what did annoy them was to find themselves shut out of the material rewards of power. They wanted some of the jobs for some of their boys, and they intended to break into the official world in the same way as they were breaking into the world of the professions, which also the gentry had been inclined to regard as preserves of their own.[62]

In the pages to come the evidence will be presented to undermine this theory. The evidence indicates, I think, that the monopoly of the aristocracy and gentry was by no means as complete as Reader's argument would suggest. The changing political conditions after 1832 in fact had opened the service via political patronage to increasing numbers of middle-class clerks. At the same time, the functional pressures on the expanding bureaucracy had brought upper-middle-class professionals to some of the highest posts. Would another extension of the franchise—the lever of patronage—give the middle class an even greater chance to bargain its way into the service? As to the upper-middle-class professionals, it must be admitted that they clearly challenged the mere gentry. But they were successful, it seems to me, largely because they themselves were considered gentlemen by all but the starchy fringe of aristocratic opinion. Hence, they could present a convincing case that given the structure of English education, the reforms would maintain, indeed enhance, the monopoly of gentlemen whether they were educated gentry or educated upper-middle-class types.

Finally, there remains the question whether the reforms were provoked in part by pressures of the expanding professional status groups interested in opening up yet another sphere of honorable employment. It is interesting to note that in a later chapter Reader acknowledges that the civil service reforms were based "on a different concept from the one for which the reformers of the professions had been campaigning. It was a competitive test in *subjects of general education,* not a qualifying examination in technical specialities."[63] Nevertheless, he continues to argue his case by glossing over this crucial difference. "The two ideas, however, were sufficiently alike to appeal broadly to the same class of people, and in fact the *effect of the new system, eventually, was* to open fresh avenues of employment to the professional class to those outside who had sufficient academic ability and determination to thrust their way in."[64] Again, Jowett's examination scheme in literary subjects could not have appealed to any but those professionals who intended to send their sons to the universities. In mid-century, the members of the lower professional branches certainly did not fall into this category, even by Reader's own account. And to argue that the system would *eventually* benefit them, too, is to say merely that some time *after* the civil service proposals and reforms they would get a chance to thrust their sons into the civil service provided they had first attended the universities. To talk about remote and possibly unanticipated consequences surely is not to explain the reform. Explanations require above all analysis of immediate constraints, opportunities, interests, and motivations.

The "mechanical" ranks, it is conceded, might well have appealed to the middling sorts of people below the liberal professions. Middle-class access to this rank, once differentiated from the "intellectual" rank, might reasonably have been expected to improve with the abolition of patronage. But there is no evidence that pressure from this quarter contributed to the reform proposals.

Those who portray the reform as a middle-class victory are generally fond of pointing to the insistent complaints in the nineteenth century that the professions were overstocked and that worried parents of educated youths were unable to find suitable employment for them.[65] Musgrove argued,

> The expansion of education for middle-class boys that took place after 1830 was not matched by the expansion of middle-class employment. The educational expansion took place in spite of the lack of suitable professional openings, not in response to the growth of new fields of employment. The increasing numbers of educated young men created the need for more positions suited to their talents and expectations. The Public Services were particularly sensitive to this pressure from the schools and their structure tended to follow rather than to dictate the changing pattern of middle-class education.[66]

Looking at Musgrove's definition of "middle class," we find that he explicitly includes the "middle-middle class" as well as "upper-middle-class" professional men, well-to-do clergy, the lesser gentry, members of the diplomatic service, higher civil servants, military commanders, as well as merchants, manufacturers, and superior tradesmen. The upper-middle class "with incomes over £1,000" were also those whose children, according to Musgrove, were in the main educated at the public schools and universities. In terms of social status, this middle class was clearly a mixed lot, and Musgrove's so-called upper-middle class clearly reached into the gentry sphere of life and must have consisted mainly of Bamford's "border zone" whose members were certainly regarded as gentlemen by mid-century.

Musgrove adduces considerable literary evidence of popular anxiety over professional employment opportunities. His strongest source is a quotation from J. C. Hudson's *The Parents' Handbook* of 1842 in which the author observes that "whatever differences of opinion may prevail on the subject of increase of population, no such difference exists with respect to the difficulty of finding profitable employment, a difficulty which is felt by the middling classes quite as keenly as by the lower."[67] He might also have added the reference in a leading article of *The Times* of 1853, which stated, "Nothing is more usual than to hear people complain that the professions are overstocked, the trades monopolized, the sciences worked out, and that there is nothing for a young man to do."[68] Although the writer of this article disagreed with these popular notions, statements of such sentiments could be marshaled over and over again. But they don't seem to me to prove that anxieties of this kind produced social and political pressure and that they were, thus, causally significant.

In any case, there is nothing in the writings of the reformers that might suggest that they in any way responded to such popular anxieties. Besides, complaints of this kind are as old as the professions and may be found in the eighteenth century as much as in the nineteenth century.[69] Finally, the statistical evidence which Musgrove marshals is all drawn from the second half of the nineteenth century.

There is no question, however, that the reformers were aware of these anxieties and sentiments and even that their reform would be welcomed by the professional status group, particularly the educationists with whom they worked in close contact. Jowett told them that he could not "conceive of a greater boon which could be conferred to the university than a share in the Indian appointments."[70] He added, significantly, that "it would provide an answer to the dreary question which a college tutor so often hears 'what line of life shall I choose, with no calling to take orders and no taste for the bar, and no connections who are able to put me forward in life?' "[71] The Reverend C. E. L. Cotton, master of Marlborough College, was troubled by the same thought. "That the difficulty of making a start in life increases every year is painfully apparent to every schoolmaster and tutor, who watches with interest the career of those among his pupils who do not wish to take holy orders, and have no private friends or connections to bring them forward."[72] Dr. Charles Vaughan, headmaster of Harrow, a most aristocratic school, doubted "that the new scheme will act widely or powerfully on that class of young men with which I am best acquainted"; nevertheless, he welcomed "the opening of a new profession to the young men of liberal education," and added,

> Everyone who has had to advise, whether as parent, tutor, or friend, upon the choice of profession knows how frequently and increasingly common is the case of those young men who scruple to take orders, have no chance at the Bar, and yet possess that kind of ability, and that amount of attainment, which would be inapplicable to engineering, and thrown away upon farming.[73]

Some men even raised the specter of an educated proletariat, discontent for want of suitable employment. "One of the greatest difficulties connected with the creation . . . of so large a body of intelligent pupil teachers and schoolmasters is this," wrote the dean of Carlisle, "that such persons ought to have before them the safe outlet of some other honourable profession in which to employ their energies in case they do not wish ultimately to devote their lives to the work of a schoolmaster. Otherwise it might be found that we are training up a large and important class of discontented and dangerous men."[74] The Reverend Charles Graves, professor of mathematics at Trinity College, Dublin, expected that "parents in the middle class will hail the prospects opened to their sons" and added that measures such as Trevelyan's "are essentially conducive to the social state," depriving as it will "democrats and socialists . . . of a special grievance."[75]

Such frightful implications naturally alarmed conservatives who were disposed not only to regard the reform plan as a schoolmaster's scheme but also as a plot to democratize the service. This fear, with which we shall deal presently, was vividly expressed in an article in the *Quarterly Review* of 1860. "The object [of the reform], in point of fact, is to turn the 16,000 places in the civil service of this empire into so many places and exhibitions for poor scholars."[76]

Nothing was further from the minds of the principal reformers. Not once did they argue that the career open to talent was an end desirable in itself. On the contrary, if they did not argue in terms of purely technical-functional needs, they replied to objections such as the *Quarterly*'s by pointing to the "aristocratic" implication of their scheme. This we shall see presently. Still, when the political going became rough *after* the publication of the reform proposal, precisely because of such conservative fears, the reformers recognized that they had natural allies in all those anxious people who welcomed the opening of new employment opportunities. In a letter to Dorman B. Eaton, a reformer of the American civil service and author of a book on the British experience, Trevelyan wrote in 1877,

> the change [in England] was made by persons conversant with public affairs from a practical perception of its necessity, but these early supporters of it *might be counted upon the fingers,* and if the matter had been put to the vote in London society, or the clubs, or even in Parliament itself *by secret voting,* the new system would have been rejected by an overwhelming majority. Nevertheless, whenever adverse motions were made in the House of Commons we always had a majority in favor of the plan. This at first caused us some surprise; but on investigation the case turned out to be thus: Large as the number of persons who profited by the former system of patronage were, those who were left out in the cold were still larger, and these included some of the best classes of our population—busy professional persons of every kind, lawyers, ministers of religion of every persuasion, schoolmasters, farmers, shopkeepers, etc. These rapidly took in the idea of the new institution, and they gladly accepted it as a valuable additional privilege. We were especially interested and amused at the sudden popularity which the system acquired in Ireland, where "*the* competition," as they called it, was regarded as a very preferable alternative to the old jobbery. You will now understand that, whatever may have been the individual sentiments of members of the House of Commons, they received such pressing letters from their constituents as obliged them *to vote straight.*[77]

Trevelyan expressed a similar opinion before the Playfair Commission in 1874. He recalled that the early supporters of the plan, *once published,* were "a large and important class of clergymen and retired officers and persons of the middle class of all sorts, who are in the habit of giving a good education to their sons with a view of putting them out in life."[78] Note that both of these statements refer to support *after* the publication of the Trevelyan-Northcote report. Kingsley himself, recognizing the obvious deficiency of his earlier analysis, wrote, "I have already suggested that middle-class desire for free entry to the public offices was a factor of no little importance in civil service reform, although one which may have had more to do with the acceptance of the proposals for open competition than with their origin."[79] Historians are yet to document middle-class pressure for access as causally significant for the inception of the departmental inquiries and the writing of the Trevelyan-Northcote report.

Dress Rehearsal: The Indian Civil Service Reform

Several months before Trevelyan and Northcote were to write their organization report, Trevelyan collaborated with Macaulay, his brother-in-law, in the campaign to reform the Indian Civil Service. This campaign was a sort of dress rehearsal for the campaign to reform the home civil service. In this campaign university reform and administrative reform converged, and the small interinstitutional clique that was to be at the center of the agitation later coalesced for the first time. Moreover, it was in the Indian civil service campaign that the profile of the liberally educated gentleman administrator evolved to be implicit thereafter in all the reports and arguments of the reformers.

As early as 1837 Macaulay, sitting in the supreme council of India, had tried to get a reform bill through Parliament but was defeated. When the charter of the East India Company came up again for renewal in 1853, a new and successful attempt was made to abolish the director's patronage and instead introduce competitive examinations as a basis for appointment. Sir Charles Wood, secretary of state for India, sponsored the bill, and he was assisted by Robert Lowe, his parliamentary undersecretary and another enthusiastic advocate of open competition. According to Wright, "Trevelyan was at the center of the agitation, explaining and persuading influential people and committees of the merits of open competitive examinations, and mobilizing support for the campaign; it was he who recruited Jowett to the cause."[80]

It is here, in the Indian civil service campaign, that university reform and administrative reform converged for the first time and that the small interinstitutional clique, which "might be counted upon the fingers," was put together. Trevelyan visited Jowett at Balliol and discussed with him Wood's India bill, particularly its bearing on Haileybury, the traditional school for the training of officials in the Indian civil service. Macaulay did not wish to maintain Hailcybury as provided in Wood's India bill. He rejected the notion of a specialist school and developed that generalist theory of the liberally educated civil servant which was to become the hallmark also of the home civil service. His plan was to select university men from honor schools. In his speech during the charter debate in Parliament, he criticized Lord Ellenborough's opposition to his plan to recruit liberally educated men and, in so doing, revealed his rationale.

> If I understand the opinions imputed to that noble Lord, he thinks that the proficiency of a young man in those pursuits which constitute a liberal education is not only no indication that he is likely to make a figure in after life, but that it positively raises a presumption that he will be passed by those whom he overcame in these early contests. I understand that the noble Lord holds that young men who gain distinction in such pursuits are likely to turn out dullards, utterly unfit for an active career, and I am not sure that the noble Lord did not say that it would be wiser to make boxing or cricket a test of fitness than a liberal education. It seems to me that there never was a fact proved by a larger mass of evidence, or a more unvaried experience than this;—that men, who distinguish themselves in their youth above their contemporaries, almost always keep to the end of their lives the start which they have gained. . . . There you have the list of wranglers and of junior optimes; and I will venture to say that, for one man who has in after life distinguished himself among the junior optimes, you will find twenty among the wranglers. Take the Oxford Calendar and compare the list of first-class men with an equal number of men in the third class. Is not our history full of instances which prove this fact? Look at the Church, or the Bar. Look at Parliament, from the time that Parliamentary government began in this country;—from the days of Montague and St. John to those of Canning and Peel. Look to India. The ablest man who ever governed India was Warren Hastings, and was he not in the first rank at Westminster? The ablest civil servant I ever knew in India was Sir Charles Metcalfe, and was he not of the first standing at Eton? The most eminent member of the aristocracy who ever governed India was Lord Wellesley. What was his Eton reputation? What was his Oxford reputation?[81]

Jowett agreed with Macaulay, and he wrote to Gladstone to argue for open competition in the Indian service and, especially, to emphasize the benefit that open competition would bring to university reform. Since the bill had already passed the Commons, the campaign focused on the House of Lords, especially on Lord Granville who was to move the desired amendment. Jowett was one of the prime movers of a concentrated lobby and letter-writing campaign that included also the Reverend Dr. Charles Vaughn, headmaster of Westminster, besides Macaulay, Trevelyan, Gladstone, and Wood, who had been won over in the meantime.

The amendment to Wood's bill passed, and the reformers moved quickly to take advantage of the victory in the Lords. Jowett drafted a blueprint of the proposed examinations and was appointed with Macaulay, J. G. Shaw Lefevre, a future civil service commissioner, and two other men, to a committee advising Wood. Macaulay, the chairman, revised and expanded Jowett's blueprint into a report, which once again conveys the convergence of interests of university and administrative reformers.

> It is notorious that the examinations for [the four] Trinity fellowships [awarded annually] have, directly or indirectly, done much to give direction to the studies of Cambridge and of all the numerous schools which are the feeders of Cambridge. What then, is likely to be the effect of a competition for prizes which will be ten times as numerous as the Trinity fellowships, and for which each will be more valuable than a Trinity fellowship? We are inclined to think that the examination . . . will produce an effect which will be felt in every seat of learning throughout the realm.[82]

More significant even than this statement of convergent interests was the clear profile of the kind of civil servant the reformers wished to cultivate: the broadly, liberally educated generalist rather than the expert—the professional gentleman rather than the professional specialist, Prussian style. It is important because this preference also underlies the notion of "literary examinations" in Trevelyan and Northcote's organization report. Macaulay may be taken to have voiced the sentiments of the entire clique of reformers.

> We believe that men who have been engaged, up to one or two and twenty years, in studies which have no immediate connection with the

business of any profession, and of which the effect is merely to open,
to invigorate, and to enrich the mind, will generally be found, in the
business of every profession, superior to men who have, at eighteen or
nineteen, devoted themselves to the special studies of their calling. . . .
He should have received the best, the most liberal, the most finished
education that his native country affords. Such an education has been
proved by experience to be the best preparation for every calling which
requires the exercise of the high powers of the mind. . . . Indeed, early
superiority in literature and science generally indicates the existence of
some qualities which are securities against vice—industry, self-denial, a
taste for pleasure not sensual, a laudable desire for honorable distinction,
a still more laudable desire to obtain the approbation of friends and
relations. We, therefore, think that the intellectual test about to be
established will be found in practice to be also the best moral test that
can be devised.[83]

It takes little imagination to suppose that the moral test they envisioned
was not altogether blind to social distinctions.

The Intentions of the Reformers

In this section we will turn from the dress rehearsal to the beginning
of the campaign to reform the civil service, especially to two early
attacks on the reform plan that gave the reformers a taste of the
impending opposition. These two attacks and the replies of the
reformers will be examined in some detail because they reveal the
intentions of the reformers. For all their insistence on the practical
necessity of the reform, they were also alive to social considerations.

It was summer of 1853. The Indian civil service campaign had
been a resounding success. Trevelyan and Northcote were still making
inquiries in the home civil service and had started to write the
organization report. The *Civil Service Gazette,* in a leading article,
commented that "the end of the wedge has been inserted" and felt
that "the introduction of competition, as a test of appointment to
the civil service of India, has been forced on the discussion of its
application to the civil service at home."[84] Elated by the Indian
experience, the reformers pressed on, and, at the end of November,
the organization report landed on Gladstone's desk.[85]

Immediately, another campaign of lobbying, letter writing, and
press priming got underway as the report was circulated to contacts
in government, administration, education, and journalism. The first

round included a select group of leading educationists as well as Ralph W. Lingen, secretary of the Board of Education, J. G. Shaw Lefevre, chairman of the Board of Inland Revenue, and Captain O'Brien, editor of the *Quarterly Review*. The enthusiastic response of the educationists we have already dealt with. Lingen, who had been in favor of limited competition only, was converted by Trevelyan to the principle of open competition. "I have come to the firm conclusion," wrote Lingen to Northcote, "that perfectly free competition *is the only plan* for which it is worthwhile to incur the disorganization temporarily incident to change whatever."[86] As we will see shortly, the distinction between "open" and "limited" competition was most significant in the controversy that was about to ensue. Lingen, a former fellow of Balliol and friend of Jowett, did not like the argument of the educationists, however, and "thought it quite beside the point to discuss the organization of the civil service as if it existed for the sake of the general education of the country."[87]

Lefevre told Trevelyan that his experience with Cambridge and the University of London gave him "considerable confidence that there would be no difficulty in examining four hundred or more candidates simultaneously." He was entirely in agreement with open competition.

> The mode suggested of giving appointments . . . according to the order of merit ascertained by examination, having other securities for character, appears to me the only practicable method of preventing the exercise of patronage or favour—and to be calculated to call forth an extraordinary amount of talent and industry. I am most sanguine as to its results. I only fear that the measure will be too stimulating.[88]

And so it was. It raised the fear that radical abolition of patronage implied by "open competition" would open the service to socially inferior men. Captain O'Brien's reply, printed at the Foreign Office, the most aristocratic of all departments, struck the keynote of the preservative opposition.[89] The captain admitted "the general mediocrity of the civil servants with respect to ability, acquirements, and energy in conducting business"; he also admitted the need "to test the qualifications of the candidates as to ability and acquirement by a previous examination and, moreover, with a view to obtain a high average of qualification largely to increase the number of candidates"; he also "expected that the highest attainable qualifications will be secured if the right to compete at the examinations be entirely thrown open"; but an open competition in literary subjects, he objected, would not reveal the necessary social qualifications.

> If such an examination duly and fairly carried out were practicable, it would undoubtedly secure the proposed object, but there are other qualifications, perhaps more essential, which must be sought for by other means. I believe it is an acknowledged fact that as a body, the civil service in the public offices in London are remarkable for their fidelity and trustworthiness. The general prevalence of this high sense of honour among a set of men can, I believe, be ensured only by selecting them from the class of society where it exists. . . . From our mothers we derive religion, from our fathers our chivalrous sense of honour. In the society we meet at *home,* we gradually become imbued with the more enlarged liberal views which gradually fit the mind for dealing practically with human affairs. Mere school learning will not do this. . . .
>
> I believe therefore that the high character for moral worth enjoyed by the civil service in the principal public offices results from their having been selected generally by the high officers of state who naturally nominate the sons of their relations, friends and acquaintances.
>
> . . . .
>
> In short, I would have gentlemen in the public offices and I believe they can be obtained only by being selected as at present.

Captain O'Brien saw no reason why the advantage of patronage could not be combined with testing "high mental qualification." He suggested that these were already combined in the army and the Royal Military Academy at Woolwich, whose selection system he described and held out as a model for the civil service to emulate. Such a system would ensure, first, that candidates are nominated by patrons and, second, that they pass a *fixed* test of minimum qualification. "The minimum qualification might be as high as you please, and a number of candidates might be nominated sufficiently large to ensure the sharpest competition."[90]

The captain's critical position on the question of patronage was not unexpected, but his argument that the proposed plan would displace gentlemen in public office evidently came as a surprise, for not once had the reformers argued that equality of opportunity would be valuable in itself. In his "Thoughts on Patronage," written before Captain O'Brien's remarks, Trevelyan had urged that the civil service "be employed in stimulating the education of our youth instead of corrupting our constituencies," and had promised that in this manner "the *governing class* would cease to be on the side of corruption."[91] Had not Macaulay argued that so high an intellectual test would also constitute the best moral test? In the judgment of Moses, Macaulay knew perfectly well to whom he was opening the examination system.

> He knew perfectly well that open competition did not involve attracting the ill-bred and ill-balanced middle class into the Indian service. Macaulay meant to open the competition to undergraduates of the great universities, and he expected that in an open competition with a high standard based on the Oxford and Cambridge honor schools, Oxford and Cambridge would more than hold their own. The scheme was not quite as democratic as it looked. Like the English cabinet and the English aristocracy, the Indian civil service was to be opened to gentlemen who had inherited breeding and culture, and to those of the middle class who had made themselves gentlemen by acquiring the same breeding and culture.[92]

In any case, this is precisely what Trevelyan and Northcote argued in their reply to Captain O'Brien. Twenty copies with extensive remarks by both of them were sent to Gladstone with the presumption that he might like to circulate them. They pointed out that the captain's argument "assumes that the young men selected by open competition will be less gentlemen than those who are appointed by close patronage, *but the real case will . . . be exactly reverse.*"[93] Here is how Trevelyan put it.

> The effect of a system of open competition will be to secure for the public offices generally and especially for the principal offices the best portion of the best educated of our youth.
> Who are so successful in carrying off the prizes at competing scholarships, fellowships, etc. as the most expensively educated young men? Almost invariably, the sons of gentlemen, or those who by force of cultivation, good training and good society have acquired the feelings and habits of gentlemen. The tendency of the measure will, I am confident, be decidedly *aristocratic,* but it will be so in a good sense by securing for the public service those who are, in a true sense ομχριστοι. At present a mixed multitude is sent up, a large proportion of whom, owing to the operation of political and personal patronage, are of an inferior rank of society . . . *and they are in general, the least eligible of their respective ranks.* The idle and useless, the fool of the family, the con-

sumptive, the hypochondriac, those who have a tendency to insanity, are the sort of young men commonly "provided for," as the term is, in a public office. I could mention off-hand scores of instances, some of which are of so wholesale a character as must command conviction. All this will be remedied by the proposed arrangement.[94]

To this Northcote added,

> To this I would add that the advantages which a university training would give in the competition would almost insure the selection of a large majority from among those who have received it; and there is no kind of education, so likely to make a man a gentleman, to fit him to play his part among other gentlemen and to furnish him forth for the world, as that of an English University. At present a large number of the recruits for the Civil Service are drawn from among young men who have not attained the age of entering the University or whom their parents do not think it worthwhile to send there, because their future prospects are already secured in the public service by the promise of appointment.[95]

Captain O'Brien's argument in favor of limited competition appears to have been a catalyst for the reformers' conviction, expressed by Lingen, to accept nothing short of open competition. In the letter to Gladstone, which accompanied the above replies, Trevelyan revealed, "We have now worked up to the standard prescribed by Parliament last session for India; and the selection for the home and Indian services may be made by the same examiners from the same body of young men."[96] In a separate letter to Gladstone, Northcote once more highlighted the position.

> The more I think of this question [of open competition], the more earnestly I hope that you will not allow it to be prejudiced by any partial attempt at combining nomination and examination. This I know is your own view, and I therefore only say what I do in order to assist you in meeting what is the first idea that seems to present itself to every mind. Captain O'Brien, the Editor of the *Quarterly*, Lingen, Trevelyan and even for a short time myself, have all thought at first of limited competition among nominees, but the last three have all given it up as worse than useless. If you cannot have open competition for all appointments, at least try it for some; and if you cannot have it really open (i.e., free from nomination), do not introduce it at all.[97]

This shift in the reformers' attitude is of utmost significance. If they started out with a soft position on the question of patronage, they could scarcely have favored to democratize the service; nor could their reply to O'Brien be interpreted as merely a clever argument designed to placate conservative opinion. And if O'Brien's paper was the catalyst for the reformer's new attitude on competition, then the arguments in that paper must have convinced them that anything short of "open competition" would preserve the worst of the patronage system. This seems to be borne out by Trevelyan's reply to O'Brien's suggestion of a compromise and the model of Woolwich. Trevelyan referred to two cases where limited competition had not worked in the past and suggested, "When patronage and competition go together, patronage will almost always trip up competition for this simple reason—that patronage is always supported by strong personal interests, while merit has only an abstract sense of duty to the public in its favor." As to the notion of a simple pass-fail system rather than a ranking of candidates according to their relative merit, Trevelyan argued that it "is habitually crammed up to, and the parents who have been assured by the cramming master that their sons come up to the mark, are naturally discontented when they fail. With a competing examination, the case is entirely different. There is no fixed standard to refer to." Finally, concerning the Woolwich model suggested by O'Brien, Trevelyan wrote,

> As it is not proposed to establish a college for the education of Civil Servants, the analogy of the Royal Military Academy does not apply. All our public schools and universities are seminaries of training and discipline for the civil service of the state. . . . Why, therefore, do we maintain a barrier of patronage between our public schools and universities and the public service?[98]

A few days after Trevelyan had written these lines, still in January 1853, Gladstone went to the cabinet with a motion "that a bill be prepared providing for admission to the civil service by free competition."[99] Gladstone recorded the votes. The ayes had it, with all the Whigs against and the Peelites for the resolution. Trevelyan was relieved. "I thank God for this decision . . . . I shall immediately proceed to draw the bill in communication with Northcote and Jowett."[100] Although Gladstone assumed that Trevelyan would "not communicate with any other person on the subject," the latter primed the press, particularly *The Times,* canvassed the support of educators, and along with Jowett solicited letters to be written to influential men.[101] Thus, the dean of Hereford got a letter from Jowett as well as Trevelyan asking him to write on behalf of the reform project. Trevelyan, backing Jowett's request, wrote,

> In its bearing on education, this is *your* subject and a public expression of your approbation, however short, at the present time will be of great assistance to the Government—but if your observations are cast in the form of a letter, I would suggest that it should be addressed to the Earl of Aberdeen and not to Lord John Russell—for Lord John, although he is as honourable and public minded a man as ever lived, is too deeply imbued with the traditional habits of Parliamentary management to be favourable to the plan, although willing to give it a fair trial. If, therefore, you wrote him, he might give you an answer we should not like.[102]

Two weeks before the organization report was submitted to Parliament, *The Times,* which had been supplied with confidential letters and editorial material, published a leading article hailing the reform plan.[103] Other papers followed suit, and by March 9, Trevelyan could write to Gladstone, "As the *Times* and *Morning Advisor* are completely on our side, besides the *Examiner, Spectator* and other less important papers, we have three-quarters of the press and probably a much larger proportion with us."[104]

George Arbuthnot, auditor of the civil list and second in command at the Treasury, as well as Lord Monteagle in the House of Lords were extremely critical of Trevelyan's "external agitation" and the fact that the press had discussed the issue before the report was presented to Parliament. Arbuthnot complained to Gladstone "that instead of beginning with this external agitation, the internal organization of the Departments had first been looked into in an impartial manner and with the aid of those who have had long experience of the working of the details of the Public Service."[105] Similarly, Lord Monteagle held that the report was "partial and ex parte" and demanded to know what instructions Trevelyan and Northcote had received.[106]

Trevelyan had encouraged Arbuthnot to commit his views to paper but had simultaneously warned Gladstone to be wary of the results. "His true point of view is that of a respectable and able representative of the old school opinions; and when you have heard what he has to say against the proposed improvements, you have heard the worst that can be said of them."[107] Angered by the unflattering references to the indolence and incompetence of civil servants, Arbuthnot applied for "a committee to inquire into the allegations contained in the report on the civil service" but withdrew under pressure from Northcote and Gladstone. Instead, it was suggested that he address a letter to the lords of the Treasury remonstrating against the attack on the civil service.

His letter as well as a reply by Trevelyan and Northcote were to be laid before Parliament. In that reply, Trevelyan and Northcote retreated considerably from their strong language and in fact wrote a letter of apology.

> We beg leave to express our sincere regret that the language of any portion of our Report should have been such as to create a painful feeling in the midst of the able and honourable body of men comprising the Service to which we ourselves belong, and with which we cannot but feel it an honour to be connected. . . .We admit that, looking to the effect which the publication of our remarks was likely to have upon the minds of persons less well acquainted with the Civil Service than your Lordships, it was an error on our part that we did not more distinctly express the sense we entertain of its merits; and we regret that we failed to do so.[108]

Arbuthnot's letters are important for two reasons. First, they exemplify another type of attack on the reform scheme. Second, like Captain O'Brien's attack, Arbuthnot's was decisive in clarifying the position of the reformers. Unlike Captain O'Brien, Arbuthnot was not a spokesman for aristocratic opponents to the abolition of patronage but a spokesman for the interests of civil servants who quickly realized the elitist implications of recruitment based on "literary" examinations and of the division of the service into "mechanical" and "intellectual" ranks. Arbuthnot argued not only that most of public business was in fact routine work but also that previous apprenticeship in the "inferior classes" of routine work was essential as a training for superior offices.

> In order to become acquainted with technical or legal phraseology, the young clerk must begin by copying documents. As in professional pursuits, the efficient Civil Servant is formed by making him in the first instance

a good workman. The most distinguished officers of this class commenced early in life at the drudgery of the desk. It is upon this principle that the system of promotion which has worked so well in the Customs has been established, and the value of the theory which would disturb that system has yet to be tested.

Therefore, "the real practical education of an official man must be within the office." The Trevelyan reform scheme, by introducing a highly educated elite into superior positions, would produce men without the necessary practical training in departmental routines, and the routine clerks, "by acquiring a superior mastery of the details of an office, may become its most efficient servants, and be really more eligible for promotion (from which they will yet be debarred) than the class who are to be admitted with the recommendation of superior mental cultivation."[109]

Finally, Arbuthnot claimed, Trevelyan's scheme would tend to give rise to two shortcomings. Because the majority of civil servants work in routine positions and will not be able to rise to higher positions,

> there will be, on the one hand, danger lest persons having high claims on the ground of intellectual attainment, and stimulated by the expectation of a prize, find themselves condemned among the mass to a life of hopeless drudgery. On the other hand, if to avoid this result the best appointments are reserved for an intellectual class, the general body of the Civil Servants will be disheartened and degraded in character.[110]

As it turned out, this argument provided the model for two kinds of popular criticism. Upon reading Arbuthnot's letter, the Right Honorable Stephen Spring Rice seized the first aspect and, accordingly, advised Trevelyan,

> Your aim should be qualified by bearing in mind that the immense majority of public appointments require but slender ability for their due fulfillment for if you should appoint to these a class of Senior Wranglers and Double Firsts you would have a discontented and inefficient body of subordinates. I find this point strongly insisted on in George Arbuthnot's paper which has reached me this morning.[111]

The *Civil Service Gazette*, on the other hand, spoke for anxious civil servants when it charged that the reform "will have a *prima facie* object of benefitting the universities, instead of conferring a boon upon the service and effecting a public good in the more efficient administration of the public business."[112]

I have said that Arbuthnot's attack was important much as O'Brien's was in clarifying the reformers' position. In answer to Rice, Trevelyan held that Arbuthnot's argument was based on "an entire misconception."

> We do not propose either that the separation between intellectual and mechanical labour should be universally carried out, whether it is applicable or not, or that Senior Wranglers and Double First Class men should be appointed Tidewaiters or Landing Waiters. What we propose is that the division of labour, above mentioned, should be firmly established in the *Government* Offices to which the business comes up ready prepared and in which there is therefore a great mass of figure and copying work to be dealt with mechanically and a certain amount of superior intellectual work in dealing with this subject by passing decisions upon it and so forth—and that the same principle should be extended to other departments so far as there are masses of mechanical work, or well defined sections of intellectual work in them *and no further.*[113]

The most significant clarification, however, came with respect to educational qualifications and proper examinations of the rank below the intellectual class. The reformers evidently began to think of articulating the inferior ranks with an English and commercial type of education in much the same way as the intellectual rank had been articulated with the public schools and universities. This train of thought led to a distinction between policy-making offices in the civil, diplomatic, Indian, and consular services, on the one hand, and "executive" and account offices on the other.

> In the first, the highest attainments of English Liberal Education with all the modern improvements, of Foreign Languages and "Moral Sciences" will come into play, while in the last, familiarity with all the practical rules of Arithmetic, Bookkeeping, *English Composition* and all that constitutes the stable of good English education will be the subject of examination.[114]

The same day these words were written, Trevelyan revealed to Gladstone the new train of thought.

> We are beginning to see our way very clearly to these Second Class examinations and much good is likely to come out of it. They will apply to the great middle class, including the majority of the persons employed

on the Civil Establishments who are unable to give their sons a finished university education—and the subject matter of the examination will be what used to be the Commercial School Education but *greatly improved.* . . . In another point of view, also, this is an important point because the middle class people and the majority of public officers look with great jealousy upon our Cambridge and Oxford men to whom they cannot attain—and it is, therefore, desirable to show them that the great mass of appointments will be open to be competed for by their sons who have received a really good English education.[115]

He went on to say that this new insight was developed in communication with Dr. Jelf, the principal, and the council of King's College, London, "who have large experience with this class—and I must do them the credit of saying that they have given our plan a development beyond what we were conscious of ourselves." According to Trevelyan, they brought out the implication that the plan was based on a conception of "three grades of examinations: High (Oxford and Cambridge), Middle (superior *English* education), Low (or national school second-rate English studies)."[116]

Writers on the civil service have generally assumed that this three-class division, which eventually became institutionalized in 1870, was developed much later. But it is clear now that this conception was developed already in 1854—even before the Trevelyan-Northcote report was published. More importantly, the conception of a three-tier civil service structure articulated with a three-tier system of education, expressed in terms of social class or status, began to emerge already at the very outset of the campaign for reform. The upper classes were to receive a monopoly of the highest posts by way of their advantage in higher education; the commercial middle class was to be channeled into "second-class" appointments based on the sort of commercial-English education they, in fact, received at that time; and the lower mechanical posts were designated for men with an even lower English education that was to be formalized in the Education Act of 1870.

Opposition to the Reform Plan

The outlines of the opposition had become clear even before the organization report was presented to Parliament. Although the reform proposals were receiving a good press and Trevelyan thought that their case was "the strongest possible," the reformers were bracing themselves for a difficult task. When the report was published, the opposition was overwhelming—sweeping like a "growling and blustering [storm] through the clubs and board-rooms between Picadilly and Parliament Street."[117] Macaulay went to his club, Brooks, and found "everybody open-mouthed . . . against Trevelyan's plans about the Civil Service." Trevelyan, he thought, "has been too sanguine. The pear is not ripe. I always thought so. The time will come, but it is not come yet. I am afraid he will be much mortified."[118] Now that the opposition was in the open and in full force, it was evident that all the groups with a stake in the patronage system were up in arms. As Trevelyan wrote to Gladstone,

> The existing Corps of Civil Servants do not like it because the introduction of well-educated, active men appointed on a different principle will force them to bestir themselves, and because they cannot hope to get their own ill-educated sons appointed under the new system. The old established Political Families habitually batten on the Public Patronage. Their sons, legitimate and illegitimate, their relatives and dependents of every degree are provided for by the score. Besides the adventuring, disreputable class of members of Parliament who make, God knows what use of the Patronage, a large number of Borough Members are mainly dependent on it for their seats.—What, for instance, are the members to do who have been sent down by the Patronage Secretary to contest Boroughs in the interest of the Government and who are pledged twenty deep to their constituents? And then there is the very large class of persons who have received or who expect to receive promises of places. All these orders of men, remember, are entrenched in the strongholds of political power.[119]

Interestingly enough, at this point Trevelyan moved to mobilize middle-class interests on behalf of the scheme. He asked Gladstone for permission to send copies of the report and Jowett's letter to all the Mechanics Institutes and added, "The classes interested in the maintenance of Patronage are so powerful that unless we can get our Plan read and understood by the rest of the community, I shall begin to fear for its success."[120] Ten days later he was beginning to see his way clear to the second-class examinations and their relevance to middle-class interests.

By far the most urgent fear of the opposition was that the reforms would lower the moral tone and social composition of the service.[121]

Edward Romilly, chairman of the Board of Audit, feared "that the ultimate result of open competition will be a democratical civil service, side by side with an aristocratical legislature."[122] James Booth, secretary to the Board of Trade, also feared an invasion of low people: "The tendency of your system," he wrote to Trevelyan,

> gradually to fill the public offices with a lower class of men, I consider one of the strongest objections to it. The lower you descend in the social scale, the less is the probability that the candidate for the civil service will possess those moral qualifications which I have already insisted on as being more important than the intellectual ones in the practical business of official life.[123]

The queen, too, let it be known that she had misgivings lest competitive examinations "fill the public offices with low people without the breeding or feelings of gentlemen."[124]

Another fear, which is of some interest in a comparative study of bureaucratization, was neatly summed up by an anonymous subaltern official who quoted from *The Daily News.*

> We want no official priesthoods. To support any scheme for converting the sixteen thousand clerks in public offices into a Prussian or Austrian phalanx of red tapists would be a most dangerous error. Downing Street does quite enough mischief as it is. . . . They can do nothing for the people as well as the people can do it for themselves; and to permit any new organization, or facilities for meddling with national interest, would be a suicidal blunder.[125]

He quite agreed with the paper that the Trevelyan scheme was a sinister plot for converting the civil service into a bureaucracy on the continental model. He quoted passage after passage from *The Daily News,* which evidently was the leading mouthpiece of the argument that an educated bureaucratic elite would surely usurp the power of Parliament and thus destroy the liberty guaranteed by the English constitution.

Next, the objections which Arbuthnot had raised were widely taken up by interested officials who, lacking the educational qualification for membership in the "intellectual rank," saw their chances of promotion dwindle with the introduction of university trained men. "It is upward of forty-six years since I first entered the Civil Service of the Crown in its humblest ranks," wrote A. Y. Spearman, an Assistant Secretary at the Treasury, "and I speak from practical experience and personal knowledge, when I express my opinion that such a system would be injurious as well as unjust."[126] Like many critics, he thought that the qualifications for high office could be acquired only by a man coming up the ranks through faithful service. "To split the civil service, it seems to me, would greatly impair its efficiency as a whole and would besides be unjust to those who enter into the lower class."[127] Much the same argument had been advanced by Arbuthnot in his letter to the Lords of the Treasury.

> I will refer to the case of the three officers of your Lordship's Board, acting immediately under the Secretaries, *viz.*, myself and the two principal clerks. We obtained our appointments to the public service, originally, by the favour of the First Lord of the Treasury for the time being. None of us was distinct in any respect by extraordinary educational attainments; and we have had no other recommendation for the preference shown to us in our promotion than that knowledge of the business of office which we had opportunities of acquiring in the course of a long and faithful service.[128]

These writers were not alone in supposing that the necessary qualification of a higher civil servant would not be indicated by a "literary" examination. "The qualities absolutely required," wrote Sir Thomas Fremantle, chairman of the Board of Customs, "are physical strength, sound health, honesty and sobriety, and a docile and contented disposition."[129] The chairman of the Emigration Board put it even more bluntly. "Unusual educational attainments are not the first requisite for a clerk in a public office."[130] The secretary of the Board of Trade could not agree more. Commanding talents and educational achievements "would, in fact, be misplaced in almost every department of government. It is rather a steady and persevering devotion to the everyday business of the department that is to be desired."[131] If the secretary of the Board of Control did "not believe the best scholars would necessarily make the best clerks," his counterpart at the Board of Trade feared that overeducation would destroy diligence and evoke indolence.[132] Partisans of the old patronage system and the traditional management style which the reformers wanted to change, they characteristically argued in terms of an undifferentiated group of clerks from which a small minority would distinguish itself by superior diligence and knowledge of departmental business. They did not think highly of Trevelyan's proposal to differentiate clerks into a group of routine workers and a group of candidates for the higher civil service.

There were, however, a number of distinguished men who shared Trevelyan's basic conception. They spoke in favor of abolishing patronage and in favor of competitive examinations, but they were not convinced that a classical education would be the best indicator of the qualities needed in the higher civil service. Edwin Chadwick and John Stuart Mill were the most prominent among them. Chadwick, as we have seen earlier, was well aware that a "literary" examination would select gentlemen rather than people of low condition. So was Mill. But like Mill, Chadwick thought that they would select "the gentleman who is, *par excellence,* an instructor in the abstract sciences and who wrote articles in the Reviews to show the impracticability of steam navigation across the Atlantic, and . . . [would exclude] those who accomplished the feat." Indeed, they would give

> precedence for the Poor Law Service to a gentleman who could tell me the names of Actaeon's hounds, but who could not tell me the names of the chief statutes to be dealt with, and whose education had grounded him neither in the older principle of public policy nor in law or political economy applicable to them, and . . . [they] would have excluded a candidate who was pre-eminent in the practical administrative reform, although he had never taken an academic degree."[133]

Nor did Chadwick doubt that Trevelyan's literary examination would furnish evidence of capability for work sufficiently similar to academic work, only that the evidence would be the weaker the more removed departmental requirements might be from academic studies. John Stuart Mill, who shared these sentiments, nevertheless defended Trevelyan by turning the critique of civil service examinations into a critique of the prevailing state of higher education. "To test a candidate," he wrote,

> to ascertain whether he has been well educated, he must be interrogated in the things which he is likely to know if he has been well educated, even though not directly pertinent to the work to which he is to be appointed. Will those who object to his being questioned in classics and mathematics, in a country where the only things regularly taught are classics and mathematics, tell us what they would have him questioned in?[134]

These, then, were the major arguments against the reform. The patronage mongers among the opponents of the plan came up with a host of other arguments, which need not concern us here and which in any case were easily shown to be superficial or altogether false. The major arguments, however, were seriously considered, and the reformers lost no time to clarify their intentions. Against the first objection, they had already clarified their position in responding to Captain O'Brien's remarks. Chadwick agreed with them, and so did John Stuart Mill. "Another objection" the latter wrote,

> is that if appointments are given to talent, the public offices will be filled with low people, without the breeding or the feelings of gentlemen. If, as this objection supposes, the sons of gentlemen cannot be expected to have as much ability and instruction as the sons of low people, it would make a strong case for social changes of a more extensive character. If the sons of gentlemen would not, even under the stimulus of competition, maintain themselves on an equality of intellect and attainments with youths of a lower rank, how much more below the mark must they be with their present monopoly; and to how much greater an extent than the friends of the measure allege, must the efficiency of the public service be at present sacrificed to their incompetency. And more: if, with advantages and opportunities so vastly superior, the youth of the higher classes have not honour enough, or energy enough, or public spirit enough, to make themselves as well qualified for the station which they desire to maintain, they are not fit for that station, and cannot too soon step out of it and give place to better people. I have not this unfavourable opinion of them: I believe that they will fairly earn their full share of every kind of distinction when they are no longer able to obtain it unearned.[135]

Gladstone tried to convince Lord John Russell that the reform plan, rather than democratize the service, was designed to *strengthen* the hold of the higher classes on the higher civil service—exactly as Chadwick saw it would and was calculated to do.

> I do not hesitate to say that one of the great recommendations of the change in my eyes would be its tendency to strengthen and multiply the ties between the higher classes and the possession of administrative power. . . . I have a strong impression that the aristocracy of this country are even superior in natural gifts, on the average, to the mass: but it is plain that with their acquired advantages, their *insensible education*, irrespective of book learning, they have an immense superiority. This

applies in this degree to all those who may be called gentlemen by birth and training; and it must be remembered that an essential part of any plan as is now under discussion is the separation of *work,* wherever it can be made, into mechanical and intellectual, a separation which will open to the highly educated class a career and give them command over all the higher parts of the civil service, which up to this time they have never enjoyed.[136]

The second objection, referring to the political danger in cultivating a bureaucratic elite, was disposed of by Trevelyan in a communication to *The Times.*

> I have heard the objection that the adoption of the proposed plan would establish a bureaucratic system like that of Prussia. To this I reply that in countries like Prussia and France the bureaucratic system is the growth of ages, while their Parliamentary system has neither practice nor pre-scription in its favour—in fact is still in its germ—whereas here in England we have, thank God, a Parliamentary System which is so firmly rooted in the very minds and natures of our people, that it may be said to form part of ourselves; and no new Bureaucracy, nor anything else that I can anticipate, can seriously endanger it. If any of our young Civilians were to take too much upon themselves, a word in Parliament, to say nothing of a hint from the chief of their Department, would set all right. Besides, if the Civil Establishments were improved as we propose, men would be continually leaving them to go into Parliament.[137]

The superior education required for entry into the higher civil service would, in fact, establish a sense of social equality and solidarity between higher civil servants and members of Parliament, and Trev-elyan might well have thought this prospect as politically advantageous as Robert Lowe did in his testimony before the Civil Service Inquiry Commission of the 1870s. "That is very advantageous, particularly when an office has to deal with members of Parliament and many people outside. Those who have to deal with them would be persons who are on a sort of equality with them . . . ."[138] Facilitating social intercourse and interchange of personnel between these branches, the education of the higher civil service might even strengthen the system of parliamentary government.

The third objection, that the reform would produce an officialdom versed in scholastic learning rather than knowledge of practical affairs, was least satisfactorily answered. The reformers held fast to Macaulay's formula that distinguished achievements in the subjects taught at public schools and universities were most likely to indicate also superior achievements in a civil service career. As Greaves suggested, the very criticisms of the bulk of the opposition, celebrating as it did the characteristics of clerks under the old management style, may well have reinforced the reformers' insistence on those qualities which they expected to catch in the net of literary examinations.[139] Finally, if we recall their agreement with the educators' expectation that the reform would stimulate university reform, we might expect that they were not altogether unsympathetic to the arguments of Chadwick and Mill. But as Mill pointed out, what examination other than a literary one could they propose on the eve of reform, especially when it was to do double duty as a moral and social test?

From Limited to Open Competition

The reformers had underestimated the opposition. The civil service reform bill promised in the speech from the throne at the opening of Parliament in 1854 had to be shelved, at least for the time being. Instead, a compromise solution was worked out to give the Civil Service Commission only limited authority and to preserve the patronage system to the extent that nomination and final selection would remain within the province of department heads. In practice, this solution turned out to be precisely that form of limited competition to which Trevelyan and Northcote had preferred no change at all. When Gladstone resigned in February of 1855, a draft of an Order in Council, nearly finished, was handed over to his successor at the Treasury.

Spurred by the Crimean disclosures of official mismanagement, middle-class agitation for reform, led by the newly founded Administrative Reform Association, went into high gear three months later.[140] The aim of the association was to infuse practical ability and a business sense into the government machinery so as to bring that "bungling" system up to the efficiency of private management. Indeed, the leaders of the association went so far as to agitate for open examinations and certificates of ability that would be honored by public as well as private employers. As might be expected, they rejected out of hand those academic subjects on which Trevelyan's "literary" examinations turned. It is not altogether clear, however, whether Palmerston's government was moved by this resurgent middle-class pressure. Still, the Order in Council was issued at the height of the agitation and laid before the House, where it was voted down. Evidently, the Commons was still not prepared to accept even the slightest invasion upon the domain of patronage by an independent Civil Service Commission, however limited its authority.

Nevertheless, the government proceeded with the reform.[141] The new civil service commissioners went to work and pursued their mandate with unexpected independence and purpose, rejecting even one of Palmerston's nominees for want of ability. During their first year in office, they rejected almost a third of the young men sent to them by departments. When their first annual report was issued, the House of Commons, obviously disposed to look favorably on the record, resolved to commend their work by a vote of 108 to 87. The demonstrated impartiality of the commission seemed to have gone a long way in allaying the fear, expressed earlier, that the commission would turn into just another powerful patron doling out benefices on behalf of faction and family.

Entitled to examine the age, health, character, and ability of candidates nominated by departments, the commission was empowered neither to set standards nor to compel recalcitrant departments to send nominees for examination. Still, the commission worked informally to establish uniform standards. By the late sixties, they were successful with respect to health and moral standards, and some progress was made with respect to age and ability. However, hardly any progress was achieved in advancing the cause of competitive examinations. Although a select committee of the House of Commons recommended in 1860 that three to five candidates normally compete for one or more vacancies, few limited competitions were in fact held in the 1860s because the government never sanctioned the recommendations of the select committee, and the Civil Service Commission was powerless to decide the matter on its own. A happy and, most likely, unanticipated circumstance augmented the power of the commission in 1859. The Superanuation Act of that year stipulated that pension claims would henceforth be verified by means of civil service certificates. Since the commission would not issue a certificate without an examination, it had in fact gained considerable leverage to compel recalcitrant departments to have its nominees examined.

When the Liberals were returned in the first general election following the second extension of the franchise (1867) and Gladstone's government took office, patronage was still very much alive. Since 1855, over 70 percent of the certificates issued by the Civil Service Commission had been awarded without competition.[142] In the first year of Gladstone's administration, the record became even bleaker, for almost 95 percent of all nominations were made without any competition at all. Clearly, family and faction still held sway—and when it touched his interest, even a reformer like Northcote was not above playing the game in traditional ways.[143]

If the political establishment in 1854–1855 tended on balance to oppose open competition, how was the situation altered in 1870, when Gladstone's Liberal government established open competition by an Order in Council? There was little public pressure, virtually no agitation by the press—certainly none comparable with that in 1855—and scarcely any mention of civil service reform in Parliament. The matter came up twice in a motion that "appointments to the Civil and Diplomatic Services ought to be obtained by open competition."[144] The first, in April 1869, was defeated 281 to 30 but only because Gladstone himself asked the House to give his government more time "to see whether we are or are not disposed to act upon the principle we have previously announced."[145] On this occasion, he assured Mr. Henry Fawcet, who had moved the resolution, that "many members of the Government have declared opinions on this subject very much in the direction of the views held by the member for Brighton. They have not altered those opinions; they are desirous to move forward in that direction."[146] The second time that motion came up, in February of 1870, it was withdrawn after Gladstone ventured to say, "unless our present expectations are very much disappointed, it will be within a limited period in our power to announce the establishment of a system of open competition on an extended scale."[147]

In the interval between these motions, the government had indeed moved to act on the reform. In June of 1869, a subcommittee of the cabinet had been formed to deal with the question of open competition and the division of the service into several ranks. A confidential paper by this committee in support of open competition was circulated and discussed by a divided cabinet. In order to overcome that opposition, which included Bright and Clarendon, Gladstone proposed a compromise that would leave the introduction of open competition to the discretion of individual ministers for the time being.

Robert Lowe, Gladstone's Chancellor of the Exchequer, was very much interested in reform and, though an ardent supporter of unqualified competition, he eventually joined Gladstone in pushing the compromise. In November he pressed Gladstone himself.

> As I have so often tried in vain will you bring the question of the Civil Service before the Cabinet to-day. Something must be decided. We cannot keep matters in this discreditable state of abeyance. If the Cabinet will not entertain the idea of open competition, might we not at any rate require a larger number of competitors for each vacancy—five or seven or ten?[148]

A month later, the cabinet approved the compromise scheme and authorized Lowe to solicit departmental views. Early in 1870, the replies came back to the Treasury. The home and foreign offices were clearly against the scheme, but most of the other departments gave their approval, qualified though it was in some cases. There was still concern lest open competition reduce the "high tone of honor" or the "habits of subordination and moral character that are essential to the well-working of a department like the Foreign Office."[149] Similarly, the secretary of state was disposed to think that "much of the business done at the Home Office is of such a character that great trustworthiness is required in those through whose hands it passes and any betrayal of confidence might prove very detrimental to the Public Service."[150] Some of those who approved the scheme raised similar concerns, which are clearly reminiscent of the arguments that had been advanced in 1854–1855 by "aristocratic" opponents who feared a democratization of the service. Gladstone, who was convinced that democratization was no likely outcome of the reform, engineered a shrewd move when he accepted the few recalcitrant opponents to the scheme and let subsequent experience in other departments speak for itself. In June of 1870, finally, the Order in Council was issued to become law after August 31.

Why, then, did Gladstone's great axe fall in 1870? This question—that is, why it was especially opportune or even politically necessary to complete the civil service reform at that time—has never been answered satisfactorily. Although the state of historical research does not allow well-founded conclusions, I will nevertheless venture some plausible suggestions. Many of the exaggerated fears of 1854–1855 had no doubt been allayed by the however scant experience with limited competition and the effective and impartial work of the Civil Service Commission. Even the *Civil Service Gazette* had turned around to support open competition, though it made another turn about when the Order in Council of 1870 was published. Evidently the old fear that university men would be appointed above the heads of deserving clerks cropped up again when it became clear that open competition would be coupled not only with tests of academic knowledge but also with a thoroughgoing differentiation of higher and lower service ranks, as foreshadowed by Trevelyan's "mechanical" and "intellectual" grades.

It is likely that many erstwhile opponents had quietly come around to see the merits of the arguments of Trevelyan, Northcote, and Gladstone himself—that the proposed reforms would have rather "conservative" results in the context of English higher education. Surely, it was not so difficult to share Sir Francis Baring's doubt whether "the practical operation of their much vaunted competitive system, which was to be open to all the world, would not ultimately be to throw all the best appointments in the public Service into the hands of the richer portion of the community."[151] And how many of the formerly apprehensive men might now agree with Thomas Farrer, permanent secretary of the Board of Trade, that the conjunction of costly education and civil service testing must give a system of recruitment a plutocratic character? On the middle class, certainly, that aspect of the reform was not lost.[152]

It is true, such prospects would scarcely console a man who had several sons to place in some living and who might have reason to expect some patronage. The "conservative" implications of the reform might have appealed, however, to an ever-widening circle of men who were worried about the democratizing effects of the second extension of the franchise. If Chadwick had been able to report that the patronage system after 1832 was pulling in increasing numbers of men from the middling orders of society, how much more dangerous must that prospect have loomed after the second extension of the franchise! Contemporaries were not then and historians are not now of one mind how the Second Reform Act might have conditioned the social results of the patronage system had it been maintained.[153] Yet there are some good reasons to suspect that in an enlarged electorate that system would have given men of the middling and lower ranks of society greater leverage to bargain their way into the service. For, as Wright argued, "after 1867 more of the middle class could turn to their local M.P.'s to secure places for their sons in the Civil Service."[154] In addition, the Second Reform Act, it must be remembered, also enfranchised the civil service, and there is evidence that the dangerous political implications were not lost on the members of Parliament or Gladstone's government. "The whole House," Gladstone revealed, "naturally feel, after the Act has been passed which gives the franchise to the Civil Service at large, an increased anxiety for an alteration in those very direct relations which have heretofore subsisted between the Members of this House individually and the disposal of first admission to the Civil Service."[155] If by Gladstone's own account, his government was "perfectly alive" to this circumstance, it can scarcely be doubted, though it has never been suggested nor proved, that it was also alive to the social and political consequences which the direct link between politics and civil service recruitment might spawn if patronage were retained while voting was extended to the lower social orders.

Gladstone had always been concerned to preserve the hold of gentlemen on the civil service, and so it is, perhaps, not too fanciful to suggest that many among the "political aristocracy" in 1870 were more likely to recognize the virtues of open civil service examinations than in 1854 when the leading supporters of reform had tried to convince a fearful opposition that the reform would, in Gladstone's words, "strengthen and multiply the ties between the higher classes and the possession of administrative power."[156] Subsequent experience certainly confirmed his expectation. After 1870 social critics would attack the social bias in the selection of higher civil servants, echoing T. H. Farrer's comment before the Select Committee on Civil Service Expenditures of 1873.

> Another point in the scheme referred to is the aristocratic or rather plutocratic character. It selects men by competitive examination, demanding an expensive education in high subjects which only the rich can afford. It offers no opportunity to those who cannot afford this early education of afterwards making good their way. It professes to

carry out the principle "La carrière ouverte aux talents." But while it follows this principle in the original selection by competition . . . it ignores a far more important and practical means of carrying out this principle.[157]

No matter how competitive the examinations at the point of entry into the civil service, the results had to be ascriptive so long as they were based on the status education of a social group whose public schools and universities remained socially exclusive.

6. Summary and Conclusion

Until the middle of the seventeenth century, the possessions of the Brandenburg rulers were widely scattered, each territory dominated by local aristocratic oligarchies ruling through territorial parliaments and administrative bodies. Unlike England, where national unification was achieved early under the auspices of a feudal monarchy and a single national parliament, the Prussian state was unified several centuries later and then entirely by means of absolutist, military-bureaucratic institutions. Whereas the English Parliament eventually rose above the crown, the Prussian crown defeated the divided estates and proceeded to monopolize sovereign power through military dominance and bureaucratic administration.

During the hundred years before the accession of Frederick II, personnel policies in the civil administration were dictated by the politics of overcoming aristocratic resistance to Prussification. Frederick William I preferred middle-class men and foreigners as commissars and councillors because they were more dependent and hence more pliable in discharging the king's antiaristocratic business. And so in nearly every part of the dynastic civil service, excepting district councillors and presidents of provincial boards, the middle class predominated in the first half of the eighteenth century. Even in the highest ministerial posts, men with nonnoble parents had a slight advantage over scions of old aristocratic families. Yet traditional sentiments were still equating high political-administrative office with noble birth. To reconcile the disjunction between theory and practice, Frederick William I ennobled commoners who had risen to the highest posts.

Meanwhile, the judicial service remained a stronghold of the aristocracy and of nepotism, venality, and patronage characteristic of the "politics of notables." By the middle of the eighteenth century, however, this traditional branch of the service was reformed by means of examinations based on academic qualifications. As a result, councillorships in the judicial service, too, increasingly fell to university-trained commoners. This change of personnel was aided by the reform of the military, especially the reshaping of the officer corps into a monopoly and virtual extension of the aristocratic status group. Since educational qualifications were low in the officer corps and since the incentive was great to start soldiering early in life, gentlemen did not aspire to a higher education that would have qualified them for positions in the reformed judiciary.

While the judicial service was, thus, modernized, the civil service continued to be recruited much as it had been in the first half of the eighteenth century. The king wanted loyal and practical men, versed in estate management, bookkeeping, and the like. Although references to academic qualifications are more frequent in the second half of the eighteenth century, practical experience outweighed academic qualifications throughout the century. Even the civil service reform of 1770 did not recommend, much less require, particular academic studies.

If Frederick William I had explicitly favored bourgeois civil servants, Frederick II forged a new alliance with the old aristocracy and sought to keep nonnobles down. He systematically favored aristocrats and virtually stopped ennobling commoners in the bureaucracy. Competition based on merit, so far as it had advanced under his father, became more limited again. If promoted, commoners rose much later than nobles, and their careers fell short of the highest posts. Despite his aristocratic sentiments and commitments, however, Frederick II needed technically qualified men; and although he constantly requested that vacancies be filled with noblemen to a larger extent than before, he could not get his way very often because the aristocracy, oriented to military service, was neglecting education. Hence, the trend toward employment of middle-class professionals was not altered drastically in all but the highest posts. On the bottom of the higher civil service, bourgeois bureaucrats predominated and even advanced.

Although specific educational qualifications were not yet institutionalized in the civil service, formal education became in fact increasingly significant in the second half of the eighteenth century. This may have been due not only to a growing need for technically qualified men but also to a need for some kind of objective criterion of judgment that would limit patronage and faction building. During the early part of the century the king, attending to every single appointment, even of subaltern officials, had exercised his discretion so as to suppress nepotism and patronage. In the second half of the century, however, the service expanded so much that it became impossible for the king to supervise all appointments. Forced to delegate authority in this crucial area, he may have become more receptive to educational qualifications as a means of checking the reemergence of the old system of family jobbery and patronage appointments.

Since educational qualifications and a series of examinations had transformed the old judiciary from a hotbed of these traditional practices to the most efficient service branch under the crown, there was every reason to expect that the same method would work in the civil service. However that may be, the new examination system of the civil service, introduced in 1770, was modeled after the examination system of the judicial service. It differed from the judicial system only in that it did not require a particular course of academic studies. Hence, the new system gave the examiners considerable discretion in defining what was meant by a good education and, thus, could be used also by the aristocratic top echelon for screening out unwanted men.

Thus, the first phase of the Prussian civil service reform bears a superficial resemblance to the English reform a hundred years later. Both reforms got on the agenda because of functional problems with significant political implications. Both schemes were thought of and were used as devices for maintaining established inequalities. Yet here the similarity ends. The English elite introduced educational tests based on the curricula of Oxford and Cambridge because it was better prepared educationally than any other status group. In Prussia, by contrast, the examinations of 1770 could work in favor of the aristocratic elite in the bureaucracy only because educational qualifications were as yet a matter of discretion.

In England, even more than in Prussia, recruitment in the unreformed civil service was based on patronage appointment. By the middle of the eighteenth century, England was ruled by a single "party" of wealthy landed oligarchs. The intense party feelings of the seventeenth century had dissolved in a stable system of political patronage. At the center, the parliamentary cabinet under the crown managed parliamentary majorities and local elections with sinecures, pensions, and jobs in court and administrative offices. Except for the fact that the heavy hand of the crown in these matters was becoming a thing of the past in the nineteenth century, the patronage system remained intact to the eve of the civil service reforms in mid-century. With the expansion of civil administration in the first half of the nineteenth century, well-educated men were increasingly brought into the top rungs of the hierarchy. Although these men, too, advanced by patronage, theirs was the patronage of notables who appreciated their professional competence and zealous work habits as much as their political reliability and family connections. The majority of them came from upper- and upper-middle-class homes and were in fact regarded as gentlemen.

The professional, liberally educated intelligentsia, to which most of them belonged, were rather distinct from the middle-class careerists in Prussia's unreformed civil service. Many of them were recruited from the status group of landed gentlemen. Unlike in Prussia, younger sons and nephews of gentlemen did not face legal impediments to entering the professions and trade. Whereas trade, certainly retail trade, was socially proscribed, the liberal professions were considered honorable and worthy of a gentleman's calling. Thus, young gentlemen in need of a living would enter the liberal professions precisely so as to maintain their gentlemanly status. Other members of the liberal professions were recruited from families whose connections with landed status were more remote but who had been identified with the honorable professions for generations. Still others, though not very many, entered from below. All of them had to pass through expensive public schools, universities, and Inns of Court. This professional status group was the link between the aristocracy and gentry, on the one hand, and the commercial middle class, on the other. But as members of the universities and the liberal professions, they ranked themselves much closer to the higher orders than to the world of industry, commerce, and trade; and by the middle of the nineteenth century, only very old-fashioned people would dispute that they were gentlemen.

Naturally, this status group of gentlemen had its share of conflicts, and there were many middle-class intellectuals who were proud of their bourgeois origins and did not confuse themselves with the landed gentry. But in the context of a nobility with a tradition of accepting families grown wealthy in commerce or industry, conflicts were comparatively mild within the camp of gentlemen who had received the proper status education at Oxford or Cambridge. If the near-gentry professionals in and out of the service had much to gain from civil service reform and were, indeed, the most eloquent advocates, they were also arguing with conviction that the proposed civil service reforms were decidedly aristocratic and would benefit all who were gentlemen by birth and cultivation.

In Prussia, by contrast, the great social divide lay between the hereditary, militarist nobility and the bourgeoisie of property and education. Nobles were legally barred from entering the professions and trade so that they might fulfill their obligation of service in the army. Wealthy bourgeois, moreover, were legally prevented from acquiring manorial estates. True, employment in the bureaucracy would raise bourgeois careerists to a status group with many quasi-aristocratic exemptions and privileges, but the social cleavage between aristocrats and seminoble bourgeois was a perennial source of conflict and bitterness within the service. In society at large, middle-class intellectuals with a fine education smarted under the discrimination by mere aristocrats claiming an inborn superiority to men whose only claim to recognition was their talent, cultivation, and professional expertise. The continuous experience of personal humiliation inclined many to a deep sense of inferiority coupled with a disposition to ape aristocratic manners and to flare up occasionally in defiant self-assertion.

German idealism and neohumanism in the decades around the turn of the eighteenth century ushered in a sort of cultural revolution giving the educated middle class a more independent social consciousness. It offered not only a political theory legitimating the rule of enlightened bureaucratic professionals but also a new standard for judging a man's worth. The doctrines of German idealism, particularly the concept of *Bildung*, strengthened the defiant attitude of middle-class intellectuals to noble rank, and it moved some men even to reverse traditional notions of aristocratic superiority and bourgeois humility. Educated burghers who were attracted to this ideology even thought of themselves as the true aristocrats of a new enlightened age. Theirs was an aristocracy of cultivation and personal refinement.

This new ideology penetrated the bureaucratic ranks in the last decades of the eighteenth century, enhancing the crisis of the aristocracy which had been brewing ever since talented commoners might be placed above aristocrats of old lineage in the chain of command. It was the age of the French Revolution and of reactionary defense of aristocratic rights, of literary challenges by bourgeois ideologists and quasi-medieval pretensions by aristocratic apologists. It was a time also when the nobility advanced on balance at the expense of burghers in many positions in the bureaucracy. The Prussian General Code of 1794 even went so far as to restrict legally the highest state dignities to men of aristocratic rank, only to force a liberalized policy of ennoblement. The growing rate of ennoblements, moreover, caused an inflation of honors and fanned the crisis of the aristocracy. Add to this the economic problems that swelled the ranks of poor and landless nobles who sought relief in the form of subaltern offices scarcely adequate for upholding the honor and dignity of the *Herrenstand*. Many bourgeois civil servants, especially younger men in the lower rungs of the higher civil service, rejected the old aristocratic social standards while some enlightened noblemen adopted the new middle-class standard of *Bildung* and began to accept their bourgeois colleagues as social equals. Thus, the long-standing social cleavage shifted to align the new aristocracy of intellect, on the one side, and mere aristocrats, on the other. Whereas the members of the English liberal professions on the eve of reform moved in the orbit of the aristocracy and gentry and were aligned against nongentlemen, the professionals in the Prussian bureaucracy, mostly of bourgeois origin, were aligned against the landed aristocracy. The concept of *Bildung* and the notion of a *Bildungsaristokratie* might assume a conservative cast after the reforms; but on the eve of those reforms this ideology challenged the claims of aristocratic privilege in the name of "the career open to talent."

Among the historical reasons for the divergent social positions of the professional intelligentsia of England and Prussia, one is particularly significant: the relationship of the aristocracy to education, especially to universities. Unlike the Prussian nobility, the English landed aristocracy and gentry were linked to higher education by a tradition that goes back to the second half of the sixteenth and the first half of the seventeenth centuries. It was then that the aristocracy had turned to education on a scale that almost certainly dwarfed a comparable move on the continent. Although the level of attendance might have dropped in the latter part of the seventeenth and during most of the eighteenth centuries, a public school and university education was to remain compatible with high social rank. It even became a badge of it. Compared with the English universities, the Prussian universities on the eve of reform were rather plebeian places; and the fate of the Prussian nobiliary academies, their inexorable transformation into plain military academies or mere riding schools, contrasts strikingly with the flourishing public schools catering to the best of English landed society.

The defeat of Prussia at the hands of Napoleon precipitated the coalescence of a reform party, led by a small band of enlightened bureaucrats. Aristocrats no less than the discredited old military and bureaucratic elite, the new men at the top shared and were responsive to the interests of middle-class careerists. The new ministers, who wrested ministerial responsiblity from the crown and who once again reduced the judiciary to interpreting rather than making the law, surrounded themselves with highly qualified young councillors. Acting much like permanent state secretaries and ministerial directors today, these councillors assisted the ministers in developing political guidelines. If it was a marriage of convenience between the new aristocratic top echelon of enlightened officials and equally educated middle-class careerists, their common orientation to the ideology of *Bildung* and to a new conception of enlightened bureaucratic absolutism also bridged whatever divergent interests they may have had and certainly contrasted sharply with the ideology of the representatives of the old status order under the crown. The bureaucracy emerged from the reform period as a sort of political-administrative corporation vested with near absolute power of the state. Fortified with the right to permanent tenure and pension, its members were now recruited exclusively by co-optation and examination from the graduates of the reformed universities.

Humboldt's reform of secondary schools and universities aligned education with the purposes of this professionalized bureaucracy. The standardization of curricula and the establishment of uniform state examinations went hand in hand with a redefinition of employment conditions in the higher civil service. In line with the idealist ideology, which cast the elite as an enlightened "universal status group" (Hegel) over and above the pulling and hauling of interest groups in civil society, the emphasis shifted away from practical experience. The regulations of 1817, finally, required a prolonged classical education culminating in the study of law as qualification for in-service training. These regulations completed the monopolization of access by owners of higher educational certificates, which, to paraphrase Max Weber, had become what the test for ancestors had been in the past: a prerequisite for equality of birth as well as a qualification for state office.

In England, the reform movement was precipitated by several conditions and events internal and external to the civil service. Externally, the Chartist movement followed by the European uprisings of 1848 created a disposition among the ruling class to put their house in order. This disposition was heightened by continuous pressure in Parliament for economy in and reduction of the civil establishment. The reformers thought that the professionalization of the service might increase the efficiency of the civil administration and, at the same time, achieve greater economies. Internally, the pressure for reform was building up too. The administration had expanded and had become so complex that it became evident that the government could not be carried on without a professional higher civil service. The reform was to provide such a corps of higher civil servants and to divide the administration into "mechanical" and "intellectual" service ranks. Finally, there were a number of changes in English society which furnished models for the professionalization of the service: the reform of the universities, which established competitive examinations for fellowships so as to improve higher education; the reforms in the legal and medical professions, which featured new associations devoted to raising qualifications of practitioners by means of examinations and licenses; and the reform of the Indian civil service, which established open competition based on the curricula of Oxford and Cambridge.

When the Trevelyan-Northcote proposals became public, the establishment of the day was opposed to the abolition of patronage and to the idea of competitive examinations. The reforms had to be shelved for the time being. The abolition of patronage threatened the very levers of power of what Trevelyan called the "political aristocracy." In many minds the reform proposals raised the specter of a democratic civil service alongside an aristocratic legislature, of a civil service overrun by the lower rank of society, and of a lowering of the moral tone if low people without the breeding and feelings of gentlemen were to be admitted. The introduction of competitive examinations based on curricula of public schools and universities also raised concern among the old-type officials who had not received a classical education and who had been recruited by patronage. They feared that the division of the service into "mechanical" and "intellectual" ranks and the assignment of young university-trained men to the latter would diminish their opportunity to rise to higher posts. In any case, it was against objections of this kind that the reformers argued time and again that the reforms would be decidedly aristocratic. Instead of displacing gentlemen, they would give them even better access to the higher civil service than they were presently enjoying. Wasn't the patronage system, as it was operating in the political context after 1832, drawing in an increasing number of men from the lower orders? And would not competitive examinations based on the curricula of Oxford and Cambridge select the sons of gentlemen and those who had acquired the education and cultivation of gentlemen? The reformers made it clear that they wanted to squeeze out the spoilsmen, aristocratic or not, but they wanted to replace this increasingly mixed group with educated, university-trained gentlemen.

If the political establishment in 1854–1855 tended on balance to oppose open competition between university-trained men interested in civil service jobs, how was the situation different in 1870 when Gladstone's Liberal government established open competition by an Order in Council? There was no apparent public pressure, no agitation by the press comparable to 1854–1855, scarcely any mention of civil service reform in Parliament. Perhaps, some of the exaggerated fears of 1854–1855 had been allayed by now especially since the new Civil Service Commission was widely credited with having done a fine job in upgrading the service by means of limited competition. The more favorable climate of opinion, I have suggested, may well have been the result of worries about the effects of the second extension of the franchise, which had returned the Liberals in the election of 1868. Would the patronage system in an enlarged electorate give men of the middling and lower ranks of society greater leverage to bargain their way into the civil service? Gladstone had always been concerned to preserve the hold of gentlemen on the civil service, and it is quite likely that the "political aristocracy" in 1870 was more receptive to his arguments of 1854, when he, much like Trevelyan and Northcote, had tried to convince Lord John Russell that the proposed reforms would strengthen and multiply the ties between the higher-status groups and the possession of administrative power.

Thus it was that in the varying social, educational, and political circumstances of Prussia and England, civil service reform appeared in a very different light to the contemporary actors with an educational advantage. To the Prussian middle-class careerists, it meant gaining administrative power. To the English gentlemen administrators it meant holding on to it. In both cases, the strategy to monopolize the higher civil service by means of educational certificates and civil service examinations could work, however, only so long as the social structure of education remained unchanged. Once aristocrats here and middling sorts of people there were pushing into the universities in anticipation of government employment, the social composition of the civil service was liable to change—in Prussia in favor of the aristocracy and in England in favor of the middle class.

Looking back, it is important to keep in mind that the road to meritocracy in the two countries was not a single highway but two distinct roads. These roads linked up here and there, to be sure; and they shared a common direction, especially when viewed from the abstract heights of concepts contrasting tradition and modernity. Yet the sense of similarity becomes spurious when one assumes unwittingly that similar institutions must have been introduced for similar reasons or that similar institutions must have had the same meaning to actors in different countries. Amidst the historical detail we understand much better Weber's admonition that ideal types are not theories themselves but only tools for formulating theories— and also that such theories are incomplete unless they contain terms referring to the meanings, intentions, strategies, and legitimations of historical actors. It is an admonition to be wary not only of the shortcomings of functional analyses and dichotomous concepts but also of the hazard of historical hindsight tempting us to treat as subjective intention what is only an unanticipated historical consequence. If in the end civil service examinations were linked with the values of equity and equality, so much so that we now regard them as direct descendants of democracy, we should not forget that those supposedly "democratic" institutions owed their inception to the interests associated, on the one hand, with the expansion of autocracy and, on the other, with the preservation of aristocracy.

Notes

Preface

1. Max Weber, *Economy and Society* (New York: Bedminster Press, 1968), III, 998.
2. Reinhard Bendix et al., eds., *State and Society: A Reader in Comparative Political Sociology* (Berkeley: University of California Press, 1973; 1st ed., Boston: Little, Brown, 1968).

Introduction

1. Weber, *Economy and Society*, III, 998ff.
2. See especially Henry Parris, *Constitutional Bureaucracy* (London: Allen & Unwin, 1969); and Maurice Wright, *Treasury Control of the Civil Service 1854–1874* (Oxford: Clarendon Press, 1969).
3. Especially Hans Rosenberg, *Bureaucracy, Aristocracy, and Autocracy* (Boston: Beacon Press, 1958), to which this study owes more than one inspiration.
4. Emmeline W. Cohen, *The Growth of the British Civil Service 1790–1939* (Hamden, Conn.: Archon Books, 1965), first published in 1941, frequently uses a model of external middle-class pressure. J. Donald Kingsley, *Representative Bureaucracy* (Yellow Springs, Ohio: Antioch Press, 1944) is a typical rise-of-the-bourgeoisie interpretation. W. J. Reader, *Professional Men* (London: Weidenfeld & Nicolson, 1966), p. 73, interprets the reform in terms of middle-class pressure for more professional positions.
5. "Preservative" interests are emphasized in Edward Hughes, "Civil Service Reform 1853–1855," *History*, 27 (1942): 51–83; Edward Hughes, "Notes and Documents: Sir Charles Trevelyan and Civil Service Reform,

1853–1854," *English Historical Review,* 64 (1949): 53–88, 206–34; Edward Hughes, "Postscript to Civil Service Reforms of 1855," *Public Administration,* 33 (1955): 299–306. See also H. R. G. Greaves, *The Civil Service in the Changing State* (London: Harrap, 1947); H. J. Hanham, *The Nineteenth Century Constitution* (London: Cambridge University Press, 1969), pp. 314–20; and Robert Moses, *The Civil Service of Great Britain* (New York: Columbia University Press, 1914).

6. The older literature under the leadership of Gustav Schmoller and Otto Hintze is quite extensive, but deals largely with the seventeenth- and eighteenth-century reforms. The literature of the Stein-Hardenberg reform period does not have comparable depth in the area of administrative reform.

7. Alexis de Tocqueville, *The Old Regime and the French Revolution* (Garden City, N.Y.: Doubleday, 1955), p. 15.

Chapter 1

1. Talcott Parsons, *The Social System* (New York: Free Press, 1951), p. 204.

2. Weber, *Economy and Society,* III, 1000; compare also Max Weber's analysis of the Chinese literati in *The Religion of China* (Glencoe, Ill.: Free Press, 1951), pp. 107ff; the "nonfunctional" aspects of the German "mandarin tradition" are discussed in Fritz K. Ringer, *The Decline of the German Mandarins* (Cambridge, Mass.: Harvard University Press, 1969). The social and political significance of the "public school tradition" is analyzed in Rupert Wilkinson, *Gentlemanly Power: British Leadership and the Public School Tradition* (London: Oxford University Press, 1964). In the literature on the reform of the classical gymnasia, "nonfunctional" and even "dys-functional" aspects of the "classical tradition" have been discussed extensively. For a convenient introduction see Hermann Röhrs, ed., *Das Gymnasium in Geschichte und Gegenwart* (Frankfurt/Main: Akademische Verlags-gesellschaft, 1969). In England, the Fulton Report on the civil service touched repeatedly on the "nonfunctional" aspects of the Macaulay-Trevelyan tradition of the classically educated generalist. See *Fulton Report on the Civil Service,* I (1968). In both countries, social criticism has constantly singled out the nontechnical social functions of the type of education required in the higher civil service.

3. Randall Collins, "Functional and Conflict Theories of Educational Stratification," *American Sociological Review,* 36 (December 1971): 1002–19.

4. Ibid., 1002–03.

5. Ibid., 1009ff.

6. Max Weber, " 'Objectivity,' in Social Science and Social Policy," in *Max Weber on the Methodology of the Social Sciences,* ed. Edward Shils

and Henry A. Finch (Glencoe, Ill.: Free Press, 1949), p. 77.

7. Weber, *Economy and Society,* III, 999.

8. Weber, " 'Objectivity,' " p. 83. The passage continues: "From our viewpoint, purpose is the conception of an *effect* which becomes a *cause* of an action. Since we take into account every cause which produces or can produce a significant effect, we also consider this one. Its specific significance consists only in the fact that we not only *observe* human conduct but can and desire to understand it."

9. Weber, *Economy and Society,* III, 998–1002.

10. Ibid., 1000.

11. Michael Young, *The Rise of the Meritocracy* (Harmondsworth: Penguin Books, 1963), p. 30.

12. Neil J. Smelser and Seymour Martin Lipset, eds., *Social Structure and Mobility in Economic Development* (Chicago: Aldine, 1966), p. 12.

13. Reinhard Bendix and Bennett Berger, "Images of Society and Problems of Concept Formation in Sociology," in *Symposium on Sociological Theory,* ed. Llewellyn Gross (New York: Harper & Row, 1959), pp. 92–118. See also the revised form in Reinhard Bendix, *Embattled Reason* (New York: Oxford University Press, 1970), pp. 116–138; also Reinhard Bendix, "Tradition and Modernity Reconsidered," in *Embattled Reason,* pp. 250–314; and several related essays in Reinhard Bendix and Günther Roth, *Scholarship and Partisanship* (Berkeley: University of California Press, 1971).

14. Parsons, *The Social System,* p. 64.

15. Ibid., pp. 58ff.

16. Ibid., p. 200.

17. "Contextual" analysis would describe series of interrelated selection processes (careers, mobility channels, status passages, etc.) and classify selection processes in terms of social results.

18. Morton White, *Social Thought in America* (Boston: Beacon Press, 1966), p. 12. I might add here that Parsons is aware that role analysis can tell us nothing about the broader contextual social significance of a particular pattern-variable arrangement: "In analyzing the components of any particular action system, one must also consider the larger system within which it is embedded . . . ." Talcott Parsons, "Pattern Variables Revisited: A Response to Robert Dubin," in his *Sociological Theory and Modern Society* (New York: Free Press, 1967), p. 196. It turns out, however, that Parsons is aiming to articulate his pattern variables with his paradigm of the four universal problems of social systems—adaptation, goal attainment, integration, and pattern maintenance. Ibid., p. 197. Variously patterned roles, he argues, are functionally significant, indeed necessary, to "solve" just these systems problems. In any case, his recommended contextual analysis once again involves merely functional analysis rather than causal-historical

explanation.

19. Parsons, *The Social System,* p. 177.

20. Ibid., p. 168.

21. This is also one of the central notions of the Davis and Moore theory, brought out in the debate that followed the initial version. See Reinhard Bendix and S. M. Lipset, eds., *Class, Status, and Power* (2nd ed., New York: Free Press, 1966), pp. 47–96, especially p. 60.

22. Talcott Parsons and Edward A. Shils, *Toward a General Theory of Action* (New York: Harper Torch, 1951), pp. 15, 17.

23. Parsons, *The Social System,* p. 182.

24. Talcott Parsons, *Societies: Evolutionary and Comparative Perspectives* (Englewood Cliffs, N.J.: Prentice-Hall, 1966). The graphs and legends on pp. 28–29 are rather interesting. "Ultimate reality" is evidently the "environment" of cultural systems and ranks highest in the "hierarchy of controlling factors." How, philosophically, is one to understand the suggestion that cultural systems are controlled "in the cybernetic sense" by "ultimate reality"?

25. Weber, " 'Objectivity,' " p. 90.

26. As Parsons put it plainly in *The Social System* (pp. 180–81), "We will proceed . . . under the assumption that this pattern [of value orientation] *is* the dominant value pattern of a society" (emphasis mine).

27. Weber, " 'Objectivity,' " pp. 102–03.

28. Ibid., pp. 94–95.

29. Ibid., p. 94.

30. Cf. Kingsley, *Representative Bureaucracy,* passim.

31. George Homans, "Bringing Men Back In," *American Sociological Review,* 29 (December 1964): 809–18.

32. Ibid., 815.

33. For example, Herbert Blumer, "Society and Symbolic Interaction," in *Human Behavior and Social Process,* ed. Arnold M. Rose (Boston: Houghton Mifflin, 1962); Harold Garfinkel, *Studies in Ethnomethodology* (Englewood Cliffs, N.J.: Prentice-Hall, 1967); and any of the works of Erving Goffman.

34. Cf. Randall Collins, *Conflict Sociology* (New York: Academic Press, 1975), who comes to historical sociology with an interactionist perspective; Jeffrey Lionel Berlant, *Profession and Monopoly* (Berkeley: University of California Press, 1975), whose work shares with mine a theoretical focus on group formation and the strategies of monopolization by professional groups; and Irving M. Zeitlin, *Rethinking Sociology* (New York: Appleton-Century-Crofts, 1973), who speaks of a "Marx-Weber model of social and historical analysis" and goes some way in mapping this historical, conflict-group approach (p. 136).

35. For this neologism and a number of other suggestions I am indebted to Reinhard Bendix, "Inequality and Social Structure: A Comparison of Marx and Weber," *American Sociological Review*, 39 (April 1974): 149–61.

36. Weber, *Economy and Society*, II, 926ff.

37. Ibid., 938. The passage continues: "And every slowing down of the change in economic stratification leads, in due course, to the growth of status structures and makes for a resuscitation of the important role of social honor."

38. Ibid., 935ff.

39. Karl Marx and Friedrich Engels, "Manifesto of the Communist Party" in Robert Freedman, ed., *Marxist Social Thought* (New York: Harcourt, Brace, 1968), pp. 178–79.

40. Cf. Sally Bould Van Til and Jon Van Til, "The Lower Classes and the Future of Inequality," *Growth and Change*, IV (January 1973):10–16.

41. Joseph Bensman and Arthur J. Vidich, *The New American Society* (Chicago: Quadrangle Books, 1971), pp. 119ff.

42. Weber, *Economy and Society*, II, 930.

43. In this vast field we also find the formation of those interinstitutional cliques which, Bensman and Vidich have recently suggested, are significant in coordinating the plurality of private and public bureaucracies in contemporary society. Cf. Bensman and Vidich, *New American Society*, pp. 87ff. As to Weber's concept of "party," it may be said that party action is oriented toward acquisition of social power in an imperatively coordinated association, to use Dahrendorf's phrase. Whereas group action based on class situation or status situation does not necessarily entail that the group has an associational character, whenever such action does take place in and through an imperatively coordinated association, Weber denotes that as the action of a party. Nor does he confine the term to an association aiming to gain power in the state. For parties may exist in a social club as well as in the state. In other words, parties are groups with an associational character representing interests arising out of class situation or status situation, usually a combination of the two, and they are groups who are striving to realize these class or status interests by gaining power within a more encompassing association.

44. Cf. Bendix, *Embattled Reason*, pp. 126–30.

45. Bendix, "Inequality and Social Structure," p. 160.

Chapter 2

1. Among the English literature, the following deal with various aspects of the pattern: Walter L. Dorn, *Competition for Empire, 1740–1763* (New York: Harper Torch, 1963): Walter Dorn, "The Prussian Bureaucracy in

the Eighteenth Century," *Political Science Quarterly*, 46 (1931): 403–23; Reinhold A. Dorwart, *The Administrative Reforms of Frederick William I of Prussia* (Cambridge, Mass.: Harvard University Press, 1953); Sidney B. Fay, *The Rise of Brandenburg-Prussia to 1786* (New York: S. Holt, 1937); Rosenberg, *Bureaucracy;* and F. L. Carsten, *The Origins of Prussia* (Oxford: Clarendon Press, 1954).

2. Cf. Otto Hintze, *Die Hohenzollern und ihr Werk* (Berlin: Paul Parey, 1915), pp. 148ff.

3. Carsten, *Origins of Prussia,* p. 169.

4. Cf. Curt Jany, *Geschichte der Preussischen Armee* (Osnabrück: Biblio Verlag, 1967), I, 148ff.

5. Hintze, *Die Hohenzollern,* p. 211.

6. As quoted in Rosenberg, *Bureaucracy,* p. 40.

7. Cf. Dorwart, *Administrative Reforms,* especially pp. 109ff.

8. These *Amtskammern* are often referred to simply as *Kammern.*

9. For a comparative-historical study of the institution of the commissar, see Otto Hintze, "Der Commissarius and seine Bedeutung in der allgemeinen Verwaltungsgeschichte" in his *Staat und Verfassung* (Göttingen: Vandenhoeck & Ruprecht, 1962), pp. 242–74.

10. Cf. *Acta Borussica. 2. Die Handels-, Zoll- und Akzisepolitik Preussens,* I, 769ff.

11. Cf. Otto Hintze, "Behördenorganisation und allgemeine Verwaltung in Preussen," *Acta Borussica. 1. Die Behördenorganisation,* VI, part 1, 260ff (hereafter cited as *A.B.B.,* etc.).

12. The present section is indebted especially to Otto Büsch, *Militärsystem und Sozialleben im alten Preussen 1713–1807* (Berlin: Walter de Gruyter, 1962).

13. Jany, *Preussischen Armee,* I, 546ff.

14. Ibid., I, 561.

15. Büsch, *Militärsystem,* p. 16.

16. Those who were inducted to serve spent one or two years on active duty but afterwards lived and worked at home for some nine or ten months out of the year. During the eighteenth century about 4 percent of the population and roughly 16 percent of all eligible males were serving in the army. See ibid., p. 1.

17. Hintze, "Staatsverfassung und Heeresverfasung" in his *Staat und Verfassung,* p. 70.

18. *A.B.B.,* III, 450.

19. *A.B.B.,* IX, 162. Frederick II was also against the customary cavalier's tour. As he put it in a marginal comment: "The goose travels, the goose returns—and then they don't want to serve. I am not for it." As quoted in Elsbeth Schwenke, "Friedrich der Grosse und der Adel," inaugural dis-

sertation, University of Berlin, 1911, p. 21.
20. As quoted in Schwenke, "Friedrich der Grosse," p. 20.
21. *A.B.B.*, II, 266.
22. *A.B.B.*, V, part 2, 817.
23. *A.B.B.*, VI, part 2, 151.
24. As quoted in Schwenke, "Friedrich der Grosse," p. 23.
25. *A.B.B.*, V, part 2, 817.
26. Jany, *Preussischen Armee*, I, 728.
27. Ibid., I, 722.
28. As quoted in Rosenberg, *Bureaucracy*, p. 60.
29. Büsch, *Militärsystem*, p. 83.
30. Ibid., pp. 94–95.
31. Fritz Martiny, *Die Adelsfrage in Preussen vor 1806* (Stuttgart: Kohlhammer, 1938), p. 113; Büsch, *Militärsystem*, pp. 95, 96.
32. Martiny, *Die Adelsfrage*, p. 113.
33. Karl Demeter, *The German Officer-Corps in Society and State 1650–1945* (London: Weidenfeld & Nicolson, 1965), pp. 6–7.
34. Büsch, *Militärsystem*, p. 93.
35. Jany, *Preussischen Armee*, II, 221–22.
36. Ibid., II, 220–21.
37. *A.B.B.*, XIII, 27ff.
38. As quoted in Büsch, *Militärsystem*, p. 104.
39. *A.B.B.*, VI, 562ff.
40. *A.B.B.*, IX, Nr. 78.
41. As quoted by Martiny, *Die Adelsfrage*, p. 44, from an opinion voiced in 1803. According to the *Allgemeines Landrecht* (Berlin: 1796), II, title 9, pph. 1, that function was "to defend the state as well as uphold its external honor and internal constitution."
42. As quoted in Friedrich-Karl Tharau, *Die geistige Kultur des preussischen Offiziers von 1640 bis 1806* (Mainz: Hase & Koehler, 1968), pp. 126–27.
43. Gordon A. Craig, *The Politics of the Prussian Army 1640–1945* (New York: Oxford University Press, 1964), pp. 25–26.
44. As quoted in ibid., p. 25n.
45. As quoted in Rosenberg, *Bureaucracy*, p. 53.
46. Ibid., p. 52.
47. *Urkunden und Aktenstücke zur Geschichte des Kurfürsten Friedrich Wilhelm von Brandenburg*, XVI, 1058.
48. As quoted in Gustav Schmoller, "Der Preussische Beamtenstand unter Friedrich Wilhelm I," *Preussische Jahrbücher*, 26 (1870): 159.
49. Hintze, "Behördenorganisation," p. 276.
50. As quoted in Schmoller, "Preussische Beamtenstand," p. 158.

51. As quoted in ibid., p. 164.

52. Rosenberg, *Bureaucracy,* pp. 55–56.

53. Ibid., pp. 89ff.

54. The quotations in this paragraph are taken from various cabinet orders, instructions, regulations, and memoranda. *A.B.B.*: I, 163, 392; III, 577–78; V, part 2, 432, 532, 537, 565, 614; VII, 130; VIII, 327, 657; IX, 161, 414, 417, 445; XIII, 683. Cf. also Schmoller, "Preussische Beaimtenstand," p. 168; and Rosenberg, *Bureaucracy,* p. 76.

55. *A.B.B.*: VII, 649; X, 34.

56. *A.B.B.,* IV, part 2, 401.

57. *A.B.B.,* VII, 168–70.

58. *A.B.B.,* IX, 153.

59. Much the same argument could be made with respect to merit as against seniority. When an official petitioned Frederick II for promotion on account of seniority, the king is said to have replied: "I have a number of mules in my stables who have served me long and well, yet none of them has any prospect of becoming master of the stables." As quoted in Herman Weill, *Frederick the Great and Samuel von Cocceji* (Madison: State Historical Society, 1961), p. 136. The argument certainly applies also to merit as against payments to the recruiting chest. Cf. Rosenberg, *Bureaucracy,* pp. 75ff.

60. *A.B.B.,* V, part 1, 34.

61. As quoted in Gustav Schmoller, "Einleitung," *A.B.B.,* I, 131.

62. Cf. A. Goodwin, "Prussia" in Albert Goodwin, ed., *The European Nobility in the Eighteenth Century* (London: Adam & Charles Black, 1953), p. 85.

63. As quoted in Schmoller, "Preussische Beamtenstand," p. 154.

64. Rosenberg, *Bureaucracy,* p. 67.

65. Ibid., p. 68.

66. *A.B.B.,* VI, part 1, 283.

67. Schmoller, "Preussische Beamtenstand," p. 163.

68. Rosenberg, *Bureaucracy,* p. 68.

69. Schmoller, "Preussische Beamtenstand," p. 163.

70. Rosenberg, *Bureaucracy,* p. 69.

71. *A.B.B.,* VIII, 528.

72. *A.B.B.,* IX, 361.

73. Ibid.

74. As quoted in Schwenke, "Friedrich der Grosse," p. 36.

75. Ibid., pp. 14, 33.

76. *A.B.B.,* VII, 183.

77. *A.B.B.,* XV, 81; see also X, 445.

78. *A.B.B.,* IX, 726–27.

79. Schwenke, "Friedrich der Grosse," p. 38.

80. Ibid., p. 39; Rosenberg, *Bureaucracy*, p. 160; see also Henri Brunschwig, *La crise de l'état prussien à la fin du XVIIIe siècle* (Paris: Presses Universitaires, 1947), pp. 153ff.

81. Rosenberg, *Bureaucracy*, pp. 169–70.

82. Ibid., p. 96.

83. Ibid., p. 97.

84. Ibid., p. 108.

85. Schmoller, "Preussische Beamtenstand," p. 167.

86. *A.B.B.*, V, part 2, 370–71.

87. Weill, *Frederick the Great*, p. 127–28.

88. As quoted in Rosenberg, *Bureaucracy*, p. 94.

89. *A.B.B.*, V, part 2, 370.

90. *A.B.B.*, IX, 235.

91. *A.B.B.*, X, 321–22.

92. *A.B.B.*, IX, 234–35.

93. Rosenberg, *Bureaucracy*, p. 130.

94. Christian Otto Mylius, ed., *Novum Corpus Constitutionum Prussico-Brandenburgensium* (Berlin: Kunst, 1751), I, part 3, col. 1023.

95. Weill, *Frederick the Great*, p. 138.

96. *A.B.B.*, VII, 45.

97. *A.B.B.*, VIII, 45.

98. Ibid., VIII, 45–46.

99. *A.B.B.*, VII, 47.

100. Rosenberg, *Bureaucracy*, p. 131.

101. Ernst Rudolph Huber, *Deutsche Verfassungsgeschichte seit 1789* (Stuttgart: Kohlhammer, 1957), I, 235ff.

102. *A.B.B.*, XII, 4–7.

103. *A.B.B.*: III, 684; IV, 34.

104. Clemens O. Delbrück, *Die Ausbildung für den höheren Verwaltungsdienst in Preussen* (Jena: Gustav Fischer, 1917), p. 4.

105. *A.B.B.*, VII, 702.

106. Hintze, "Behördenorganisation," p. 280.

107. *A.B.B.*, V, part 2, 627–28.

108. *A.B.B.*, IX, 85.

109. *A.B.B.*, X, 55.

110. *A.B.B.*, VIII, 665.

111. *A.B.B.*, X, 220.

112. Ibid., X, 349.

113. *A.B.B.*, XIII, 565–66.

114. *A.B.B.*, XV, 243.

115. *A.B.B.*, XVI, 244.

116. *A.B.B.*, XV, 251.

117. Ibid., XV, 260.

118. Ibid., XV, 262.

119. Ibid., XV, 255.

120. Rosenberg, *Bureaucracy*, p. 178.

121. Ibid., p. 179.

122. Ibid., p. 180.

123. Ibid., p. 63.

124. As quoted in ibid., p. 181.

125. Ibid., p. 178.

126. Demeter, *German Officer-Corps*, p. 66.

127. Friedrich Paulsen, *Geschichte des gelehrten Unterrichts* (Berlin and Leipzig: Walter de Gruyter, 1919), I, 521.

128. B. Poten, "Geschichte des Militär-Erziehungs- und Bildungswesens in den Landen deutscher Zunge," *Monumenta Germaniae Paedagogica,* XVII (1896): 11.

129. Ibid., 26.

130. As quoted in ibid., 33.

131. Ibid., 32, 62. According to Martiny, in 1806, there were 721 places in the corps of cadets when the entire officer corps numbered between 7,000 and 8,000 men. Martiny, *Die Adelsfrage,* pp. 68-69.

132. Tharau, *Die geistige Kultur,* p. 73. Tharau thinks that military training did not have priority in the corps of cadets. He bases this judgment on the published lesson plans according to which the cadets were to receive forty hours of education and sixteen hours of military drill per week.

133. Martiny, *Die Adelsfrage,* p. 113.

134. Ibid., p. 113.

135. It is interesting to note in this context that the University of Halle developed out of a nobiliary academy. When Magdeburg fell to the House of Hohenzollern in 1670, the vacant residence including stables, riding arena, ballroom, fencing floor, and much of the personnel was turned over to a new nobiliary academy. Invited to lecture at the new academy in 1690, the already famous Thomasius attracted so much interest that an older plan to convert the academy into a university ripened rapidly. The year following its formal foundation in 1694, there were fifteen professors, including Thomasius and Franke, both leading scholars and veterans of the University of Leipzig, where they had to leave because of their unorthodox views. Thus, ironically, a nobiliary academy contributed to the creation of one of the two German universities in the eighteenth century (the other was Göttingen) which challenged the traditional school wisdom in the name of rationalism, pietism, and neohumanism.

136. Alexander Kluge, *Universitäts-Selbstverwaltung* (Frankfurt/Main:

Klostermann, 1958), p. 72.

137. Paulsen, *Geschichte,* II, 10.

138. Ibid., II, 11.

139. Johann Christoph Hofbauer, *Geschichte der Universität zu Halle bis zum Jahre 1805* (Halle: Schimmelpfenning, 1805), p. 32.

140. As cited in Paulsen, *Geschichte,* II, 11.

Chapter 3

1. For a concise outline of the Elizabethan system and an outline of the present state of scholarship, see Alan G. R. Smith, *The Government of Elizabethan England* (New York: Norton, 1967). The relationship between the power of Parliament and royal finance is explored in Conrad Russel, "Parliament and the King's Finance" in *The Origins of the English Civil War,* ed. Conrad Russel (New York: Harper & Row, 1973), pp. 91–116.

2. This section is indebted to J. H. Plumb, *The Growth of Political Stability in England 1675–1725* (Baltimore: Penguin Books, 1967).

3. Ibid., p. 94.

4. Ibid., p. 118.

5. Quoted in Kingsley, *Representative Bureaucracy,* p. 26.

6. Quoted in Lewis Namier, *The Structure of Politics at the Accession of George III* (London: Macmillan, 1968), p. 219.

7. Quoted in Kingsley, *Representative Bureaucracy,* p. 27.

8. *Political Register* (March 1, 1806), as quoted in Elie Halévy, *A History of the English People in the Nineteenth Century* (London: Benn, 1949), I, 15.

9. Quoted in Parris, *Constitutional Bureaucracy,* p. 54.

10. W. F. Moneypenny and G. E. Buckle, *Life of Benjamin Disraeli* (London: Murray, 1929), I, 1163.

11. Sir Charles Trevelyan and Sir Stafford Northcote, "On the Organization of the Permanent Civil Service" in "Reports and Papers Relating to the Reorganization of Civil Service," *Parliamentary Papers,* 20 (1854–1855): 4.

12. Trevelyan to Delane, February 6, 1854, *British Museum, Gladstone Papers,* Add. Mss. 44333, nr. 138 (hereafter cited as B.M.G.P., Add. Mss.).

13. See Parris, *Constitutional Bureaucracy,* p. 55, for example.

14. B.M.G.P., Add. Mss. 44333, Nr. 138.

15. As quoted in Parris, *Constitutional Bureaucracy,* p. 57.

16. Moneypenny and Buckle, *Disraeli,* I, 388.

17. Ibid.

18. B.M.G.P., Add. Mss. 44333, Nr. 216.

19. As quoted in Parris, *Constitutional Bureaucracy,* p. 58.

20. Ibid.

21. See Plumb, *Political Stability*, p. 81.

22. Namier, *Structure of Politics*, pp. 16ff and passim.

23. Ibid., p. 5.

24. Ibid., passim.

25. Ibid., p. 423.

26. Ibid., p. 107.

27. Ibid., p. 374.

28. Cornelius O'Leary, *The Elimination of Corrupt Practices in British Elections 1868–1911* (Oxford: Clarendon Press, 1962), p. 15.

29. Peter G. Richards, *Patronage in British Government* (Toronto: University of Toronto Press, 1963), p. 20.

30. O'Leary, *Elimination of Corrupt Practices*, pp. 15–19.

31. Richards, *Patronage*, p. 27.

32. Quoted in Cohen, *British Civil Service*, p. 38.

33. Select Committee on Sinecure Offices, "Report," *Parliamentary Papers*, 6 (1834): 347–48.

34. Quoted in Hughes, "Civil Service Reform 1853–1855," p. 19.

35. Quoted in Hughes, "Notes and Documents," p. 67.

36. The latter point of view is taken in Cohen, *British Civil Service*, passim.

37. Halévy, *English People*, I, 17; cf. D. L. Keir, *The Constitutional History of Modern Britain Since 1485* (Princeton: D. Van Nostrand, 1966), p. 373. Keir writes, "The process by which the central executive was subjected to investigation and reform by Parliament was begun . . . not in order to increase administrative efficiency, but to diminish the royal influence based on patronage which threatened to impair the balance of the constitution and the independence of the legislature." Cf. also Richard Pares, *King George III and the Politicians* (Oxford: Clarendon Press, 1953), p. 130. He writes, "When Fox and Burke reformed administration or expenditure, they did so (as they were careful to point out) without any desire to increase efficiency or to save money, but solely to reduce the political influence of the crown."

38. Keir, *Constitutional History*, p. 373.

39. Norman Gash, *Politics in the Age of Peel* (London: Longmans, Green, 1953), p. x. See especially Chapters 8 and 9, as well as Chapter 13 on political patronage, where the argument concerning decline in quality and quantity of patronage jobs is discussed.

40. Cf. W. H. Aydelotte, "The House of Commons of the 1840's," *History*, 39 (1954): 248–62. See also W. L. Guttsman, *The British Political Elite* (London: Macgibbon & Kee, 1963), pp. 34ff.

41. Derek Beales, *From Castlereagh to Gladstone, 1815–1885* (London: Nelson, 1969), p. 117.

42. The number of baronets or sons of peers was 180 in 1865. Ibid., p. 117. This constitutes about 31 percent of the House of Commons; roughly another 45 percent were gentry, and about 23 percent manufacturers, merchants, and bankers without territorial interests. See Guttsman, *Political Elite,* p. 41.

43. Ibid., p. 39.

44. Quoted in Gash, *Age of Peel,* p. 15.

45. Among the obstacles to middle-class representation, two factors stand out. On the one hand, the cost of elections was very high, reaching in the tens of thousands of pounds. On the other hand, the middle class did not hook into that other resource for advancing in politics—the web of cousinhood and memberships in clubs and cliques, which depended on genealogical ramifications. See Guttsman, *Political Elite,* pp. 41ff.

46. Ibid., pp. 58–59.

47. G. M. Trevelyan, *The Life of John Bright* (London: Constable & Co., 1913), p. 274.

48. Cf. Chapter 5, below.

49. Lawrence Stone, *The Crisis of the Aristocracy* (Oxford: Clarendon Press, 1965), passim.

50. Ibid., p. 672. By this movement, Stone continues, "the propertied classes exploited and expanded the higher educational resources of the country. By doing so they fitted themselves to rule in the new conditions of the modern state, and they turned the intelligentsia from a branch of the clergy into a branch of the laity."

51. Lawrence Stone, "Social Mobility in England, 1500–1700," *Past and Present,* 33 (1969): 16–55. See also Mark H. Curtis, "The Alienated Intellectuals of Early Stuart England," *Past and Present,* 23 (1962): 25–43.

52. Quoted in ibid., 25.

53. Lawrence Stone, "The Educational Revolution in England, 1560–1640," *Past and Present,* 28 (1964): 68.

54. Ibid., 45. See also Stone's critique of Jordan's argument that even the poor must have profited from the expansion. See W. K. Jordan, *The Charities of Rural England, 1480–1660* (London: George Allen & Unwin, 1961), p. 319; and Stone, "Educational Revolution," pp. 44–45.

55. See ibid., pp. 47ff; and Joan Simon, "The Social Origins of Cambridge Students, 1603–1640," *Past and Present,* 26 (1963): 58–67.

56. Stone, "Educational Revolution," pp. 63–64.

57. Ibid., p. 65; Simon, "Social Origins," pp. 60ff.

58. Stone, "Social Mobility," p. 19.

59. Ibid., p. 20.

60. G. S. R. Kitson Clark, *The Making of Victorian England* (Cambridge, Mass.: Harvard University Press, 1962), p. 259.

61. Thomson D. F. Edgeworth, *What Should my Son be?* (London: 1870). As quoted in Reader, *Professional Men*, p. 13.

62. Stone, "Educational Revolution," p. 75.

63. Cf. Ian Weinberg, *The English Public Schools: The Sociology of Elite Education* (New York: Atherton Press, 1967), pp. 32ff.

64. Ibid., p. 34.

65. Nicholas Hans, *New Trends in Education in the Eighteenth Century* (London: Routledge & Kegan Paul, 1951), p. 78.

66. Dissenters, however, were not admitted to Oxford and Cambridge until the second half of the nineteenth century.

67. Cf. Sheldon Rothblatt, *The Revolution of the Dons* (New York: Basic Books, 1968), pp. 38ff.

68. Cf. T. W. Bamford, *The Rise of the Public Schools* (London: Thomas Nelson, 1967), passim.

69. Calculated from numbers presented in T. W. Bamford, "Public Schools and Social Class, 1801–1850," *British Journal of Sociology*, 12 (1961): 225.

70. Calculated from numbers in ibid. Here the unclassifiable "others" have been excluded and the proportions are calculated relative to totals excluding the "others."

71. Ibid., 230.

72. Bamford, *Rise of the Public Schools*, p. 7.

73. Bamford, "Public Schools and Social Class," p. 233.

74. Tables 5 and 6 are calculated from numbers in ibid., p. 225.

75. John Burke and Sir John B. Burke, *A Genealogical and Heraldic History of the Landed Gentry; or Commoners of Great Britain and Ireland* (London: Colburn, 1846); Edward Walford, *County Families of the United Kingdom* (London, 1860).

76. Rothblatt, *Revolution of the Dons*, pp. 86ff.

77. See Reader, *Professional Men*, pp. 25ff.

78. Kitson Clark, *Victorian England*, p. 262.

79. As quoted in Reader, *Professional Men*, p. 14.

80. Ibid.

81. Hester Jenkins and D. Caradog Jones, "Social Class of Cambridge University Alumni of the 18th and 19th Centuries," *British Journal of Sociology*, 1 (1950): 99. See also Rothblatt, *Revolution of the Dons*, p. 87.

82. Ibid., p. 66.

83. Ibid., pp. 84–85.

84. Ibid., p. 68.

85. Harold Perkin, *The Origins of Modern English Society, 1780–1880* (London: Routledge & Kegan Paul, 1969), pp. 252ff.

86. N. G. Annan, "The Intellectual Aristocracy," in J. H. Plumb, ed., *Studies in Social History* (London: Longmans, Green, 1955), p. 247.

87. W. L. Burn, *The Age of Equipoise* (New York: Norton, 1964), p. 263.

88. "Reports and Papers Relating to the Reorganization of the Civil Service," *Parliament Papers,* 20 (1854–1855): 181.

Chapter 4

1. Minister Freiherr von Hardenberg, "Über die Reorganization des Preussischen Staats, verfasst auf höchsten Befehl Seiner Majestät des Königs," in Georg Winter, ed., *Die Reorganisation des Preussischen Staates unter Stein und Hardenberg* (Leipzig: S. Hirzel, 1931), Vol. I, p. 305.

2. Ibid., p. 306.

3. Ibid., p. 313.

4. Ibid.

5. Ibid.

6. Ibid., p. 314.

7. Cf. Wilhelm Treue, *Deutschland und Europa* (Düsseldorf: Droste, 1951).

8. For a review of liberal and other interpretations in German historiography of the period, see Ernst Klein, *Von der Reform zur Restauration* (Berlin: Walter de Gruyter, 1965), pp. 166ff.

9. Reinhard Koselleck, *Preussen zwischen Reform und Revolution* (Stuttgart: Ernst Klett Verlag, 1967), pp. 153–54.

10. Chief Councillor von Altenstein, "Uber die Leitung des preussischen Staats an Seine des Herrn Staatsministers Freiherrn von Hardenberg Exzellenz," in Winter, *Die Reorganisation,* p. 391.

11. Ibid., p. 392.

12. Ibid., p. 396.

13. Ibid., p. 404.

14. Hardenberg, "Über die Reorganisation," p. 404.

15. Altenstein, "Über die Leitung," p. 406.

16. Minister Freiherr von Stein, "Über die zweckmässige Bildung der obersten und der Provinzial-, Finanz- und Polizeibehörden in der preussischen Monarchie," in Winter, *Die Reorganisation,* p. 199.

17. Ibid.

18. Ibid.

19. Ibid.

20. Walter Görlitz, *Stein: Staatsmann und Reformator* (Frankfurt/Main: Frankfurter Hefte, 1949), pp. 178–80.

21. Stein, "Über die Zweckmässige Bildung" in Winter, *Die Reorganisation,* p. 200.

22. Ibid., p. 201.

23. Ibid.

24. Ibid., p. 202.

25. As quoted in Koselleck, *Reform und Revolution,* p. 176.

26. For a more detailed account of the reorganization of administration, see Willard R. Fann, "The Consolidation of Bureaucratic Absolutism in Prussia, 1817–1827," Ph.D. dissertation, University of California, Berkeley, 1965, pp. 39–199.

27. Minister Freiherr vom Stein, "Darstellung der fehlerhaften Organisation des Kabinetts und der Notwendigkeit der Bildung einer Ministerialkonferenz" in Winter, *Die Reorganisation,* p. 10.

28. Cf. Fann, *Consolidation,* pp. 200–43.

29. Altenstein, "Über die Leitung" in Winter, *Die Reorganisation,* pp. 302ff., 346ff.

30. As quoted in Ernst von Meier, *Die Reform der Verwaltungsorganisation unter Stein und Hardenberg* (München: Duncker & Humblot, 1912), pp. 246–47.

31. Fann, *Consolidation,* pp. 174ff.

32. Hardenberg, "Über die Reorganisation" in Winter, *Die Reorganisation,* pp. 302ff., 346ff.

33. As quoted in Koselleck, *Reform und Revolution,* p. 165.

34. Altenstein, "Über die Leitung" in Winter, *Die Reorganisation,* p. 520.

35. Chief Councillor Freiherr von Altenstein, "Die des Königs Majestät vorzuschlagende Veränderung in der Verfassung betreffend," in Winter, *Die Reorganisation,* p. 66.

36. Ibid., p. 67.

37. Stein, "Darstellung der fehlerhaften Organisation" in Winter, *Die Reorganisation,* p. 12.

38. Ibid.

39. Cf. John R. Gillis, *The Prussian Bureaucracy in Crisis* (Stanford, Calif.: Stanford University Press, 1971), especially pp. 51ff. Cf. also Ringer, *German Mandarins,* pp. 1–80.

40. Johanna Schultze, *Die Auseinandersetzung zwischen Adel und Bürgertum in den Deutschen Zeitschriften der letzten drei Jahrzehnte des 18. Jahrhunderts (1773–1806)* (Berlin: Ebering, 1925).

41. Cf. Hans Weil, *Die Entstehung des deutschen Bildungsprinzips* (Bonn: Bouvier, 1967).

42. As quoted in Rosenberg, *Bureaucracy,* p. 184.

43. Martiny, *Die Adelsfrage,* p. 30.

44. Büsch, *Militärsystem*, p. 106.
45. Martiny, *Die Adelsfrage*, p. 35.
46. Hans Rosenberg, *Probleme der deutschen Sozialgeschichte* (Frankfurt/Main: Suhrkamp, 1969), p. 17.
47. Koselleck, *Reform und Revolution*, p. 84.
48. Martiny, *Die Adelsfrage*, p. 65.
49. As quoted in Georg H. Pertz, *Das Leben des Ministers Freiherrn vom Stein* (Berlin: Reimer, 1849–1855), II, 500.
50. Jany, *Geschichte*, III, 37–38.
51. Martiny, *Die Adelsfrage*, p. 71.
52. Quoted in ibid.
53. Frederick William II in Christian Otto Mylius (ed.), *Novum Corpus Constitutionum Prussico-Brandenburgensium*, 10 (1798), p. 1701.
54. Ibid., p. 1704.
55. Martiny, *Die Adelsfrage*, p. 77.
56. Craig, *Politics of the Prussian Army*, p. 26.
57. As quoted in ibid., p. 43.
58. As quoted in ibid.
59. Koselleck, *Reform und Revolution*, pp. 82–83.
60. Hans Gerth, "Die Sozialgeschichtliche Lage der Bürgerlichen Intelligenz um die Wende des 18. Jahrhunderts," Ph.D. dissertation, University of Frankfurt/Main, 1935, p. 16.
61. As quoted in Theodor Bach, *Theodor Gottlieb von Hippel* (Breslau: Tremendt, 1863), p. 117.
62. Koselleck, *Reform und Revolution*, p. 172.
63. Huber, *Deutsche Verfassungsgeschichte*, I, 99.
64. *Berlinische Monatsschrift*, 2 (1788): 251ff.
65. Anonymous, "Mittel und Vorschläge, die Menge derer zurückzuhalten, die sich jetzt aus den niederen Ständen, ohne natürlichen Beruf zum Studiren auf Universitäten, und in die Stände der Gelehrten eindrängen," *Deutsches Magazin* (Altona: Hammerich, 1797), pp. 80ff.
66. Justus Möser, "Also soll man das Studieren nicht verbieten," *Sämmtliche Werke* (Berlin: Nicolai, 1842), 3, 125–28.
67. *Minerva*, 26 (1836): 169–70.
68. Wilhelm Dilthey, *Die Jugendschriften Hegels: Gesammelte Schriften* (Stuttgart: Kohlhammer, 1959), IV, 16.
69. Adolph Freiherr von Knigge, *Über den Umgang mit Menschen* (Gera: C. B. Griesbach, 1929), p. 229.
70. Cf. Gerth, *Die Sozialgeschichtliche*, pp. 80ff.
71. Wilhelm Naudé, "Zur Geschichte des preussischen Subalternbeamtentums," *Forschungen zur Brandenburgischen und Preussischen Geschichte*, 18 (1905): 359.

72. Martiny, *Die Adelsfrage*, p. 83.
73. Naudé, "Zur Geschichte . . .," p. 374.
74. See also Chapter 4, first section, above.
75. Calculated from data presented by Brunschwig, *La crise de l'état prussien*, pp. 326–27.
76. Ibid., p. 154.
77. Ibid., pp. 328–29.
78. Ibid., p. 330.
79. Koselleck, *Reform und Revolution*, p. 108.
80. As quoted in ibid.
81. Rosenberg, *Bureaucracy*, pp. 186–87.
82. G. W. F. Hegel, *Philosophy of Right* (London: Bell, 1958), p. 193.
83. Huber, *Deutsche Verfassungsgeschichte*, I, 127ff.
84. Ibid., p. 126.
85. Clemens Theodor Perthes, *Der Staatsdienst in Preussen* (Hamburg: Perthes, 1838), p. 45.
86. Gillis, *Prussian Bureaucracy*, pp. 26, 34.
87. Albert Lotz, *Geschichte des deutschen Beamtentums* (Berlin: Decker, 1909), p. 374.
88. Delbrück, *Die Ausbildung*, p. 6.
89. See C. J. Friedrich, "The Continental Tradition of Training Administrators in Law and Jurisprudence," *Journal of Modern History*, 11 (1939): 129–48.
90. Delbrück, *Die Ausbildung*, p. 7.
91. Ibid.
92. Ibid., p. 9.
93. Friedrich, "Continental Tradition," p. 141.
94. Altenstein, "Über die Leitung" in Winter, *Die Reorganisation*, p. 507.
95. Meier, *Die Reform*, p. 339.
96. Huber, *Deutsche Verfassungsgeschichte*, I, 258ff.
97. Koselleck, *Reform und Revolution*, p. 164.
98. *Allegemeines Landrecht*, II, title 12, pph. 1. Cf. also Huber, *Deutsche Verfassungsgeschichte*, p. 264.
99. Cf. Alfred Heubaum, "Die Reformbestrebungen unter dem Preussischen Minister Julius von Massow (1798–1807) auf dem Gebiete des höheren Bildungswesens," *Mitteilungen der Gesellschaft für deutsche Erziehungs- und Schulgeschichte*, 14 (1904): 186–225.
100. Wilhelm von Humboldt, "Uber die Liegnitzer Ritterakademie," in *Werke* (Stuttgart: Cotta, 1964), IV, 145.
101. Wilhelm von Humboldt, "Uber Kadettenhäuser, in *Werke*, IV, 91.
102. Paulsen, *Geschichte*, II, 544ff.

103. Naudé, "Zur Geschichte . . .," p. 13.

104. Ibid. It may be noted in this connection that Gillis writes, "in the 1820's only the judiciary was recruiting solely from among those who held university degrees; the administration had just begun to establish formal educational standards and until 1846 did not require university graduation as a prerequisite to entry." At this point he makes reference to Naudé. Gillis has obviously confused the higher civil service (*höheren Bamtendienst*) with the higher subaltern service (*höheren Bürodienst*), which is the subject of Naudé's discussion. In the 1920s the requirement of a university education was already firmly established in the higher civil service. Cf. Gillis, *Prussian Bureaucracy*, pp. 26, 34.

105. Wilhelm von Humboldt, as quoted in Huber, *Deutsche Verfassungsgeschichte*, I, 287. On the reform of the universities, see also Frederick Lilge, *The Abuse of Learning* (New York: Macmillan, 1948), pp. 1–56.

106. Ringer, *German Mandarins*, p. 33.

107. Paulsen, *Geschichte*, II, 433.

108. Cf. Max Weber, *Gesammelte Politische Schriften* (Tübingen: J. C. B. Mohr, 1958), pp. 235–36.

109. Otto Camphausen to Ludolf Camphausen, November 10, 1843, in Joseph Hansen, ed., *Rheinische Briefe und Akten zur Geschichte der politischen Bewegung 1830–1850* (Essen: Baedeker, 1919), I, 609.

110. Friedrich Paulsen, *Die deutschen Universitäten und das Universitätsstudium* (Berlin: Asher, 1902), pp. 149–50.

111. Nikolaus von Preradovich, *Die Führungsschichten in Österreich und Preussen* (Wiesbaden: Steiner, 1955), pp. 121–22.

112. Koselleck, *Reform und Revolution*, p. 245.

113. Preradovich, *Die Führungsschichten*, p. 122.

114. Koselleck, *Reform und Revolution*, p. 436.

115. Ibid.

116. "Statistische Übersicht des öffentlichen Unterrichts im preussischen Staate im Jahre 1816 und im Jahre 1846," *Mitteilungen des Statistischen Bureau's in Berlin*, 1 (1848): 38–45. Also Johannes Conrad, *Das Universitätsstudium in Deutschland während der letzten 50 Jahre* (Jena: Fischer 1884), pp. 12–16.

117. Calculated from data presented in Johannes Conrad, "Die Statistik der Universität Halle," in *Festschriften* (Halle: Universitäat, 1894), p. 30.

118. Herman Finer, *Theory and Practice of Modern Government* (New York: H. Holt, 1949); Eckart Sturm, "Die Entwicklung des öffentlichen Dienstes in Deutschland," in C. H. Ule, ed., *Die Entwicklung des öffentlichen Dienstes* (Köln: Heymann, 1961), pp. 33–35; Koselleck, *Reform und Revolution*, p. 245.

119. Koselleck, *Reform und Revolution*, p. 245.

120. Cf. Paul Drews, *Der evangelische Geistliche in der deutschen Vergangenheit* (Jena: Diederichs, 1924), pp. 126–28; Paul Diepgen, *Geschichte der Medizin* (Berlin: Walter de Gruyter, 1951), I, part 1, 69–82.

121. G., "Woher kommt es, dass es sich jetzt alles so zum studieren drängt, und wie ist dem möglichst absuhelfen," *Hannoveranisches Magazin* (1828), pp. 730–38; J. D. Goldhorn, "Was sollten Prediger bedenken, welche junge Leute aus niederen Ständen zum studieren veranlassen?" *Journal für Prediger,* 69 (1826): 302ff; J. D. Goldhorn, "Wer soll studieren?" *Neues Journal für Prediger,* 53 (1828): 277–93; "Mittel gegen die Studiermanie," *Der Gesellschafter,* 1840, p. 676; W. Mönnich, "Einige Bemerkungen zur Erklärung der vorhandnehmenden Studiersucht in Deutschland," *Hesperus,* 1828, pp. 577ff; Albrecht Reugger, "Von der Übersetzung der höheren Berufsarten, oder von der Berufsnot," *Kleine, meistens ungedruckte Schriften,* 1828, pp. 169–76; "Über den Andrang junger Leute zum Studieren von Jünglingen aus niederen Ständen," *Schlesische Provinzialblätter,* 100 (1834): 545ff. "Die unverhältnismässig zunehmende Anzahl der Studierenden im Deutschland," *Hesperus,* 1832, pp. 363–64.

122. Gillis, *Prussian Bureaucracy,* pp. 39, 41.

123. *Justizministerialblatt,* 1839, p. 414. See also Jonathan H. T. Behr, *Einige Gedanken über den Zudrang zum Studieren in unseren Tagen* (Gera: Heinsius, 1826).

124. Gillis, *Prussian Bureaucracy,* pp. 41, 233.

125. Ibid., pp. 43, 234.

126. Ibid., passim; and Koselleck, *Reform und Revolution,* pp. 398ff.

Chapter 5

1. Trevelyan and Northcote, "Organization of the Permanent Civil Service," in "Reports and Papers Relating to the Civil Service." *Parliamentary Papers,* 20 (1854–55). When quotations are clearly from this report, they will not be footnoted each time.

2. As quoted in Wright, *Treasury Control,* p. xiv.

3. Quoted in ibid.

4. In addition to the general literature cited in Chapter 1, see also Ernest Barker, *The Development of Public Services in Western Europe, 1660–1930* (London: Oxford University Press, 1944), p. 35.

5. From W. J. M. Mackenzie and J. W. Grove, *Central Administration in Britain* (London: Longmans, Green, 1957), p. 7. See also Herman Finer, *The British Civil Service* (London: Allen & Unwin, 1937), p. 24.

6. Wright, *Treasury Control,* p. xxiii.

7. Especially ibid., passim; see also Parris, *Constitutional Bureaucracy,* passim.

8. Memorandum by C. E. Trevelyan, April 26, 1848, as quoted in Parris, *Constitutional Bureaucracy*, pp. 84–85.

9. Ibid., pp. 86–87.

10. Quoted in H. C. F. Bell, *Lord Palmerston* (London: Longmans, Green, 1936), I, 28.

11. Ibid., I, 9.

12. Quoted in Parris, *Constitutional Bureaucracy*, p. 110.

13. Trevelyan and Northcote, "Organization of the Permanent Civil Service," p. 2.

14. Quoted in Hughes, "Notes and Documents," p. 56.

15. Quoted in Parris, *Constitutional Bureaucracy*, p. 115.

16. Quoted in ibid.

17. Quoted in Hughes, "Notes and Documents," pp. 56–57.

18. Quoted in ibid., p. 57.

19. Trevelyan to Gladstone, B.M.G.P. Add. Mss. 44578, Nr. 139.

20. Cf. Burn, *Age of Equipoise*, Kitson Clark, *Victorian England*, as well as the latter's *An Expanding Society: Britain 1830–1900* (London: Cambridge University Press, 1967), especially pp. 30ff.

21. Especially Anthony Trollope, *The Three Clerks* (1858; London: Oxford University Press, 1943); and Charles Dickens, *Little Dorrit* (1855–1857; London: J. M. Dent, 1908).

22. Quoted in Hughes, "Civil Service Reform 1853–1855," p. 60.

23. Ibid.

24. Ibid., p. 61.

25. As quoted in ibid., pp. 61–62.

26. See Kingsley, *Representative Bureaucracy*, pp. 50ff.; Cohen, *British Civil Service*, pp. 87ff.

27. S.E. Finer, *The Life and Times of Sir Edwin Chadwick* (London: Methuen, 1952), pp. 476–77.

28. Jeremy Bentham, *Official Aptitude Maximized, Expense Minimized, as Shown in the Several Papers Comprised in This Volume* (London: R. Heward, 1830).

29. Cf. O. MacDonagh, "The Nineteenth-Century Revolution in Government: A Reappraisal," *Historical Journal*, 1 (1958): 52–67; Henry Parris, "The Nineteenth-Century Revolution in Government: A Reappraisal Reappraised," *Historical Journal*, 3 (1960): 17–37; Jenifer Hart, "Nineteenth-Century Social Reform: A Tory Interpretation of History," *Past and Present*, 31 (1965): 39–61; Valerie Cromwell, "Interpretations of Nineteenth-Century Administration: An Analysis," *Victorian Studies*, 9 (1966): 245–55.

30. Cf. Perkin, *The Origins*, pp. 267–78.

31. Ibid., pp. 269–70; emphasis mine.

32. Moneypenny and Buckle, *Disraeli*, I, 1432–33.

33. Ibid., I, 1435–36.
34. Civil Service Inquiry Commission, "Second Report," *Parliamentary Papers*, 23 (1875), Appendix F, 100.
35. Cf. Olive Anderson, "The Janus Face of Mid-Nineteenth-Century English Radicalism: The Administrative Reform Association of 1855," *Victorian Studies*, 7 (1964–1965): 231–42.
36. Olive Anderson, *A Liberal State at War* (London: Macmillan, 1967), pp. 101ff.
37. Trevelyan to Gladstone, March 3, 1954, B.M.G.P. Add. Mss. 44333, Nr. 244.
38. Bamford, *Rise of the Public Schools*, pp. 40–41.
39. Cf. Perkin, *The Origins*, pp. 259–60.
40. Ibid., p. 298.
41. Philippe Ariès, *Centuries of Childhood* (New York: Vintage Books, 1962), p. 328.
42. S. I. Curtis, *History of Education in Great Britain* (London: University Tutorial Press, 1967), p. 423.
43. Reader, *Professional Men*, p. 18.
44. Rothblatt, *Revolution of the Dons*, pp. 181ff.
45. Quoted in A. M. Carr-Saunders and P. A. Wilson, *The Professions* (London: Cass, 1964), p. 310.
46. Rothblatt, *Revolution of the Dons*, p. 118.
47. Ibid., p. 185.
48. Ibid., p. 207.
49. Quoted in Carr-Saunders and Wilson, *The Professions*, p. 310.
50. Other recommendations are described in V. H. H. Green, *The Universities* (Harmondsworth: Penguin Books, 1969), p. 66.
51. Quoted in Hughes, "Civil Service Reform, 1853–1855," p. 63.
52. Ibid.
53. Quoted in ibid.
54. Quoted in ibid., p. 62.
55. Green, *The Universities*, pp. 67–68.
56. Cf. Wright, *Treasury Control*, p. 56.
57. Cf. Reader, *Professional Men*, pp. 85ff; Carr-Saunders and Wilson, *The Professions*, pp. 311ff.
58. E. Chadwick, August 1, 1854, "Reports and Papers," *Parliamentary Papers*, 20 (1854–1855), p. 186.
59. Carr-Saunders and Wilson, *The Professions*, p. 311.
60. Reader, *Professional Men*, passim.
61. Ibid., pp. 51–52.
62. Ibid., p. 73.
63. Ibid., p. 86, emphasis mine.

64. Ibid., emphasis mine.

65. Kingsley, *Representative Bureaucracy,* pp. 60ff; F. Musgrove, "Middle-Class Education and Employment in the Nineteenth Century," *Economic History Review,* 12 (1959): 99–111. See also H. J. Perkin, "Middle-Class Education and Employment in the Nineteenth Century: A Critical Note," *Economic History Review,* 14 (1961): 122–30; and F. Musgrove, "Middle-Class Education and Employment in the Nineteenth Century: A Rejoinder," ibid., pp. 320–29.

66. F. Musgrove, "Middle-Class Education," p. 99.

67. Ibid., p. 109.

68. *The Times,* February 16, 1853.

69. Cf. Perkin, *The Origins,* p. 127.

70. As quoted in R. Symonds, *The British and Their Successors* (London: Faber & Faber, 1966), p. 44.

71. Ibid.

72. C.E.L. Cotton, March 18, 1854, "Reports and Papers," p. 61.

73. Rev. Dr. Vaughan, May 13, 1854, "Reports and Papers," pp. 87, 89.

74. Quoted in Hughes, "Civil Service Reform, 1853–1855," p. 64.

75. Rev. Charles Graves, February 21, 1854, "Reports and Papers," pp. 22–23.

76. "Competitive Examinations," *Quarterly Review,* 108 (1860): 568.

77. Dorman B. Eaton, *Civil Service in Great Britain* (New York: Harper Brothers, 1880), pp. 430–31. This passage, partially quoted, was of "utmost significance" to Kingsley's thesis that the civil service reforms in England were due to pressure of the rising middle class. Cf. Kingsley, *Representative Bureaucracy,* pp. 63–64.

78. Civil Service Inquiry Commission, "Second Report," Appendix F, p. 102.

79. Kingsley, *Representative Bureaucracy,* p. 60.

80. Wright, *Treasury Control,* p. 55.

81. Quoted in Moses, *Civil Service of Great Britain,* p. 55.

82. Ibid., p. 56.

83. Ibid., pp. 56–57.

84. *Civil Service Gazette,* July 2, 1853.

85. The report was dated November 23, 1853, and cover letter to Gladstone November 28, 1853, B.M.G.P. Add. Mss. 44333, Nr. 30.

86. Lingen to Northcote, January 21, 1854, B.M.G.P. Add. Mss. 44333, Nr. 118.

87. Quoted in Hughes, "Civil Service Reform, 1853–1855," p. 64.

88. Lefevre to Trevelyan, January 23, 1854, B.M.G.P. Add. Mss. 44333, Nr. 109.

89. "Remarks by Capt. H. H. O'Brien, R. A., on Sir Stafford Northcote's and Sir Charles Trevelyan's Report upon the Reorganization of the Civil Service," B.M.G.P. Add. Mss. 44580, Nr. 103.

90. Ibid.

91. Sir Charles Trevelyan, "Thoughts on Patronage," January 17, 1854, B.M.G.P. Add. Mss. 44333, Nr. 91; emphasis mine.

92. Moses, *Civil Service of Great Britain*, p. 61. About Northcote, he wrote,

> Northcote was a typical product of Eton and of Balliol College, firmly convinced of the superiority of such an education to any other as a preparation for Parliament or the public service. He was, like Gladstone, shrewdly aware that in an examination based on the Oxford and Cambridge schools, the upper class would more than hold its own; but like Macaulay, he seems to have had the idea that a man who was distinguished in the humane letters would probably be capable and a gentleman, no matter what his antecedents or who his sponsors.

Ibid., p. 67.

93. B.M.G.P. Add. Mss. 44580, Nr. 130; emphasis mine.

94. Ibid.

95. Ibid.

96. Trevelyan to Gladstone, January 20, 1854, B.M.G.P. Add. Mss. 44333, Nr. 103.

97. Northcote to Gladstone, January 23, 1854, B.M.G.P. Add. Mss. 44333, Nr. 224.

98. "Remarks by Capt. O'Brien," Nr. 103.

99. Quoted in Hughes, "Civil Service Reform, 1853–1855," p. 62.

100. Trevelyan to Gladstone, January 27, 1854, B.M.G.P. Add. Mss. 44333, Nr. 121.

101. Ibid.

102. Trevelyan to the dean of Hereford, February 6, 1853, B.M.G.P. Add. Mss. 44333, Nr. 143.

103. For the controversy concerning Trevelyan's indiscretion, see Wright, *Treasury Control*, pp. 61ff.

104. Trevelyan to Gladstone, March 9, 1854, B.M.G.P. Add. Mss. 44333, Nr. 251.

105. Arbuthnot to Gladstone, February 10, 1854, B.M.G.P. Add. Mss. 44333, Nr. 24.

106. Cf. Wright, *Treasury Control*, p. 62.

107. Trevelyan to Gladstone, February 9, 1954, B.M.G.P. Add. Mss. 44333, Nr. 158.

108. Trevelyan and Northcote in "Reports and Papers," p. 416.

109. Ibid., pp. 411, 413.

110. Ibid., p. 413.

111. Rice to Trevelyan, March 3, 1854, B.M.G.P. Add. Mss. 44333, Nr. 257.

112. Quoted in Wright, *Treasury Control,* p. 62. Leading article in *Civil Service Gazette,* February 23, 1854; other leading articles attacking civil service reform appeared on March 4, 11, 18, 1854.

113. Trevelyan to Rice, March 10, 1854, B.M.G.P. Add. Mss. 44333, Nr. 262.

114. Ibid., Nr. 262.

115. Trevelyan to Gladstone, March 10, 1854, B.M.G.P. Add. Mss. 44333, Nr. 225.

116. Ibid.

117. G. Otto Trevelyan, *The Life and Letters of Lord Macaulay* (New York: Harper & Brothers, 1876), II, 317.

118. Ibid., II, 314.

119. Trevelyan to Gladstone, February 27, 1854, B.M.G.P. Add. Mss. 44333, Nr. 216.

120. Trevelyan to Gladstone, March 1, 1854, B.M.G.P. Add. Mss. 44333, Nr. 226.

121. Cf. Greaves, *The Civil Service,* p. 27.

122. Edward Romilly, August 22, 1854, "Reports and Papers," p. 258.

123. James Booth, Augut 1854, ibid., p. 133.

124. Quoted in Asa Briggs, *Victorian People* (Harmondsworth: Penguin Books, 1967), p. 119.

125. Anonymous, *Observation upon the Report by Sir C. E. Trevelyan, K.C.B. and Sir S. H. Northcote, Bart., on the "Organization of the Permanent Civil Service"* (London: Painter, 1854), p. 14.

126. A. Y. Spearman, no date, "Reports and Papers," p. 400.

127. Ibid., p. 339.

128. G. Arbuthnot, March 6, 1854, "Reports and Papers," p. 403.

129. Thomas Francis Freemantle, November 24, 1854, "Reports and Papers," p. 327.

130. T. W. C. Murdoch, September 9, 1954, "Reports and Papers," p. 298.

131. James Booth, August 1854, "Reports and Papers," p. 134.

132. Ibid.

133. E. Chadwick, August 1, 1854, "Reports and Papers," pp. 165, 166.

134. John Stuart Mill, *Considerations on Representative Government* (London: Longmans, Green, 1907), p. 110.

135. John Stuart Mill, May 22, 1854, "Reports and Papers," p. 94.

136. Gladstone to Russel, January 20, 1854; reprinted in John Morley, *The Life of William Edward Gladstone* (London: Macmillan, 1903), I, 649.

137. Trevalyan to Delane, February 6, 1854, B.M.G.P. Add. Mss. 44333, Nr. 138.

138. Quoted in Kingsley, *Representative Bureaucracy*, p. 83.

139. Greaves, *The Civil Service*, p. 33.

140. Cf. Anderson, "The Janus Face."

141. An Order in Council does not require parliamentary sanction.

142. Wright, *Treasury Control*, p. 75.

143. Ibid., pp. 74–75:

Sir Stafford Northcote, hard put to it to place his seven sons, had been promised a clerkship for one of them in the Colonial Office, but on the resignation of the minister it had been cancelled. In March 1867 he appealed anxiously to Disraeli, Chancellor of the Exchequer, to find a place for his son in the civil service. Another who benefited from his party and family connections was George Kekewich, who entered service in March 1868. His father, an M.P., asked Northcote, who was at that time president of the Board of Trade, and to whom he was related by marriage, to obtain an appointment in the service for his son. Northcote interceded on Kekewich's behalf with the Duke of Malborough, newly appointed lord president of the council, and wrote to Kekewich that if he called at the privy council office and asked for an interview, the Duke of Marlborough would appoint him to an examinership in the education department. Kekewich called at the office, where he was interviewed by both the lord president and the secretary to the education department, Ralph Lingen. Both interviews were of "exceedingly short duration," and no inquiry was made of his knowledge of education or the system then in operation.

144. *Hansard Parliamentary Debates*, 3rd series (1869), pp. 480ff, and (1870), pp. 808ff.

145. *Hansard* (1869), p. 497.

146. Ibid., pp. 494–95.

147. *Hansard* (1870), p. 815.

148. Quoted in Wright, *Treasury Control*, p. 74.

149. Quoted in ibid., pp. 82, 83.

150. Quoted in ibid., p. 83.

151. Quoted in Hughes, "Civil Service Reform, 1853–1855," p. 64.

152. Hence the agitation of the Administrative Reform Association and of the lower civil servants against "literary" examinations.

153. Cf. K. C. Wheare, *The Civil Service in the Constitution* (London: Athlone Press, 1954).

154. Wright, *Treasury Control,* p. 79.

155. *Hansard* (1869), p. 495.

156. Gladstone to Russel in Morley, *Gladstone,* p. 649.

157. Select Committee on Civil Service Expenditures, "Report," *Parliamentary Papers,* 7 (1873): 292.

Bibliography

Abel, Wilhelm. *Geschichte der deutschen Landwirtschaft*. Stuttgart: Ulmer, 1962.

Abramovitz, Moses, and Vera F. Eliasberg. *The Growth of Public Employment in Great Britain*. Princeton: Princeton University Press, 1957.

Acta Borussica. Denkmäler der Preussischen Staatsverwaltung im 18. Jahrhundert.
1. *Die Behördenorganisation und die allgemeine Staatsverwaltung in Preussen.* Vols. 1–15, 1892ff.
2. *Die Handels-, Zoll- und Akzisepolitik Preussens.* Vols. 2 and 3, 1922ff.

Allgemeines Landrecht für die Preussischen Staaten. Berlin, 1796. 2 vols.

Altmann, Wilhelm. *Ausgewählte Urkunden zur Brandenburgisch-Preussischen Verfassungs- und Verwaltungsgeschichte*. Berlin: Weidmann, 1915. Vol. 2.

Anderson, Eugene N. *The Social and Political Conflict in Prussia, 1858–1864*. Lincoln: University of Nebraska Press, 1954.

Anderson, Eugene N., and Pauline R. Anderson. *Political Institutions and Social Change in Continental Europe in the Nineteenth Century*. Berkeley: University of California Press, 1967.

Anderson, Olive. *A Liberal State at War: English Politics and Economics During the Crimean War*. London: Macmillan, 1967.

———."The Janus Face of Mid-Nineteenth-Century English Radicalism: The Administrative Reform Association of 1855." *Victorian Studies,* 7 (1964–1965), 231–42.

Annan, Noel G. "The Intellectual Aristocracy." In *Studies in Social History*, edited by J. H. Plumb. London: Longmans, Green, 1955.

Anonymous. "Die unverhältnismässig zunehmende Anzahl der Studierenden in Deutschland." *Hesperus*, 1832, pp. 363–64.

Anonymous. "Mittel und Vorschläge, die Menge derer zurückzuhalten, die sich jetzt aus den niederen Ständen, ohne natürlichen Beruf zum Studiren auf Universitäten, und in die Stände der Gelehrten eindrängen." *Deutsches Magazin.* Altona: Hammerich, 1797.

Anonymous. *Reform of the Civil Service: Being a Reply to a Pamphlet Entitled "The Civil Service: by a Practical Man."* London: Ridgway, 1861.

Anonymous. *The Civil Service: Examinations for, and Promotions Therein Considered by a Practical Man.* London: Pigott, 1855.

Anonymous. *The Common Sense of Competition: A Plea for an Open Civil Service.* London: Ridgway, 1861.

Anonymous. "Über den Andrang junger Leute zum Studieren von Jünglingen aus niederen Ständen." *Schlesische Provinzialblätter,* 100(1834): 545ff.

Anschütz, Gerhard. *Die Verfassungs-Urkunde für den Preussischen Staat vom 31. Jan. 1850.* Berlin: Haering, 1912.

Archer, Richard L. *Secondary Education in the Nineteenth Century.* London: Cass, 1966.

Aries, Philippe. *Centuries of Childhood.* New York: Vintage Books, 1962.

Arndt, Adolf. "Der Anteil der Stände an der Gesetzgebung in Preussen von 1812 bis 1848." *Archiv für öffentliches Recht,* 17 (1902).

Aronson, Sidney H. *Status and Kinship in the Higher Civil Service.* Cambridge, Mass.: Harvard University Press, 1964.

Ashworth, William. *An Economic History of England, 1870–1939.* London: Methuen, 1960.

Aydelotte, William H. "The House of Commons of the 1840's." *History,* 39 (1954):248–62.

———. "Voting Patterns in the British House of Commons in the 1840's." *Comparative Studies in Society and History,* 5 (January 1963), 134–63.

Bach, Theodor. *Theodor Gottlieb von Hippel.* Breslau: Tremendt, 1863.

Badger, Alfred B. *The Public Schools and the Nation.* London: Hale, 1944.

Bagehot, Walter. *The English Constitution.* Boston: Little, Brown, 1873.

Bamford, Thomas W. "Public Schools and Social Class, 1801–1850." *British Journal of Sociology,* 12(1961): 224–35.

———. *The Rise of the Public Schools.* London: Thomas Nelson, 1967.

Banks, Olive. *Parity and Prestige in English Secondary Education.* London: Routledge & Kegan Paul, 1955.

Barker, Ernest. *The Development of Public Services in Western Europe, 1660–1930.* London: Oxford University Press, 1944.

Barnard, Howard C. *A History of English Education from 1760.* London: London University Press, 1961.

Beales, Derek. *From Castlereagh to Gladstone, 1815–1885.* London: Thomas Nelson, 1969.

Bendix, Reinhard et al., eds. *State and Society: A Reader in Comparative*

Political Sociology. Berkeley: University of California Press, 1973.

Benecke, Wolf-Guenther. *Stand und Stände in Preussen vor den Reformen.* Dissertation, University of Berlin, 1935.

Bensman, Joseph, and Arthur J. Vidich. *The New American Society.* Chicago: Quadrangle Books, 1971.

Bentham, Jeremy. *Official Aptitude Maximized, Expense Minimized, as Shown in the Several Papers Comprised in This Volume.* London: R. Heward, 1830.

Berlant, Jeffrey Lionel. *Profession and Monopoly.* Berkeley: University of California Press, 1975.

Best, Samuel. *Thoughts on the Proposals for the Improvement of the Civil Service, and for the Granting of Diplomas Through the Agencies of the Institution in Union with the Society of Arts.* London: Groombridge, 1854.

Bishop, Thomas J. H. *Winchester and the Public School Elite.* London: Faber, 1967.

Blattner, Fritz. *Das Gymnasium.* Heidelberg: Quelle & Meyer, 1960.

Blumer, Herbert. "Society and Symbolic Interaction." In *Human Behavior and Social Process,* edited by Arnold M. Rose. Boston: Houghton Mifflin, 1962.

Born, Stephen. *Erinnerungen eines Achtundvierzigers.* Leipzig: Meyer, 1898.

Bramstëd, Ernest K. *Aristocracy and the Middle Classes in Germany: Social Types in German Literature 1830–1900.* Chicago: University of Chicago Press, 1964.

Brandt, Hartwig. *Landständische Repräsentation im deutschen Vormärz: Politisches Denken im Einflussfeld des monarchischen Prinzips.* Neuwied: Luchterhand, 1968.

Brebner, John. "Laissez Faire and State Intervention in Nineteenth-Century Britain." In *The Making of English History,* edited by R. L. Schuyler and H. Ausubel. New York: Dryden, 1952.

Briggs, Asa. *The Age of Improvement.* London: Longmans, Green, 1959.

———. *Chartist Studies.* New York: St. Martin's Press, 1959.

———.*Victorian People: A Reassessment of Persons and Themes, 1851–1867.* Harmondsworth: Penguin Books, 1967.

Briggs, Asa, and John Saville, eds. *Essays in Labour History.* New York: St. Martin's Press, 1960.

British Museum-Gladstone Papers (Add. Mss. 44333).

Brown, R. G. S. *The Administrative Process in Britain.* London: Methuen, 1970.

Brunner, Otto. *Adeliges Landleben und Europäischen Geist.* Salzburg: Müller, 1949.

———. *Land und Herrschaft.* Wien: Rohrer, 1959.

———. *Neue Wege der Verfassungs- und Sozialgeschichte.* Göttingen: Vandenhoeck & Ruprecht, 1968.

Brunschwig, Henri. *La crise de l'état prussien à la fin du XVIIᵉ siècle et la genèse de la mentalité romantique.* Paris: Presses Universitaires, 1947.

Buller, James. *The Civil Service: Letter to R. M. Bromley, Esq.* London: Bickers & Bush, 1855.

Burke, John, and Sir John B. Burke. *A Genealogical and Heraldic History of the Landed Gentry; or Commons of Great Britain and Ireland.* London: Colburn, 1846.

Burn, William L. *The Age of Equipoise.* New York: Norton, 1964.

Busch, Alexander. *Die Geschichte des Privatdozenten, eine soziologische Studie zur grossbetrieblichen Entwicklung der deutschen Universitäten.* Stuttgart: Enke, 1959.

Büsch, Otto. *Militärsystem und Sozialleben im alten Preussen 1713–1807.* Berlin: Walter de Gruyter, 1962.

Butterfield, Herbert. *George III, Lord North and the People.* London: Bell, 1950.

Campbell, Alexander D. P. *Educating Our Rulers.* London: Duckworth, 1957.

Camphausen, Otto. "Letters to Ludolf Camphausen of November 10, 1843." In *Rheinische Briefe und Akten zur Geschichte der Politischen Bewegung 1830–1850,* edited by Joseph Hansen. Essen: Baedeker, 1919.

Cannon, Walter F. "Scientists and Broad Churchmen: An Early Victorian Intellectual Network," *Journal of British Studies,* 4 (November 1964):65–68.

Carr-Saunders, Alexander M., and P. A. Wilson. *The Professions.* London: Cass, 1964.

Carsten, Francis L. *The Origins of Prussia.* Oxford: Clarendon Press, 1954.

Chambers, Jonathan David. *The Agricultural Revolution, 1750–1880.* New York: Schocken, 1966.

Checkland, Sydney G. *The Rise of Industrial Society in England, 1815–1885.* London: Longmans, Green, 1964.

Chrimes, Stanley B. *English Constitutional History.* London: Routledge & Kegan Paul, 1958.

Civil Service Inquiry Commission. "Reports," *Parliamentary Papers,* 23 (1875).

Clapham, John H. *An Economic History of Modern Britain.* Cambridge University Press, 1932.

Cohen, Emmeline W. *The Growth of the British Civil Service 1780–1939.* Hamden, Conn.: Archon Books, 1965.

Collins, Randall. *Conflict Sociology.* New York: Academic Press, 1975.

———. "Functional and Conflict Theories of Educational Stratification," *American Sociological Review,* 36 (December 1971):1002–19.

———. "Reassessment of Sociological History: The Empirical Validity of the Conflict Tradition," *Theory and Society*, I (1974), pp. 147–78.

Conacher, J. B. *The Aberdeen Coalition 1852–1855*. London: Cambridge University Press, 1968.

Conrad, Hermann. *Die geistigen Grundlagen des Allgemeinen Landrechts für die preussischen Staaten*. Köln und Opladen: Westdt. Verlag, 1958.

Conrad, Johannes. *Das Universitätsstudium in Deutschland während der letzen 50 Jahre*. Jena: Fischer, 1884.

———. "Die Statistik der Universität Halle." In *Festschriften zum zweihundert jährigen Jubiläum der Vereinigten Friedrichsuniversitäten Halle-Wittenberg*. Halle: Universität, 1894.

Conze, Werner, ed. *Staat und Gesellschaft im deutschen Vormärz*. Stuttgart: Ernst Klett, 1962.

Cosin, B. R., ed. *Education: Structure and Society*. Harmondsworth: Penguin Books, 1972.

Cotgrove, Stephen F. *Technical Education and Social Change*. London: George Allen & Unwin, 1958.

Cowling, Maurice. *Disraeli, Gladstone and Revolution*. London: Cambridge University Press, 1967.

Craig, Gordon A. *The Politics of the Prussian Army 1640–1945*. New York: Oxford University Press, 1964.

Cromwell, Valerie. "Interpretations of Nineteenth-Century Administration: An Analysis." *Victorian Studies*, 9 (March 1966): 245–55.

Cruickshank, Majorie. *Church and State in English Education*. London: Macmillan, 1963.

Curtis, Mark H. "The Alienated Intellectuals of Early Stuart England." *Past and Present*, 23 (1962): 25–43.

Curtis, Stanley I. *History of Education in Great Britain*. London: University Tutorial Press, 1968.

Dahrendorf, Ralf. *Society and Democracy in Germany*. New York: Doubleday, 1967.

Dale, Harold E. *The Higher Civil Service of Great Britain*. Oxford: Oxford University Press, 1941.

Dangerfield, George. *The Strange Death of Liberal England, 1910–1914*. New York: Smith & Haas, 1935.

Davis, Henry W. C. *The Age of Grey and Peel*. Oxford: Clarendon Press, 1929.

Dawes, Richard. *Remarks on the Reorganization of the Civil Service and Its Bearing on Educational Progress*. London: Ridgway, 1859.

Deane, Phyllis. *British Economic Growth, 1688–1959*. London: Cambridge University Press, 1967.

Delbrück, Clemens O. *Die Ausbildung für den höheren Verwaltungsdienst in Preussen*. Jena: Gustav Fischer, 1917.

Demeter, Karl. *The German Officer-Corps in Society and State 1650-1945*.

London: Weidenfeld & Nicolson, 1965.

Diepgen, Paul. *Geschichte der Medizin.* Berlin: Walter de Gruyter, 1951.

Dieterici, C. G. W. *Geschichtliche und statistische Nachrichten über die Universitäten im preussischen Staate.* Berlin: Duncker & Humblot, 1836.

Dietrich, Richard, and Gerhard Öestreich, eds. *Forschungen zu Staat und Verfassung. Festgabe für Fritz Hartung.* Berlin: Duncker & Humblot, 1958.

Dilthey, Wilhelm. *Die Jugendschriften Hegels: Gesammelte Schriften.* Stuttgart: W. Kohlhammer, 1959. Vol. 4.

Dorn, Walter L. *Competition for Empire, 1740–1763.* New York: Harper Torch, 1963.

———. "The Prussian Bureaucracy in the Eighteenth Century." *Political Science Quarterly,* 46 (1931): 403–23.

Dorwart, Reinhold August. *The Administration Reforms of Frederick William I of Prussia.* Cambridge, Mass.: Harvard University Press, 1953.

Drews, Paul. *Der evangelische Geistliche in der deutschen Vergangenheit.* Jena: Diederichs, 1924.

Dubin, Robert. "Parsons' Actor: Continuities in Social Theory." *American Sociological Review,* 25 (August 1960):457–67.

Eaton, Dorman B. *Civil Service in Great Britain: A History of Abuses and Reforms and Their Bearing upon American Politics.* New York: Harper & Brothers, 1880.

Eggert, Oskar. *Stände und Staat in Pommern im Anfang des 19. Jahrhunderts.* Köln: Böhlau, 1964.

Eichholtz, Dietrich. *Junker und Bourgeoisie.* Berlin: Akademie Verlag, 1962.

Engelsing, Rolf. "Zur politischen Bildung der deutschen Unterschichten 1789–1863." *Historische Zeitschrift,* 206 (1968).

Eulenburg, Franz. *Die Entwicklung der Universität Leipzig.* Leipzig: Hirzel, 1909.

———. *Die Frequenz der Deutschen Universitäten.* Leipzig: Teubner, 1904.

Fann, Willard Reese. *The Consolidation of Bureaucratic Absolutism in Prussia, 1817–1827.* Doctoral dissertation, University of California, Berkeley, 1965.

Fay, Sidney B. *The Rise of Brandenburg-Prussia to 1786.* New York: S. Holt, 1937.

Feuchtwanger, E. J. *Disraeli, Democracy, and the Tory Party.* Oxford: Clarendon Press, 1968.

———. *Prussia: Myth and Reality; the Role of Prussia in German History.* Chicago: Regnery, 1970.

Finck von Finckenstein, Hans Wolfram. *Die Entwicklung der Landwirtschaft in Preussen und Deutschland 1800–1930.* Würzburg: Holzner, 1960.

Finer, Herman. *The British Civil Service.* London: George Allen & Unwin, 1937.

————. *Theory and Practice of Modern Government.* New York: Holt, 1949.

Finer, Samuel E. *The Life and Times of Sir Edwin Chadwick.* London: Methuen, 1952.

Fischer, Ferdinand. *Preussen am Abschlusse der ersten Hälfte des neunzehnten Jahrhunderts.* Berlin: Reimer, 1876.

Fischer, Wolfram. *Handwerksrecht und Handwerkswirtschaft um 1800.* Berlin: Duncker & Humblot, 1955.

Fish, Carl R. *The Civil Service and the Patronage.* Cambridge: Harvard University Press, 1920.

Ford, Guy S. *Stein and the Era of Reform in Prussia, 1807–1815.* Princeton: Princeton University Press, 1922.

Forschungen zur brandenburgischen und preussischen Geschichte. Berlin, 1888–1943. 55 vols.

Freedman, Robert, ed. *Marxist Social Thought.* New York: Harcourt, Brace, 1968.

Friedrich, Carl J. "The Continental Tradition of Training Administrators in Law and Jurisprudence," *Journal of Modern History*, 11(1939): 129–48.

G. "Woher kommt es, dass es sich jetzt alles so zum studieren drängt, und wie ist dem möglichst abzuhelfen," *Hannoveranisches Magazin*, 1828, pp. 730–38.

Garfinkel, Harold. *Studies in Ethnomethodology.* Englewood Cliffs, N.J.: Prentice-Hall, 1967.

Garve, Christian. *Versuche über verschiedene Gegenstände aus der Moral, der Litteratur und dem gesellschaftlichen Leben.* Breslau: n.p., 1801.

Gash, Norman. *Politics in the Age of Peel: A Study in the Technique of Parliamentary Representation 1830–1850.* London: Longmans, Green, 1953.

————. *Reaction and Reconstruction in English Politics, 1832–52.* Oxford: Clarendon, 1965.

————. *Sir Robert Peel: The Life of Sir Robert Peel After 1830.* London: Longmans, 1972.

————, ed. *Documents of Modern History: The Age of Peel.* London: Arnold, 1968.

Gebhardt, Bruno. *Wilhelm von Humboldt als Staatsman.* Stuttgart: Cotta, 1899. 2 vols.

Gerstfeldt, Philip. "Beiträge zur Statistik der Finanzen in Preussen." *Jahrbücher für Nationalökonomie und Statistik*, 7 (1883).

Gerth, Hans. *Die Sozialgeschichtliche Lage der Bürgerlichen Intelligenz um die Wende des 18. Jahrhunderts.* Doctoral dissertation, University of Frankfurt/Main, 1935.

Gesetz-Sammlung für die Königlich Preussischen Staaten. Berlin, 1810 ff.

Gierke, Julius von. *Die erste Reform des Freiherrn vom Stein.* Darmstadt: Wissenschaftliche Buchgesellschaft, 1957.

Gierke, Otto von. *Die Steinsche Städteordnung.* Darmstadt: Wissenschaftliche Buchgesellschaft, 1957.

———. *Natural Law and the Theory of Society.* Boston: Beacon Press, 1957.

Giese, G. *Quellen zur deutschen Schulgeschichte zeit 1800.* Göttingen: Musterschmidt, 1961.

Gillis, John R. *The Prussian Bureaucracy in Crisis.* Stanford, Calif.: Stanford University Press, 1971.

Gladden, Edgar N. *British Public Service Administration.* London: Staple Press, 1961.

———. *Civil Service or Bureaucracy?* London: Staple Press, 1956.

———. *Civil Service of the United Kingdom 1855–1970.* London: Case, 1967.

Glaser, Barney, and Anselm Strauss. *Status Passage.* Chicago: Aldine, 1971.

Glass, David V. "Education and Social Change in Modern England." In *Education, Economy and Society,* edited by A. H. Halsey et al. New York: Free Press, 1961.

Gneist, Rudolf. *Die preussische Kreis-Ordnung in ihrer Bedeutung für den inneren Ausbau des deutschen Verfassungsstaates.* Berlin: Springers, 1870.

Goffman, Erwin. *Encounters.* Indianapolis: Bobbs Merrill, 1961.

———. *Interaction Ritual.* Chicago: Aldine, 1967.

———. *Strategic Interaction.* Philadelphia: University of Pennsylvania Press, 1969.

Goldhorn, J. D. "Was sollten Prediger bedenken, welche junge Leute aus niederen Ständen zum Studieren veranlassen?" *Journal für Prediger,* 69 (1826): 302ff.

———. "Wer soll studieren?" *Neues Journal für Prediger,* 53 (1828): 277–93.

Gollwitzer, Heinz. *Die Standesherren, die politische und gesellschaftliche Stellung der Mediatisierten 1815–1918, ein Beitrag zur deutschen Sozialgeschichte.* Stuttgart: Vorwerk, 1957.

Goltz, J. Frhr. von der. *Auswirkungen der Stein-Hardenbergschen Agrarreform im Laufe des 19. Jahrhunderts.* Dissertation, University of Göttingen, 1936.

Goodwin, Albert, ed. *The European Nobility in the Eighteenth Century.* London: Adam & Charles Black, 1953.

Görlitz, Walter. *Die Junker, Adel und Bauer im deutschen Osten.* Glücksberg: Starke, 1957.

———. *Stein: Staatsmann und Reformator.* Frankfurt/Main: Frankfurter Hefte, 1949.

Grabower, Rolf. *Preussens Steuern vor und nach den Befreiungskriegen.* Berlin: Beck, 1932.

Greaves, Harold R. G. *The Civil Service in the Changing State.* London: George G. Harrap, 1947.

Green, V. H. H. *The Universities.* Harmondsworth: Penguin Books, 1969.

Griewank, Karl. *Deutsche Studenten und Universitäten in der Revolution von 1848.* Weimar: H. Böhlaus Nachf, 1949.

———. *Gneisenau, ein Leben in Briefen.* Leipzig: Koehler & Amelang, 1939.

Gross, Llewellyn, ed. *Symposium on Sociological Theory.* New York: Harper & Row, 1959.

Guttsman, Wilhelm L. *The British Political Elite.* London: Macgibbon & Kee, 1963.

———, ed. *The English Ruling Class.* London: Weidenfeld & Nicolson, 1969.

Habakkuk, Hrothgar J. "England." In *The European Nobility in the Eighteenth Century,* edited by A. Goodwin. London: Adam & Charles Black, 1953.

Halévy, Elie. *A History of the English People in the Nineteenth Century.* London: Benn, 1949.

Halsey, Albert H. "British Universities and Intellectual Life." In *Education, Economy and Society,* edited by A. H. Halsey et al. New York: Free Press, 1965.

Halsey, Albert H., Jean Floud, and C. Arnold Anderson, eds. *Education, Economy, and Society: A Reader in the Sociology of Education.* New York: Free Press, 1965.

Hamerow, Theodore S. *Restoration, Revolution, Reaction: Economics and Politics in Germany, 1815–1871.* Princeton: Princeton University Press, 1958.

Hanham, Harold J. *Elections and Party Management: Politics in the Time of Disraeli and Gladstone.* London: Longmans, 1959.

———. *The Nineteenth-Century Constitution: Documents and Commentary.* London: Cambridge University Press, 1969.

———. *The Reformed Electoral System in Great Britain, 1832–1914.* London: London Historical Association, 1968.

———. "The Sale of Honours in Late Victorian England." *Victorian Studies,* 3 (March 1960): 277–89.

Hans, Nicholas. *New Trends in Education in the Eighteenth Century.* London: Routledge & Kegan Paul, 1951.

Hansemann, David. *Das preussische und deutsche Verfassungswerk.* Berlin: Schneider, 1850.

———. *Preussen und Frankreich.* Leipzig: Brüggemann, 1834.

Hansen, Joseph, ed. *Rheinische Briefe und Akten zur Geschichte der politischen Bewegung 1830–1850.* Essen: Baedeker, 1919. 2 vols.

Harnisch, W. *Die deutsche Bürgerschule, eine Anweisung, wie für den gesamten Mittelstand zweckmässige Schulen zu begründen . . . sind.* Halle: Anton, 1830.

Harrison, Royden J. *Before the Socialists*. London: Routledge & Kegan Paul, 1965.

Hart, Jenifer. "Nineteenth-Century Social Reform: A Tory Interpretation of History." *Past and Present*, 31 (July 1965):39–61.

Hartung, Fritz. *Deutsche Verfassungsgeschichte vom 15. Jahrhundert bis zur Gegenwart*. Stuttgart: Koehler, 1950.

———. *Staatsbildende Kräfte der Neuzeit, Gesammelte Aufsätze*. Berlin: Duncker & Humblot, 1961.

———. *Studien zur Geschichte der preussischen Verwaltung*. Berlin: Walter de Gruyter, 1942.

Haussherr, Hans. *Die Stunde Hardenbergs*. Hamburg: Hanseatischer Verlag Anstalt, 1943.

———. *Hardenberg, eine politische Biographie*. Köln: Böhlau, 1963.

———. *Verwaltungseinheit und Resorttrennung vom Ende des 17. bis zum Beginn des 19. Jahrhunderts*. Berlin: Akademischer Verlag, 1953.

Havighurst, Robert J. *Comparative Perspectives on Education*. Boston: Little, Brown, 1968.

Heffter, Heinrich. *Die deutsche Selbstverwaltung im 19. Jahrhundert*. Stuttgart: Koehler, 1950.

Hegel, G. W. F. *Philosophy of Right*. London: G. Bell & Sons, 1958.

Heinzen, Karl. *Die preussische Bürokratie*. Darmstadt: Leske, 1845.

Henderson, William O. *The State and the Industrial Revolution in Prussia, 1740–1870*. Liverpool: University Press of Liverpool, 1958.

Heubaum, Alfred. "Die Reformbestrebungen unter dem Preussischen Minister Julius von Massow (1778–1807) auf dem Gebiete des höheren Bildungswesens." *Mitteilungen der Gesellschaft für deutsche Erziehungs- und Schulgeschichte*, 14 (1904):186–225.

Hintze, Otto. "Behördenorganisation und allgemeine Verwaltung in Preussen." *Acta Borussica. 1. Die Behördenorganisation*, 4 (1901): part 1, 260ff.

———. "Der oesterreichische und preussische Beamtenstaat im 17. und 18. Jahrhundert." *Historische Zeitschrift*, 86 (1901).

———. *Die Hohenzollern und ihr Werk*. Berlin: Paul Parey, 1915.

———. *Geist und Epochen der Preussischen Geschichte: Gesammelte Abhandlungen*. Leipzig: Koehler & Amelang, 1943.

———. *Regierung und Verwaltung*. Göttingen: Vandenhoeck & Ruprecht, 1967.

———. *Soziologie und Geschichte*. Göttingen: Vandenhoeck & Ruprecht, 1964.

———. *Staat und Verfassung*. Göttingen: Vandenhoeck & Ruprecht, 1962.

Hinze, Kurt. *Die Arbeiterfrage zu Beginn des Modernen Kapitalismus in Brandenburg-Preussen*. Berlin: Walter de Gruyter, 1963.

Hobsbawn, Eric J. *Industry and Empire*. New York: Pantheon Books, 1968.

———. *Laboring Men.* London: Weidenfeld & Nicolson, 1964.

———. *The Age of Revolution (1789–1848).* London: Weidenfeld & Nicolson, 1962.

Hofbauer, Johann Christoph. *Geschichte der Universität zu Halle bis zum Jahre 1805.* Halle: Schimmelpfennig, 1805.

Hoffman, J. G. *Die Bevölkerung des preussischen Staates.* Berlin: Nicolai, 1839.

Holborn, Hajo. "Der deutsche Idealismus in sozialgeschichtlicher Beleuchtung." *Historische Zeitschrift,* 174(1952): 85–108.

Homans, George. "Bringing Men Back In." *Americal Sociological Review,* 29 (December 1964): 809–18.

Houghton, Walter E. *The Victorian Frame of Mind: 1830–1870.* New Haven: Yale University Press, 1957.

Hovell, Mark. *The Chartist Movement.* London: Longmans & Green, 1925.

Hoven, Jupp. *Der preussische Offizier des 18. Jahrhunderts.* Dissertation, University of Leipzig, 1936.

Huber, Ernst Rufolf. *Deutsche Verfassungsgeschichte seit 1789.* Stuttgart: W. Kohlhammer, 1957. 3 vols.

Hughes, Edward. "Civil Service Reform, 1853–1855." *History,* 27(1942): 51–83.

———. "Notes and Documents: Sir Charles Trevelyan and Civil Service Reform, 1853–1854." *English Historical Review,* 64 (1949):53–88, 206–34.

———. "Postscript to Civil Service Reforms of 1855." *Public Administration,* 33 (1955): 299–306.

Humboldt, Wilhelm von. *Über Einrichtung landständischer Verfassungen in den Preussischen Staaten.* Heidelberg: Universitätsverlag, 1949.

———. "Über die Liegnitzer Ritterakademie." In *Werke.* Stuttgart: Cotta, 1964. Vol. 4.

———. "Über Kadettenhäuser." In *Werke.* Stuttgart: Cotta, 1964. Vol. 4.

Ibbeken, Rudolf. *Preussen 1807–1813. Staat und Volk als Idee und in Wirklichkeit.* Köln & Berlin: Grote, 1970.

Imhof, Maximus. *Rede über das dringende Zeitbedürfnis in unserem Vaterlande die Anzahl der Studierenden zu vermindern, und ihre Zurückweisung ins bürgerliche Leben durch angemessene Mittel zu erleichtern.* Müchen: Joseph Leutner, 1804.

Jany, Curt. *Geschichte der Preussischen Armee vom 15. Jahrhundert bis 1914.* Osnabrück: Biblio Verlag, 1967. 4 vols.

Jeismann, Karl-Ernst. *Staat und Erziehung in der Preussischen Reform 1807–1819.* Göttingen: Vandenhoeck & Ruprecht, 1969.

Jenkins, Hester, and D. Caradog Jones. "Social Class of Cambridge University Alumni of the 18th and 19th Centuries." *British Journal of Sociology,* 1 (1950): 93–116.

Jennings, Sir Ivor. *Cabinet Government.* Cambridge University Press, 1959.

———. *Party Politics.* Cambridge University Press, 1961. 2 vols.

Jones, Wilbur D. *Lord Derby and Victorian Conservatism.* Athens: University of Georgia, 1956.

Jordan, Wilbur K. *The Charities of Rural England, 1480–1660.* London: George Allen & Unwin, 1961.

Kaehler, Siegfried A. *Wilhelm von Humboldt und der Staat.* Göttingen: Vandenhoeck & Ruprecht, 1963.

Kamptz, Karl A. von, ed. *Annalen der Preussischen inneren Staats-verwaltung.* Berlin: Dümmler, 1813–1839. 24 vols.

Kehr, Eckart. "Zur Genesis der preussischen Bürokratie und des Rechtsstaats." In *Primat der Innenpolitik,* edited by Hans-Ulrich Wehler. Berlin: Walter de Gruyter, 1965.

———. "Zur Genesis des Koeniglich Preussischen Reserve-offiziers." In *Primat der Innenpolitik,* edited by Hans-Ulrich Wehler. Berlin: Walter de Gruyter, 1965.

Keir, David L. *The Constitutional History of Modern Britain Since 1485.* Princeton: D. Van Nostrand, 1966.

Kelsall, Roger K. *Higher Civil Servants in Britain from 1870 to the Present Day.* London: Routledge & Kegan Paul, 1955.

Kingsley, J. Donald. *Representative Bureaucracy: An Interpretation of the British Civil Service.* Yellow Springs, Ohio: Antioch Press, 1944.

Kitson Clark, G. S. R. *An Expanding Society: Britain 1830–1900.* Cambridge University Press, 1967.

———. " 'Statesmen in Disguise': Reflexions on the History of the Neutrality of the Civil Service." *Historical Journal,* 2 (1959):19–39.

———. *The Making of Victorian England.* Cambridge, Mass.: Harvard University Press, 1962.

Klein, Ernst. "Funktion und Bedeutung des Preussischen Staatsministeriums." *Jahrbuch für die Geschichte Mittel- und Ostdeutschlands,* 9–10 (1961):195–261.

———. *Von der Reform zur Restauration: Finanzpolitik und Reformgesetzgebung des preussischen Staatskanzlers Karl August von Hardenberg.* Berlin: Walter de Gruyter, 1965.

Klotzbach, Kurt. *Das Eliteproblem im politischen Liberalismus.* Köln and Opladen: Westdeutscher Verlag, 1966.

Kluge, Alexander. *Universitäts-Selbstverwaltung.* Frankfurt/Main: Klostermann, 1958.

Knemeyer, Franz-Ludwig. *Regierungs- und Verwaltungsreformen in Deutschland zu Beginn des 19. Jahrhunderts.* Köln & Berlin: Grote, 1970.

Knigge, Adolph Freiherr von. *Über den Umgang mit Menschen.* Gera: C. B. Griesbach, 1929.

König, René. *Vom Wesen der deutschen Universität.* Darmstadt: Wissenschafliche Buchgesellschaft, 1970.

Koselleck, Reinhard. *Preussen zwischen Reform und Revolution.* Stuttgart: Ernst Klett Verlag, 1967.

Koser, Reinhold. *Geschichte Friedrich des Grossen.* Stuttgart: Cotta, 1912. 4 vols.

Lambert, Royston. *Sir John Simon 1816–1904, and English Social Administration.* London: MacGibbon & Kee, 1963.

Lang, Andrew. *The Life, Letters, and Diaries of Sir Stafford Northcote.* Edinburgh: Blackwood, 1890. 2 vols.

Laqueur, Walter, and George L. Mosse, eds. *Education and Social Structure in the Twentieth Century.* New York: Harper Torchbook, 1967.

Laski, Harold J. *Parliamentary Government in England.* New York: Viking, 1938.

Laubert, Manfred. *Die Verwaltung der Provinz Posen 1815–1847.* Breslau: Briebatsch, 1923.

Lecky, William E. *History of England in the Eighteenth Century.* New York: D. Appleton, 1882–1887.

Lenz, Max. *Geschichte der kgl. Friedrich Wilhelm Universität zu Berlin.* Halle: Buchh andlung des Waisenhauses, 1910–1918. 5 vols.

Lewis, Richard A. *Edwin Chadwick and the Public Health Movement.* London: Longmans, Green, 1952.

Lexis, W. *Die Deutschen Universitäten.* Berlin: Asher, 1893.

———, ed. *Die Reform des höheren Schulwesens in Preussen.* Halle: Waisenhaus, 1902.

Lichtenstein, Ernst. *Zur Entwicklung des Bildungsbegriffs von Meister Eckart bis Hegel.* Heidelberg: Quelle & Meyer, 1966.

Lilge, Frederick. *The Abuse of Learning: The Failure of the German University.* New York: Macmillan, 1948.

Loewenstein, Karl. *British Cabinet Government.* New York: Oxford University Press, 1967.

Losch, Philipp. *Der Soldatenhandel.* Kassel: Bärenreiter, 1933.

Lotz, Albert. *Geschichte des deutschen Beamtentums.* Berlin: Decker, 1909.

Lynd, Helen. *England in the Eighteen-Eighties.* London: Oxford University Press, 1945.

MacDonagh, Oliver. *A Pattern of Government Growth, 1800–1860; the Passenger Acts and Their Enforcement.* London: Macgibbon & Kee, 1961.

————."The Nineteenth-Century Revolution in Government: A Reappraisal." *Historical Journal,* 1 (1958):52–67.

Macdonald, D. F. *The Age of Transition.* London: St. Martin's Press, 1967.

Macintosh, John P. *The British Cabinet.* London: Methuen, 1968.

Mack, Edward C. *Public Schools and British Opinion, 1780–1860.* London: Methuen, 1938.

Mackenzie, K. R. *The English Parliament.* Harmondsworth: Penguin Books, 1965.

Mackenzie, William J. M., and Jack W. Grove. *Central Administration in Britain.* London: Longmans, Green, 1957.

Magnus, Philip M. *Gladstone.* London: Murray, 1954.

Maitland, Frederic W. *The Constitutional History of England.* Cambridge University Press, 1908.

Mamroth, Karl. *Geschichte der Preussischen Staatsbesteuerung 1806–1816.* Leipzig: Duncker & Humblot, 1890.

Mann, Golo. *Deutsche Geschichte im 19. und 20. Jahrhundert.* Frankfurt: Gustav Fischer, 1958.

Marshall, Dorothy. *Eighteenth-Century England.* New York: McKay, 1962.

————. *English People in the Eighteenth Century.* London: Longmans, Green, 1956.

Marshall, T. H. *Class, Citizenship and Social Development.* New York: Doubleday, 1964.

Martiny, Fritz. *Die Adelsfrage in Preussen vor 1806.* Stuttgart-Berlin: Kohlhammer, 1938.

Mather, Frederick C. *Public Order in the Age of the Chartists.* Manchester: Manchester University Press, 1959.

Mathias, Peter. *The First Industrial Nation.* London: Methuen, 1969.

McCord, Norman. *The Anti-Corn Law League.* London: George Allen & Unwin, 1958.

McIlwaine, C. H. "Medieval Estates." *The Cambridge Medieval History,* 7 (1932):665–715.

McPherson, Robert G. *Theory of Higher Education in Nineteenth-Century England.* Athens: University of Georgia Press, 1959.

Meier, Ernst von. *Die Reform der Verwaltungsorganisation unter Stein und Hardenberg.* München and Leipzig: Duncker & Humblot, 1912.

Meiners, Christoph. *Über die Verfassung und Verwaltung deutscher Universitäten.* Göttingen: Roewer, 1801. 2 vols.

Meitzen, August. *Der Boden und die landwirtschaftlichen Verhältnisse des Preussischen Staates.* Berlin: Parey, 1901.

Melzer, F. "Desiderien der statistischen Nachrichten über das Verhältnis der Versorgungen zu der Zahl der Studierenden." *Jahrbuch der deutschen Universitäten.* Leipzig: Weidmann, 1842.

Merton, Robert K., et al., eds. *Reader in Bureaucracy*. New York: Free Press, 1952.

Meusel, Friedrich. *Friedrich August von der Marwitz*. Berlin: Weidmann, 1908–1913. 3 vols.

Mill, John Stuart. *Considerations on Representative Government*. London: Longmans, Green, 1907.

Millerson, Geoffrey. *The Qualifying Associations*. London: Routledge & Kegan Paul, 1964.

Möller, Helmut. *Die kleinbürgerliche Familie im 18. Jahrhundert: Verhalten und Gruppenkultur*. Berlin: Walter de Gruyter, 1969.

Moneypenny, W. F., and G. E. Buckle. *Life of Benjamin Disraeli*. London: Murray, 1929. 2 vols.

Mönnich, W. "Einige Bemerkungen Zur Erklärung der vorhandnehmenden Studiersucht in Deutschland," *Hesperus*, 1828, pp. 577ff.

Möser, Justus. "Also soll man das Studieren nicht verbieten," *Sämmtliche Werke* (Berlin: Nicolai, 1842), vol. 3, pp. 125–28.

Moore, D. C. "The Other Face of Reform." *Victorian Studies*, 5 (1961):7–34.

Morley, John. *The Life of William Edward Gladstone*. London: Macmillan, 1903. 3 vols.

Morstein Marx, Fritz. *The Administrative State: An Introduction to Bureaucracy*. Chicago: University of Chicago Press, 1957.

Moses, Robert. *The Civil Service of Great Britain*. New York: Columbia University Press, 1914.

Mosgrove, Frank. "Middle-class Education and Employment in the Nineteenth Century." *Economic History Review*, 12 (1959): 99–111.

The Migratory Elite. London: Heinemann, 1963.

Most, Otto. "Zur Wirtschafts- und Sozialstatistik der höheren Beamten in Preussen." *Schmollers Jahrbuch für Gesetzgebung, Verwaltung und Volkswirtschaft*, 39 (1915).

Müsebeck, Ernst. *Das Preussische Kultusministerium vor hundert Jahren*. Stuttgart and Berlin: Weidmann, 1918.

Musgrave, Peter W. *Society and Education in England Since 1800*. London: Methuen, 1968.

Mylius, Christian Otto, ed. *Corpus Constitutionem Marchicarum*. Berlin & Halle: 1737–1751. 6 vols.

Novum Corpus Constitutionum Prussico-Brandenburgensium, Berlin: Kunst, 1751–1810. 12 vols.

Naef, Werner. "Frühformen des 'Modernen Staates' im Spaetmittelalter." *Historische Zeitschrift*, 171 (1951): 225–43.

Namier, Lewis. *The Structure of Politics at the Accession of George III*. London: Macmillan, 1968.

Nathan, Helene. *Preussens Verfassung und Verwaltung im Urteile Rheinischer Achtundvierziger.* Bonn: Marcus & Weber, 1912.

Naude, Wilhelm. "Zur Geschichte des preussischen Subalternbeamtentums." *Forschungen zur Brandenburgischen und Preussischen Geschichte,* 18(1905): 355–86.

Neale, J. E. *Elizabeth I and Her Parliaments 1559–1581.* New York: Norton, 1966. 2 vols.

Newsome, David. *Godliness and Good Learning.* London: John Murray, 1961.

Nitsch, Wolfgang, et al. *Hochschule in der Demokratie.* Berlin: Luchterland, 1965.

O'Boyle, Lenore. "The Democratic Left in Germany, 1848." *Journal of Modern History,* 33(1961): 374–83.

O'Leary, Cornelius. *The Elimination of Corrupt Practices in British Elections 1868–1911.* Oxford: Clarendon Press, 1962.

Otto, Friedrich. *Der deutsche Bürgerstand und die deutschen Bürgerschulen.* Leipzig: Merseburger, 1871.

Pares, Richard. *King George III and the Politicians.* Oxford: Clarendon Press, 1953.

Parris, Henry. *Constitutional Bureaucracy: The Development of British Central Administration Since the Eighteenth Century.* London: George Allen & Unwin, 1969.

———. *Government and the Railways in Nineteenth-Century Britain.* London: Routledge & Kegan Paul, 1965.

———. "The Nineteenth-Century Revolution in Government: A Reappraisal Reappraised." *Historical Journal,* 3 (1960): 17–37.

Parsons, Talcott. *Sociological Theory and Modern Society.* New York: Free Press, 1967.

———. *Societies: Evolutionary and Comparative Perspectives.* Englewood Cliffs, N.J.: Prentice-Hall, 1966.

———. *The Social System.* New York: Free Press, 1951.

Parsons, Talcott, and Edward A. Shils. *Toward a General Theory of Action.* New York: Harper Torch, 1951.

Paulsen, Friedrich. *Die deutschen Universitäten und das Universitätsstudium.* Berlin: Asher, 1902.

———. *German Education Past and Present.* New York: Scribner, 1912.

———. *Geschichte des gelehrten Unterrichts.* Berlin und Leipzig: Walter de Gruyter, 1919 and 1921. 2 vols.

———. *Die höheren Schulen Deutschlands und ihr Lehrerstand.* Braunschweig: Friedrich Vieweg, 1904.

———. *Der höhere Lehrerstand und seine Stellung in der gelehrten Welt.* Braunschweig: Friedrich Vieweg, 1902.

Pelling, Henry. *Popular Politics and Society in Late Victorian Britain.* New York: Macmillan, 1968.

Perkin, Harold. *The Origins of Modern English Society, 1780–1880.* London: Routledge & Kegan Paul, 1969.

Perthes, Clemens Theodor. *Das deutsche Staatsleben vor der Revolution. Eine Vorarbeit zum deutschen Staatsrecht.* Hamburg & Gotha: Perthes, 1845.

———. *Der Staatsdienst in Preussen.* Hamburg: Perthes, 1838.

Pertz, G. H. *Das Leben des Ministers Freiherrn vom Stein.* Berlin: Reimer, 1849–1855. 6 vols.

Petermann, Theodor. *Die Gelehrtenschulen und der Gelehrtenstand.* Dresden: Zahn & Jaensch, 1904.

Plessner, Helmut, ed. *Untersuchungen zur Lage der deutschen Hochschullehrer.* Göttingen: Vandenhoek, 1956. 3 vols.

Plumb, J. H. *England in the Eighteenth Century (1714–1815).* Harmondsworth: Penguin Books, 1968.

———. *The Growth of Political Stability in England 1675–1725.* Baltimore: Penguin Books, 1967.

Plumb, J. H., ed. *Studies in Social History.* London: Longmans, Green, 1955.

Porrit, Edward, and Annie G. Porrit. *The Unreformed House of Commons.* Cambridge University Press, 1903. 2 vols.

Poten, B. "Geschichte des Militär-Erziehungs-und Bildungswesens in den Landen deutscher Zunge." *Monumenta Germaniae Paedagogica,* 17(1896).

Preradovich, Nikolaus von. *Die Führungsschichten in Österreich und Preussen.* Wiesbaden: Steiner, 1955.

Raack, R. C. *The Fall of Stein.* Cambridge, Mass.: Harvard University Press, 1965.

Ranke, Leopold. *Denkwürdigkeiten des Staatskanzlers Fürsten von Hardenberg.* Leipzig: Duncker & Humblot, 1877.

Reader, W. J. *Professional Men.* London: Weidenfeld & Nicolson, 1966.

Rein, Adolf. *Die Idee der politischen Universität.* Hamburg: Hanseatische Verlanganstalt, 1933.

"Reports and Papers Relating to the Reorganization of the Civil Service," *Parliamentary Papers,* 20(1854–1855).

Reugger, Albrecht. "Von der Überbesetzung der höheren Berufsarten, oder von der Berufsnot," *Kleine, meistens ungedruckte Schriften,* 1828, pp. 169–76.

Richards, Peter G. *Patronage in British Government.* Toronto: University of Toronto Press, 1963.

Riehl, Wilhelm H. *Die bürgerliche Gesellschaft.* Stuttgart: Göschen, 1861.

Ringer, Fritz K. "Higher Education in Germany in the Nineteenth Century." In *Education and Social Structure in the Twentieth Century,* edited by

Walter Laqueur and George L. Mosse. New York: Harper Torchbook, 1967.

———. *The Decline of the German Mandarins.* Cambridge, Mass.: Harvard University Press, 1969.

Ritter, Gerhard. *Staatskunst und Kriegshandwerk.* München: Oldenburg, 1960. 2 vols.

Ritter, Ulrich Peter. *Die Rolle des Staates in den Frühstadien der Industrialisierung: Die preussische Industrieförderung in der ersten Hälfte des 19. Jahrhundert.* Berlin: Duncker & Humblot, 1961.

Roach, J. P. C. "Victorian Universities and the National Intelligentsia." *Victorian Studies,* 3(1959): 131–50.

Roberts, David. *Victorian Origins of the British Welfare State.* New Haven: Yale University Press, 1960.

Robson, Robert. *Ideas and Institutions of Victorian Britain.* London: Bell, 1967.

Robson, William A. *The Civil Service in Britain and France.* London: Hogarth Press, 1956.

Roessler, Wilhelm. *Die Entstehung des modernen Erziehungswesens in Deutschland.* Stuttgart: W. Kohlhammer, 1961.

Röhrs, Hermann, ed. *Das Gymnasium in Geschichte und Gegenwart.* Frankfurt/Main: Akademische Verlagsgesellschaft, 1969.

Roscher, Wilhelm. *Die Ein- und Durchführung des Adam Smithschen Systems in Deutschland.* Leipzig: Sächsische Gesellschaft der Wissenschaft, 1867.

Rosenberg, Hans. *Bureaucracy, Aristocracy, and Autocracy.* Boston: Beacon Press, 1958.

———. *Probleme der deutschen Sozialgeschichte.* Frankfurt/Main: Suhrkamp, 1969.

Rössler, Hellmuth. *Reichsfreiherr vom Stein.* Göttingen: Musterschmidt, 1964.

Rostow, Walt Whitman. *The British Economy of the Nineteenth Century.* Oxford: Clarendon Press, 1948.

Rothblatt, Sheldon. *The Revolution of the Dons: Cambridge and Society in Victorian England.* New York: Basic Books, 1968.

Rüfner, Wolfgang. *Verwaltungsrechtsschutz in Preussen von 1749 bis 1842.* Bonn: Röhrscheid, 1962.

Rühle, Otto. *Idee und Gestalt der deutschen Universität.* Berlin: Deutscher Verlag der Wissenschaften, 1966.

Runge, Wolfgang. *Politik und Beamtentum in Parteistaat.* Stuttgart: E. Klett, 1965.

Russel, Conrad, ed. *The Origins of the English Civil War.* New York: Harper & Row, 1973.

Samuel, R. H., and R. Hinton Thomas. *Education and Society in Modern Germany.* London: Routledge & Kegan Paul, 1949.

Schelsky, Helmut. *Einsamkeit und Freiheit; Idee und Gestalt der deutschen Universität und ihrer Reformen.* Hamburg: Rowohlt, 1963.

Schindlmayr, Norbert. *Zur preussischen Personalpolitik in der Rheinprovinz.* Doctoral dissertation, University of Köln, 1969.

Schmoller, Gustav. "Einleitung. Die Behördenorganisation." *Acta Borussica-Behördenorganisation,* 1 (1894):15–143.

———. "Die Innere Verwaltung des Preussischen Staates unter Friedrich Wilhelm I." *Preussische Jahrbücher,* 26 (1870): 1–16.

———. "Der Preussische Beamtenstand unter Friedrich Wilhelm I." *Preussische Jahrbücher,* 26 (1870):148–72, 253–70, 538–55.

Schnabel, Franz. *Deutsche Geschichte im 19. Jahrhundert.* Freiburg: Herder, 1929 and 1923. Vols. 1 and 2.

Schultze, Johanna. *Die Auseinandersetzung zwischen Adel und Bürgertum in den Deutschen Zeitschriften der letzten drei Jahrzehnte des 18. Jahrhunderts (1773–1806).* Berlin: Ebering, 1925.

Schulze, Berthold. *Die Reform der Verwaltungsbezirke in Brandenburg und Pommern 1809–1818.* Berlin: Historische Kommission, 1931.

Schultze, Hermann. *Das Preussische Staatsrecht auf Grundlage des Deutschen Staatsrechts.* Leipzig: Breitkopf & Härtel, 1872.

Schuyler, Robert L., and Herman Ausubel, eds. *The Making of English History.* New York: Dryden, 1952.

Schwenke, Elsbeth. "Friedrich der Grosse und der Adel." Inaugural dissertation, University of Berlin, 1911.

Schwerin, Friedrich von. *Die Befähigung zum höheren Verwaltungs dienst.* Berlin: Heymann, 1908.

Seeley, J. R. *Life and Times of Stein.* Boston: Roberts, 1879.

Select Committee on Civil Service Appointments. "Report, Proceedings, Minutes of Evidence, and Appendices." *Parliamentary Papers,* 9(1860).

Select Committee on Civil Service Expenditure. "Report." *Parliamentary Papers,* 7(1873).

Select Committee on Sinecure Offices. "Report." *Parliamentary Papers,* 6 (1834).

Seymour, Charles. *Electoral Reform in England and Wales: The Development and Operation of the Parliamentary Franchise, 1832–1885.* New Haven: Yale University Press, 1915.

Shanahan, William O. *Prussian Military Reforms, 1786–1813.* New York: Columbia University Press, 1945.

Shils, Edward, and Henry A. Finch, eds. *Max Weber on the Methodology of the Social Sciences.* Glencoe, Ill.: Free Press, 1949.

Silver, Harold. *The Concept of Popular Education.* London: MacGibbon & Kee, 1965.

Simon, Brian. *Education and the Labour Movement 1870–1920.* London: Lawrence & Wishart, 1965.

———. *Studies in the History of Education, 1780–1870.* London: Lawrence & Wishart, 1960.

Simon, Joan. "The Social Origins of Cambridge Students, 1603–1640." *Past and Present,* 26(1963): 58–67.

Simon, W. M. *The Failure of the Prussian Reform Movement, 1807–1819.* Ithaca: Cornell University Press, 1955.

Sisson, C. H. *The Spirit of British Administration and Some European Comparisons.* London: Faber & Faber, 1959.

Smellie, K. B. *The British Way of Life.* New York: Praeger, 1955.

———. *A History of Local Government.* London: George Allen & Unwin, 1968.

———. *A Hundred Years of English Government.* London: Duckworth, 1950.

Smelser, Neil J. *Social Change in the Industrial Revolution.* Chicago: University of Chicago Press, 1959.

———. *Toward a Theory of Collective Behavior.* New York: Free Press, 1963.

Smelser, Neil J., and Seymour Martin Lipset, eds. *Social Structure and Mobility in Economic Development.* Chicago: Aldine, 1966.

Smith, Alan G. R. *The Government of Elizabethan England.* New York: Norton, 1967.

Smith, Francis B. *The Making of the Second Reform Bill.* Cambridge University, 1966.

Smith, Paul. *Disraelian Conservatism and Social Reform.* London: Routledge & Kegan Paul, 1967.

Society of Civil Servants (Haldane, ed.). *The Development of the Civil Service.* London: King, 1922.

Somervell, David C. *Disraeli and Gladstone: A Duo-Biographical Sketch.* London: Jarrolds, 1925.

Southgate, Donald. *The Passing of the Whigs, 1832–1886.* London: Macmillan, 1962.

Spranger, Eduard. *Wandlungen im Wesen der Universität seit 100 Jahren.* Leipzig: Wiegandt, 1913.

———. *Wilhelm von Humboldt.* Berlin: Reuther, 1910.

"Statistische Übersicht des öffentlichen Unterrichts im preussischen Staate im Jahre 1816 und im Jahre 1846." *Mittheilungen des statistischen Bureau's in Berlin,* 1 (1848):38–45.

Stephani, D. Heinrich. *System der öffentlichen Erziehung.* Erlangen: Palm, 1813.

Stern, Alfred. *Der Einfluss der Französischen Revolution auf das deutsche Geistesleben.* Stuttgart: Cotta, 1928.

Stölzel, Adolf. "Die Berliner Mittwochgesellschaft über Aufhebung oder Reform der Universitäten." *Forschungen zur Brandenburgischen und Preussischen Geschichte*, 2 (1889): 201–22.

Stone, Lawrence. *The Crisis of the Aristocracy.* Oxford: Clarendon Press, 1965.

———. "The Educational Revolution in England, 1560–1640." *Past and Present*, 28(1964): 41–80.

———, "Social Mobility in England, 1500–1700." *Past and Present*, 33(1969): 16–55.

Strauss, Anselm. *The Contexts of Social Mobility: Ideology and Theory.* Chicago: Aldine, 1971.

Sturm, Eckart. "Die Entwicklung des öffentlichen Dienstes in Deutschland." In *Die Entwicklung des öffentlichen Dienstes,* edited by C. G. Ule. Köln: Heymann, 1961.

Sturt, Mary. *The Education of the People.* London: Routledge & Kegan Paul, 1967.

Symonds, Richard. *The British and Their Successors.* London: Faber & Faber, 1966.

Tharau, Friedrich-Karl. *Die geistige Kultur des preussischen Offiziers von 1640 bis 1806.* Mainz: Hase & Koehler, 1968.

Thompson, Edward P. *The Making of the English Working Class.* New York: Vintage Books, 1966.

Thompson, Francis M. L. *English Landed Society in the Nineteenth Century.* London: Routledge & Kegan Paul, 1963.

Thomson, David. *England in the Nineteenth Century, 1815–1914.* Harmondsworth: Penguin Books, 1950.

Tocqueville, Alexis de. *The Old Regime and the French Revolution.* Garden City, N.Y.: Doubleday, 1955.

Tolchin, Martin, and Susan Tolchin. *To the Victor . . . Political Patronage from the Clubhouse to the White House.* New York: Random House, 1971.

Treitschke, Heinrich von. *Deutsche Geschichte im neunzehnten Jahrhundert.* Leipzig: Hirzel, 1890–1896. 5 vols.

Treue, Wilhelm. *Deutschland und Europa.* Düsseldorf: Droste, 1951.

———. *Wirtschaftsgeschichte der Neuzeit, 1700–1960.* Stuttgart: Kröner, 1962.

———.*Wirtschaftszustände und die Wirtschaftspolitik in Preussen 1815 bis 1825.* Berlin: W. Kohlhammer, 1937.

Trevelyan, Sir Charles, and Sir Stafford Northcote. "On the Organization of the Permanent Civil Service." In "Reports and Papers Relating to the Reorganization of the Civil Service," *Parliamentary Papers,* 20(1854–1855).

Trevelyan, George Macaulay. *British History in the Nineteenth Century and After: 1782–1919*. Harmondsworth: Penguin Books, 1968.
———. *English Social History*. London: Longmans & Green, 1946.
———. *The Life of John Bright*. London: Constable & Co., 1913.
Trevelyan, George Otto. *The Life and Letters of Lord Macaulay*. New York: Harper & Brothers, 1876. 2 vols.
Trevor-Roper, H. R. *Religion, the Reformation and Social Change*. London: Macmillan, 1967.
Troeltsch, Ernst. "The Ideas of Natural Law and Humanity in World Politics." In *Natural Law and the Theory of Society*, edited by Otto Gierke. Boston: The Beacon Press, 1957.
Tschirch, Otto. *Geschichte der öffentlichen Meinung in Preussen vom Baseler Frieden bis zum Zusammenbruch des Staates (1795–1806)*. Weimar: Böhlau, 1934. 2 vols.
Turner, Ralph H. "Modes of Social Ascent Through Education: Sponsored and Contest Mobility." In *Education, Economy, and Society*, edited by A. H. Halsey et al. New York: Free Press, 1965.
Twesten, Karl. "Der Preussische Beamtenstaat." *Preussische Jahrbücher*, 18 (1866): 1–39, 109–48.
Ule, C. H. *Die Entwicklung des Öffentlichen Dienstes*. Köln: Heymann, 1961.
Van Til, Sally Bould, and Jon Van Til. "The Lower Classes and the Future of Inequality." *Growth and Change*, 4 (January 1973): 10–16.
Vincent, John. *Formation of the Liberal Party, 1857–1868*. London: Constable, 1966.
Vollmer, F. *Friedrich Wilhelm I. und die Volksschule*. Göttingen: Vandenhoeck & Ruprecht, 1909.
Wager, Albrecht. *Der Kampf der Justiz gegen die Verwaltung in Preussen*. Hamburg: Hanseatische Verlagsanstalt, 1936.
Walford, Edward. *Country Families of the United Kingdom*. London, 1860.
Ward, W. R. *Victorian Oxford*. London, Cass, 1965.
Wardle, David. *English Popular Education 1780–1970*. Cambridge: Cambridge University Press, 1970.
Warren, John H. *The English Local Government System*. London: George Allen & Unwin, 1963.
Webb, Sidney, and Beatrice Webb. *English Local Government: The Parish and the County*. London: Longmans, Green, 1906. Vol. 1.
Weber, Max. "Agrarstatistische und sozialpolitische Betrachtungen zur Fideikommissfrage in Preussen." In *Gesammelte Aufsätze zur Sociologie und Sozialpolitik*. Tübingen: Mohr, 1924.
———. *Economy and Society*. New York: Bedminster, 1968. 3 vols.
———. *Gesammelte Politische Schriften*. Tübingen: J. C. B. Mohr, 1958.

Weber, Max. *Max Weber on the Methodology of the Social Sciences,* edited by Edward Shils and Henry A. Finch. Glencoe, Ill.: Free Press, 1949.

———. *The Religion of China.* Glencoe, Ill.: Free Press, 1951.

Wehler, Hans-Ulrich, ed. *Moderne deutsche Sozialgeschichte.* Köln: Kiepenheuer & Witsch, 1968.

———. *Primat der Innenpolitik.* Berlin: Walter de Gruyter, 1965.

Weil, Hans. *Die Entstehung des deutschen Bildungsprinzips.* Bonn: Bouvier, 1967.

Weill, Herman. *Frederick the Great and Samual von Cocceji: A Study in the Reform of the Prussian Judicial Administration 1740–1755.* Madison: State Historical Society of Wisconsin, 1961.

Weinberg, Ian. *The English Public Schools: The Sociology of Elite Education.* New York: Atherton Press, 1967.

Wheare, Kenneth C. *Modern Constitutions.* London: Oxford University Press, 1951.

———. *The Civil Service in the Constitution.* London: Athlone Press, 1954.

White, Leonard D., et al. *Civil Service Abroad.* New York and London: McGraw-Hill, 1935.

White, Morton. *Social Thought in America: The Revolt Against Formalism.* Boston: Beacon Press, 1966.

Wiese, L. *Das Höhere Schulwesen in Preussen.* Berlin: Wiegandt, 1864.

Wilhelm, Theodor. *Die Idee des Berufsbeamtentums, Ein Beitrag zur Staatslehre des deutschen Früh-Konstitutionalismus.* Tübingen: J. C. B. Mohr, 1933.

Wilkinson, Rupert. *Gentlemanly Power: British Leadership and the Public School Tradition: A Comparative Study in the Making of Rulers.* London: Oxford University Press, 1964.

Williams, Raymond. *Culture and Society, 1780–1950.* London: Chatto & Windus, 1958.

———. *The Long Revolution.* New York: Columbia University Press, 1961.

Winstanley, D. A. *Unreformed Cambridge.* Cambridge University Press, 1935.

Winter, Georg, ed. *Die Reorganisation des Preussischen Staates unter Stein und Hardenberg.* Leipzig: S. Hirzel, 1931. Vol. 1.

Woodward, Ernest L. *The Age of Reform, 1815–1870.* Oxford: Clarendon Press, 1962.

Woody, Thomas. *Fürstenschulen in Germany after the Reformation.* N.p., 1920.

Wright, Maurice. *Treasury Control of the Civil Service, 1854–1874.* Oxford: Clarendon Press, 1969.

Young, George M. *Early Victorian England, 1830–1865.* London: Oxford University Press, 1934.

——. *Victorian England: Portrait of an Age.* London: Oxford University Press, 1936.

——. *Victorian Essays.* London: Oxford University Press, 1962.

Young, Michael. *The Rise of the Meritocracy.* Harmondsworth: Penguin Books, 1963.

Zagorin, Perez. *The Court and the Country: The Beginning of the English Revolution.* New York: Atheneum, 1970.

Zeeden, E. W. *Hardenberg und der Gedanke einer Volksvertretung in Preussen 1807–1812.* Berlin: Ebering, 1940.

Zeitlin, Irving M. *Rethinking Sociology: A Critique of Contemporary Theory.* New York: Appleton-Century-Crofts, 1973.

Index

Aberdeen, Earl of, 206
Abitur (certificate of maturity), 161,
 164
Absolutism, in Europe and England,
 54, 91–92
Academic freedom, in Prussia, 163
Achievement
 achievement-ascription dichotomy,
  15, 17, 18, 25
 in American value orientation,
  19–20
 as basis for ascription in Prussian
  administration, 63–64
 defined, 15
 role assignment by, 13–23
Adaptation, as assimilation technique,
 30, 237
Administration, English. *See also* Bureaucracy; Civil service; Competition, in English civil service
 abolition of sinecures, 103, 194
 administrative boards, 175–76
 Civil Service Commission, 217, 218,
  219, 221, 233
 efficiency critique of, 180–81
 fee system and, 104
 growth of, 136, 174–75, 227, 231
 patronage system and, 23, 54, 91,
  95–108
 qualifications for office, 104–5
 reaction to Trevelyan-Northcote report in, 100, 200–210

reform of, 106–8, 167–223
 adoption of reform, under Gladstone, 217–23, 232–33
 ascriptive aspects of, 223
 beneficiaries of, 191–97
 characterization of, 167
 and educational requirements, 183
 effects of, 191–97
 in Indian civil service, 197–200
 internal pressure for, 173–78
 limited vs. open competition debate, 200–210
 middle-class pressure and,
  193–94, 257
 motivation for, 106, 219–23,
  231–33
 multi-tiered system proposed,
  170–71, 210
 opposition to, 210–17
 political pressure for, 178–83
 and professional status groups,
  192–93
 purposes of, 182–83
 reformers as clique, 188
 social composition of, 4, 107–8,
  227–28
Administration, English and Prussian,
 compared, 136, 167, 183, 216
 reform of, 126–27, 226–27, 233
Administration, Prussian. *See also* Bureaucracy; Civil service; Competition, in Prussian civil service

achievement as basis for ascription
    in, 63–64
appointment process and training
    for, 56–59, 74–77, 152–53,
    156–57
before absolutist reforms, 54–55
bureaucratization process of, 57–58
civil service commission, 77, 78,
    80–81, 126
educational standards in, 59, 74–78,
    150–53, 156–58, 162, 231
growth of, 41–42, 79–81, 136,
    226–27
outline of system, 42, 43–45, 54–55
from patronage to limited competi-
    tion, 54–81
reform of, 67–81, 159–66, 224–26,
    229, 230, 233
    background of reformers, 155
    civil service reform of 1770 as
        "reform before the reform," 38,
        67, 126
    differentiated levels within re-
        formed administration, 150–52,
        162
    judicial service reforms, 68–74,
        156
    local government reforms, 133,
        125–36
    motivation for, 230–31
    as shift in class and status rela-
        tions, 137
    Stein's reforms, 134–37
social composition of, 59–63, 65–66,
    147–48, 150–51, 152–53, 164–66
social conflict within, 66–67, 81
Administrative Reform Administration,
    217–18, 260
Admiralty, boroughs controlled by, 102
Affectivity-affective neutrality dichot-
    omy, 15, 16, 19–20
Alembert, Jean Le Rond d', 85
Altenstein, Chief Councillor Freiherr
    von
    on power of judiciary, 157–58
    reform ideas of, 129, 130–32,
        136–37
Amtskammern, 43, 44
Annan, N. G., on "intellectual aristoc-
    racy," 124–25
Anti-Corn Law League, 178

Antiformalism, White's characteriza-
    tion of, 18–19
Apothecaries, reform of, 189–90
Apothecaries Act (1855), 89
Arbuthnot, George, 177, 178
    criticizes civil service reform plan,
        206–9, 212, 213
    on need for competitive civil service,
        177
Ariès, Philippe, on social type of 19th-
    century gentleman, 184–85
Aristocracy, 27, 28
    adaptation and incorporation tech-
        niques used by, 30–31
Aristocracy, English
    administrative reform by, to limit
        royal powers, 106
    attack on monopolies of, 178, 179
    education of, 91, 109–11, 115, 115
        table, 116, 116 table, 119 table,
        120 table, 123, 230, 247
    number of, in Commons, 107, 247
    political control by, 106–8, 227–28,
        233
    and rise of gentleman professionals,
        124–25
    status-group linkages of, with landed
        gentry and middle class, 122,
        227–28
    use of patronage by, 91, 96–100
Aristocracy, English and Prussian,
    compared, 3–4
    on education, 3–4, 108, 122–23
Aristocracy, Prussian
    abolition of privileges, 128–29,
        146–47, 155
    administrative experience of, 6,
        152–53, 164–66
    and administrative reform, 132–38,
        152–53, 155, 164–66
    economic position of, 51–52,
        140–45, 229
    education of, 52–54, 82, 83–87,
        88–90, 89 table, 90 table, 230
    effect of land tenure system on,
        140–44
    effect of Napoleon's victory over,
        140, 144–45
    and ennoblement policies, 63–64,
        140, 144
    militarization of, 46–50

and monopoly on ownership of manorial estates, 28, 52
officer corps monopolized by, 49–50, 144–45, 225
professional restrictions on, 52
relations with prince and estates, 39–42
social barriers between lower classes and, 143–44, 153, 228
in Stein's plans, 132–33
Arnold, Thomas, and reform of public schools, 183–84
Ascription
  achievement as basis of, in Prussian administration, 63–64
  achievement-ascription dichotomy, 15, 17, 18, 25
  as characteristic of civil service reforms, 223
  defined, 15
  as outcome of class and status-group formation process, 34
  overemphasis of, in functional analyses, 6, 7–11
  role assignment by, 13–23
Assessoren, 152, 165–66
Auerstadt, Prussian defeat at, 154
Auskultatoren (in-service trainees), 152

Bagehot, Walter, 107
Balliol College, Oxford, 168, 258
Bamford, T. W., on English education, 115–17, 184, 194
Bamtendienst, höheren, 253
Baring, Sir Francis, 221
Bendix, Reinhard, x, 14, 34, 36
Bensman, Joseph, 32, 239
Bentham, Jeremy, and Benthamites, on educational and administrative reform, 124, 125, 173, 180–82, 184, 185
Berlin, 62, 70, 84–85
Bildung, ideology of, 150, 154, 229, 230
Bill of Rights, English, 94
Birmingham, Eng., schools in, 118
Board of Audit, English, 212
Board of Control, English, 213
Board of Customs, English, 213
Board of Trade, English, 212, 213, 221

Boards of War and Domains, Prussian, 155
  social composition of administrators, 62, 153
  Stein's reforms of, 133, 135
Boden (Prussian administrator), 61
Böhmer, Prof. J. H., 61
Booth, James, 212
Bork, Count von, 61
Bourgeoisie. *See* Middle class, English; Middle class, Prussian
Brandenburg, 39–42
Brandenburg, Elector of, 39
Bright, John, 107, 178, 219
Brookbanks (English administrator), 178
Brooks Club, London, 211
Bureaucracy, bureaucratization and, 1–4, 11, 12, 139. *See also* Administration, English; Administration, Prussian
  methods of selection in, 13–23
  "modern bureaucracy" (Weber), 34
  professionalization of, 230–31
Burke, Edmund, 97, 246
Burke, John (*Landed Gentry*), 118
Burn, W. L., on gentility in administration, 125
Bürodienst, höherer ("highest bureau service"), 162, 253
Bürodienst (subaltern "bureau service"), 162
Byron, George Gordon, Lord, 99

Cabinet, Prussian, Stein's reform of, 134
Cadet schools, Prussian, 84, 86, 244
  Humboldt's reform of, 161
Caius College, Cambridge, 110
Cambridge University, 91, 107, 108, 189, 226, 228, 232, 248, 258
  curriculum at, 185
  preparation for civil service at, 172
  reform of, 185–87
  social composition of student body, 13, 89, 110, 123
Camerlistics, education for, 46, 74, 87, 155, 157
Canning, George, 198
Capitalism, in Weber's thought, 26–27
Carlisle College, dean of, 195
Carmer (Prussian minister), 157

Carr-Saunders, H. M., 189
Causal-historical explanation, 6, 11–13, 237–38
Cecil, Lord Robert (Lord Salisbury), 188
Central value system (Parsons), 20, 238
Certificate of maturity (*Abitur*), 161, 164
Chadwick, Edwin, and reform plans, 125, 180, 189, 214, 215, 217
Change, as cause of social stratification, 26–27
Charles I, 93, 94
Chartism, 178, 179, 231
Church of England, 112, 183–84
Civil service. *See also* Administration, English; Administration, Prussian
functional analyses of, 5–13
naturalistic theory of reform, 22–23
reform of, in England and Prussia, contrasted, 3–4, 126–27, 226–27
strategies of monopolization in, 12–13
Civil Service Commission, English, 217, 218, 219, 221, 223
Civil service commission, Prussian, 77, 78, 80–81, 126
Civil service examinations, 6, 234. *See also* Education, English; Education, Prussian; Examinations, English; Examinations, Prussian
achievement-ascription elements of, 17
and bureaucratization, 11, 12
functionalist explanation for, 8–9
proliferation of, 1–4
Civil Service Gazette, 208–9, 221
Civil Service Inquiry Commission, 216
Clarendon, George Villiers, Earl of, 219
Clark, Kitson, 111–12, 121
Classes, concept of (Weber), 2, 5, 23–36
formation of, 2, 27
and Marx's concept, 26–27
and status groups, 25–36
as tendencies of group formation, 32–33
Class society, 28–29, 31–32
Clergy, Anglican

in public-school and university student bodies, 115, 115 table, 116, 116 table, 119 table, 120 table, 123
status of, 111–12
Cleves, 56, 59
Duke of, 39
Closure, of status societies, 28
Cobbett, William, 97
Cobden, Richard, 179
Cocceji, Samuel von, 90, 242
judicial reforms of, 68–74, 76
Collins, Randall, on rising educational qualifications in U.S., 9–10
Colomb (Prussian administrator), 65
Colonial Office, English, 260
Communal ethos, and class society, 31–32
Communist Manifesto, The (Marx-Engels), 29
Comparative studies, theoretical underpinnings of
functional analyses, shortcomings of, 5–13
pattern variables as methods of selection, 13–23
status groups and classes, 23–36
Competition, in English civil service, 185–87, 200–210, 212, 217–23, 232
Competition, in Prussian civil service, 54–81
Condorcet, Marie Jean, Marquis de, 85
Conflict theory, and conflict-group approach, ix, x, 1–2, 10, 12, 13
Corn Laws, 178, 182
Coronation Oath, English, 94
Corps of cadets, Prussian, 84, 86, 161, 244
Cotton, Rev. C. E. L., 195
Country Families (Walford), 118
Crafer (English administrator), 178
Creutz (Prussian administrator), 61
Crimean War, 178, 182, 217
Curriculum, in English educational institutions, 114, 184, 209, 226. *See also* Education, English
and reform of universities, 185, 187
suggested in Trevelyan-Northcote report, 172–73

Curriculum, in Prussian educational institutions, 53, 82–86, 161, 231. *See also* Education, Prussian
Customs and Excise Department, English, 174

Dahrendorf, Ralf, 239
Daily News, The, 212
Davis, Kingsley, 11, 238
Degenfeld-Schönburg, Count von, 61
Derby, Lord, 182
Dessau, Prince Leopold von, 61
Dichotomous concepts, shortcomings of analysis through, 14–23, 234
Diffuseness-specificity dichotomy, 15, 16
Dilthey, Wilhelm, 150
Disraeli, Benjamin
and patronage, 98, 99, 260
and reform of administration, 182, 189
Dohna, General Count zu, 53–53, 61

East Elbe, 40
East India Company, 197
East Prussia, 55, 70
Eaton, Dorman B., 196
Economy and Society (Weber), 12
Edgeworth, Thomson D. F ., 112
Edinburgh, University of, 172
Edinburgh Review, 183
Education
bureaucracy and, 1–4
and job requirements, 9–10
as strategy of monopolization, 12–13, 17–18
Education, English
Benthamite ideas of, 124, 125, 173, 180–82, 184, 185
cost of, 123
"cultural revolution" of 17th and 18th centuries, 110
and exams in professions, 188–97
grammar schools, 113–14
humanist ideals of, 109
as new definition of gentility, 118–25
as promoter of disaffection, 109
reform of, 183–88, 214, 216–17, 226
social structure of, 108–18, 230, 247

and status-group identity, 227–28, 233
Education, English and Prussian, compared, 108, 111, 117, 230, 233
Education, Prussian
for administrative service, 74, 76–78, 80–81, 126, 156, 158–63, 225–27
of aristocracy, 52–54, 71, 82–90, 89 table, 90 table
cadet schools, 84, 86, 161, 244
centralization of, 159, 160
curriculum of, 53, 82–86, 88, 161, 231
elementary and municipal school reform, 160, 161
Humboldt's reform of, 126, 160–63, 231
ideology of, 150, 154
and judicial service reforms, 68–71, 226, 253
Kulturstaat objective of reformers, 158–59
levels of, 82, 126, 160–63
and middle-class mobility, 138–39, 148–49
military education, 46–48, 84, 86, 144–45
nationalization aspects of, 159–60
as new force uniting status groups, 154
royal and nobiliary academies, 82, 83–87
secondary education reforms, 158, 160–62
social composition of student bodies, 71, 82–90, 89 table, 90 table, 148–49, 165
as status-group differentiator, 153, 154
teachers' salaries and status, 86, 159–60
tutoring, 149–50
university reforms, 87–90, 159–66
Education, U.S., social biases in admission to, 18
Education Act of 1870, 210
Eichmann, Privy Councillor von, 63
Elections, parliamentary, 95, 102–3, 247
Ellenborough, Lord, 198
Elliot (English administrator), 177

Engels, Friedrich, 107
Engineering, English reform of, 190
England. *See also* Administration, Eng-
    lish; Aristocracy, English; Educa-
    tion, English; Examinations,
    English; Gentry, landed; Middle
    class, English; Parliament,
    English; Patronage, English
  civil service reforms in, 126–27,
    167–223
    Indian civil service reform,
      97–200
    intentions of reformers, 200–210,
      231–33
    internal pressure for, 173–78
    from limited to open competition,
      217–23
    opposition to, 210–17
    political pressure for, 178–82
    professional education and exams,
      188–97, 230
    and reform of education, 183–88
    Trevelyan-Northcote report,
      168–73
  historical background, 3, 26, 28,
    91–125
    gentility, redefinition of, 118–25,
      138
    historical pattern, 91–96
    patronage and the unreformed
      civil service, 23, 54, 96–108
    social structure of education,
      108–18
Ennoblement, Prussian policies of,
  50–51, 63–64, 140, 144, 225, 229
Estates, Prussian, 38–42, 54–56, 92,
  132, 224
Ethnomethodology, 24
Eton, social composition of student
  body at, 115, 115 table, 116, 116
  table, 198, 258
Examinations, English, 138, 167, 218,
    231, 260. *See also* Education,
    English
  for Indian civil service, 197
  Jowett's plans for, 193
  levels of, in administrative reform,
    210
  in professions, 188–97
  reform of, in universities, 185–88
  in Trevelyan-Northcote report, 170,
    171–73

values linked to, 234
Examinations, Prussian. *See also* Edu-
    cation, Prussian
  in administrative reforms, 77–78,
    80–81, 126, 152, 163
  and judicial service, 69
  nationalization and standardization
    of, 160
Examiner, The, 206
Expertise, overemphasis on, in func-
    tional analyses, 5–7

Factory Acts, 174
Family, selection by, 13–23
Farrer, Thomas H., 221, 222–23
Fichte, Johann Gottlieb, 129, 132,
  139, 149, 153
Fideikommisse inheritance principle,
  141
Foreign Office, English, 176
Fox, Charles, 246
France, 92, 144, 162, 216. *See also*
  French Revolution
Franke, Professor, 244
Frankfurt/Oder, University of, 89, 123
Frederick I, 42, 64
Frederick II (the Great), 79, 81, 134,
    141–43, 151, 157
  administrative recruiting and service
    under, 58–60, 63, 66, 71–72,
    74–76, 80, 150–51, 225–26, 242
  aristocracy in administration of, 58,
    63, 65, 152, 225–26
  and education of aristocracy, 52–53,
    82, 84, 86, 89, 240
  ennoblement policies of, 64–65,
    144, 225
  militarization of nobility and purg-
    ing of nonnobles from officer
    corps by, 48, 49, 50, 144
Frederick William ("Great Elector"),
  41–42, 59–60, 83, 84
Frederick William I, 61, 64, 83, 157
  administration under, 56, 58, 60,
    63, 66, 74, 150–51, 224–25
  aristocratic monopolies under, 49,
    50
  militarization policies, 42, 46, 47–48
  and reform of judicial service, 68–69
Frederick William II
  and education of aristocracy, 85–86,
    134, 144

and preservation of economic position of aristocracy, 51–52, 142–43
Frederick William III, 143–44
Fremantle, Sir Thomas, 213
Freemantle (Peel's patronage secretary), 105
Free trade, Prussian, and traditional monopolies, 145
French Revolution, 4, 81, 103, 143, 229
impact on German thought, 146–47, 149, 150
Friedrich, Carl J., on legal background and administration, 157
Fuchs, Jr. (Prussian administrator), 61
Fulton Report, 236
Functional analyses, shortcomings of, 5–13, 234
Functionalism, ix, 134–36
Fürst, Minister von, 78

Gash, Norman, 106
General Board of War, Prussian, 86
General Code of 1794, Prussian, 155, 158, 159, 229
General Directory, Prussian, social composition of and recruitment for, 57, 61, 65–66, 76–77
General Financial Directory, Prussian, 61
General War Commissariat, Prussian, 61–62
Geneva, University of, 53
Gentility, 91
defined, 108–9
redefinition of, 118–25, 138
Gentry, landed
in public-school and university student bodies, 110–11, 115, 115 table, 116, 116 table, 119 table, 120 table, 123
status-group linkages of, with aristocracy and middle class, 122, 227–28
George III, abuse of patronage by, 106
Gerth, Hans, on liberal thought in Germany, 146
Gillis, John R., 166, 253
Gladstone, William, 189, 258

and abolition of patronage, 105, 108
coordination of reform efforts with Trevelyan, 174, 200, 204, 206, 207, 209–11
and reform of civil service, 100, 178, 188, 199, 204–6, 215–16, 217–23, 232–33
Glasgow, University of, 172
Gneisenau, Count August von, 133
Goal attainment (Parsons), 237
Görne (Prussian administrator), 61
Göttingen, University of, 87, 88, 129, 244
Grammar schools, English, 112, 113–14
Graves, Rev. Charles, 195
Greaves, Harold R. G., 217
Grey, Lord, 177
Grolman, General, 144–45
Groups, as units of analysis, 10, 24–25, 33
group-formation tendencies, 25–36
as alternative to Parsons' pattern variables, 33–34
ideal types as outcomes of tendencies, 34
pattern variables linked to, 25–26
Grumbkow, Count von, 61
Gundling, Professor, 61
Gymnasia, 160, 161, 162–63, 165

Hagen, Minister von, 81
Haile bury School, 198
Halévy, Elie, on motivation for English civil service reforms, 106
Halle, University of, 61, 72, 87, 88, 123
origin of, 244
social composition of student body, 88–89, 89 table, 90 table, 165
Hans, Nicholas, 113
Happen (Prussian administrator), 61
Hardenberg, Minister Freiherr von
and check on judiciary, 158
reform plans of, 126, 127–37
regulation of reforms, 156
serfdom abolished by, 128
traditional monopolies abolished by, 128–29

Harrington, Lord, 97
Harrow, 115, 115 table, 116, 116 table, 195
Hastings, Warren, 198
Hegel, G. W. F., and ideology of official intelligentsia in Prussia, 149, 155, 159, 231
Heineccius, Professor, 61
Herder, Johann Gottfried von, 149
Hereford, dean of, 206
Hintze, Otto, on Prussian reforms, 43, 234
Historical sociology, ix–x, 2, 10, 11, 24, 26
Historicism, Weber's removal of class and status concepts from, 35–36
History
    need for historical as well as functional analysis, 12
    and sociology, compared, x
    theory confused with, 22
Hofkammer, 43, 44
Hohenzollern, House of, 38–45, 54, 244. *See also individual rulers by name*
Hölderlin, Friedrich, 149
Holstein Beck, Duke von, 61
Homans, George, on sociological duty of explanation, 23–24
Honor (Weber), 32, 239
Huber, Ernst Rudolph
    on background of Prussian reformers, 155
    on impact of French Revolution on German thought, 147
Hudson, J. C., 194
Hughes, Edward, on government inquiry into civil service, 179–80
Humboldt, Alexander von, educational reforms by, 126, 154, 160–63, 231

Idealism, German, 150, 154, 228–29
Ideal types (Weber), 5, 23–36
    of institutions, 34
    of society, 27, 30
    as tools, 233–34
    warning on dichotomization, 21–22
    of Weber and Parsons, compared, 21–22

Ideological considerations, and methods of selection, 6, 7
Ideology, Prussian, liberalization of, 145–47
Illegitimacy, Prussian, and royal policies, 143–44
Incorporation, as assimilation technique, 30
Indian civil service, reform of, 167–68, 197–200, 204, 231–32
Individuals, in sociological theory, 24
Industrialization
    bureaucracy needed for, 6
    in England and Prussia, compared, 145
    and methods of selection, 13
    and redefinition of gentility, in England, 118, 121
Inheritance laws, Prussian, 20, 140, 141
Inland Revenue Department, English, 174
Inss of Court, 110, 227
In-service training, in Prussian administration, 74–77, 81, 152, 157, 231
Institutions, sociological study of, 24–25
Integration (Parsons), 237
Interactionism, symbolic, 24

James II, 94
Jelf, Dr., 188, 210
Jena, battle of, 152, 154
Jesus College, 123
Jeune, Dr., 188
Jowett, Rev. B., 187, 191, 205, 211
    exam reforms of, 172–73, 183, 193
    and Indian civil service reform, 198, 199
    and Trevelyan-Northcote report, 168, 187, 194–95, 206
    and university reform, 183, 188
Judicial Examination Commission, Prussian, 77–78
Judicial service, English, local institutions of, 92
Judicial service, Prussian
    education for, 46, 59, 89, 90 table, 253
    experience of reformers in, 155
    growing power of, 157–58

noble-nonnoble division of bench, 73
reform of, 68–74, 76, 133, 165–66, 225, 226
social composition of, 69–71, 89, 90 table, 152
Jus indigenatus, 54–55, 56
Justices of the peace
compared to Prussian *Landräte*, 135
social origin and function of, 92–93

Kammern, 65, 66
Kant, Immanuel, 129, 132, 147, 149
Keir, D. L., 246
Kekewich, George, 260
King Edward VI School, 118
King's College, London, 188, 210
Kingsley, David, analysis of civil service reform by, 23, 197, 257
Kinship, in Parsons' pattern variables, 20
Knigge, Freiherr von, 150
Königsberg, University of, 76, 89, 129
Krause, Karl Christian, 129
Kraut (Prussian administrator), 61
Kurmark, Prussa, 45, 62
Küstrin, Prussia, 62

Landed Gentry (Burke), 118
Landräte, 48
compared to justices of the peace, 135
office restricted to nobles, 62, 152, 153
Land tenure, Prussian
aristocratic monopoly over manorial estates, 52, 128–29, 228
and decline of aristocratic economic base, 140–44
division of family patrimony, 140
Laud, Archbishop, 185
Lefevre, J. G. Shaw, 199, 201
Legal profession, English, reform of, 189, 190, 231
Leipzig, University of, 123, 244
Lenin, Vladimir I., 28
Lenz (Prussian administrator), 65
Lewis, G. C., 183
Liberalism, growth of, in Prussia, 129–30, 145–46
Licensing associations, English, 167, 231

Liegnitz, nobiliary academy at, 161
Lingen, Ralph W., 201, 204, 260
Lipset, Seymour M., 13
Liverpool, politics in, 106
Liverpool Financial Reform Association, 182
Local administration, Prussian, reform of, 135–36
London, schools in, 118
London, University of, 185
Lowe, Robert, 188, 197, 216, 220
Ludewig, Professor von, 61
Luxury goods, Prussian, state regulation of, 145

Macaulay, Thomas B., 188, 203, 236
academic achievements of, 189
and civil service reform, 203, 211, 216–17, 258
and reform of Indian civil service, 168, 197, 199–200
Magdeburg, Prussia, 62, 244
Malthus, Thomas, 123
Manchester, politics in, 106
Manchester Grammar School, 118
"Mandarin tradition," German, 236
Manorial estates, Prussian
aristocratic monopoly over, 28, 52, 128–29, 228
and decline of aristocratic economic base, 140–44
Manorial system, European, 40, 46–47
Mark, Count of, 39
Mark Brandenburg, 49–50, 140
Market
class society and, 26, 28–29
and status societies, 27–28, 29
Marlborough, Duke of, 260
Marlborough College, 195
Marriage, restrictions on Prussian aristocracy regarding, 142–43
Marshall (Prussian administrator), 63
Martiny, Fritz, on education of aristocracy, 86–87
Marx, Karl, class concept of, 26–27, 29
Marxist history, Weber's approach and, 35–36
"Mass behavior" (Weber), 33

Massow, von, educational pluralism of, 162
Mechanics Institute, 211
Medical Acts (of 1858, 1886), 190
Medicine, English, teaching and reform of, 185, 189–90, 231
Merchant Taylor's school, 118
Merit, selection by, 13–23
Metcalfe, Sir Charles, 198
Middle class, English, 2, 23, 247
    criticism of thesis about rise of, and civil service reform, 193–94, 257
    gentility and co-optation of, 107–8, 227–28
Middle class, Prussian, 2
    in administration, 60, 128–29, 164–66, 224–26, 233
    barriers to, 144, 145, 153, 228
    civil service reform and, 128–29, 137–38, 164–66, 231
    rise of, 145–54
Military, Prussian, 38, 42, 46–54, 240
    aristocratic monopoly of, 49, 50, 225
    decline of officer corps, 144–45
    effect on aristocratic education, 52–54, 160
    military equipment, state regulation of, 145
    and Prussian administration, 60–61, 151–52
    recruitment for, 46–48
    size of army, 42–43, 49–50, 244
Mill, John Stuart, 214, 215, 217
Minerva (publication), 148–49
"Modern bureaucracy" (Weber's ideal type), 34
Modernization-tradition dichotomy, 13–23
Monopolies and monopolization
    abolition of, in Prussia, 128–29, 145, 155
    attack on, in England, 178
    by professionals, 238
    of status groups, 27
    strategies of, 12–13
Monteagle, Lord, 206
Morning Advisor, The, 206
Möser, Justus, 148
Moses, Robert, 203
Münchhausen, Minister von, 78, 88
Münchow, von, 63

Municipal administration, Prussian, 133, 136
Municipal school, Prussian, 161
Musgrove, F., on reforms as middle-class victory, 193–94

Namier, Lewis, on political function of patronage, 101–3
Napoleon, effect on Prussia of defeat by, 4, 127, 137, 140, 144, 162, 230
Nassau document (Stein), 132–33
Naudé, Wilhelm, on levels of Prussian bureaucracy, 151, 253
Nepotism, in Prussian administration, 59, 226
Newark, England, politics in, 106
Nobiliary academies, Prussian, 83–86, 161, 248
    compared to English public schools, 117
Northcote, Sir Stafford, 98–99, 100, 145. *See also* Trevelyan-North-cote report
    and administrative reforms, 188, 200, 217, 219, 221, 233
    background of, 258
    exchanges with reform opponents, 203–5, 207
    uses patronage, 260

Oberpräsident, 135
O'Brien, Captain H. H., 215, 258
    concern for character of administrators, 201–2
    favors limited competition, 201–2, 204, 205, 207, 209
    Trevelyan's correspondence with, 202–4
Occupational sphere, role behavior in, 19–20
Officer corps, Prussian, 49–50, 144–45, 225
Old Sarum, 106, 182
Oligarchy, English, growth of, 94–96
Oxford University, 91, 107, 108, 168, 226, 228, 232, 248, 258
    cost of, 123
    curriculum at, 185–86
    and preparation for civil service, 172

social composition of student body, 13, 89, 110

Palmerston, Lord, 176, 218
Parliament, English
  aristocracy in Commons, 107, 247
  and civil service reform, 167–68, 176, 179–80, 188, 197, 210, 218, 219, 231
  cost of elections to, 95, 102–3, 247
  and Indian civil service reform, 199
  and patronage, 91, 94, 101–3
  relations with crown, 91–96, 224, 246
  strength of institution, 38–39
Parsons, Talcott
  on equilibrium social state assumption, 7–8
  and group-formation approach, 33–34
  and ideal types, 21–22
  pattern variables of, 2, 5, 13–23, 25, 237–38
  on U.S. value structure, 19
Particularism-universalism dichotomy, 15, 16, 17
Party, political
  English system, 94–95, 100
  as unit in conflict-group theory, 10
  Weber's concept of, 239
Patronage, English, 91, 96–108, 192, 218, 260
  abolition of, 125, 138, 167, 168, 205–6, 215, 232
  as aristocratic welfare system, 96–100
  and Church, 112
  and civil service, 6, 23, 175–76, 202–3, 217, 221–22, 227
  expansion of, through franchise growth, as stimulus to reform, 217–23, 233
  in Indian civil service, 197
  parliamentary role and, 94–96
  political function of, 100–108
  and problem of quality, 175–76
  and Prussian, contrasted, 54
  symbolic of aristocratic dominance, 182
  in Trevelyan-Northcote report, 168–69
Patronage, Prussian, 54–58, 226

Pattern maintenance (Parsons), 237
Pattern variables (Parsons), 2, 25, 237–38
  dichotomous, described, 14–17
  and group formation, 25–26, 33–34
  in normative patterns, 19–23
  pitfalls in use of, 5, 13–23
  socialization of, individual, 15–16
Paulsen, Friedrich, on Prussian education, 87, 164
Peasantry, Prussian, militarization of, 46–47
Peel, Robert, 104, 105, 106, 179, 198
Pembroke College, 188
Performance-quality dichotomy, 15
Perkins, Harold, on professionalism in England, 181–82
Pestel, Judge, 58
Phenomenology, 24
Playfair Commission, 182, 196
Plumb, J. H., 95
Pocket boroughs, 106
Podewils, Minister von, 63
Pomerania, 49, 84
Poor Law Amendment Act of 1834, 174
Post Office, English, 174
Press, English, support for reforms from, 206
Primogeniture, English, and professionalization, 121–22
Proberelation, 69
Professionals, English
  and administrative reform, 181–82
  education of, 115, 115 table, 116, 116 table, 119 table, 120 table, 123
  group formation and strategies of monopolization by, 238
  licensing associations and exams, 167, 188–97, 231
  meaning of professionalization, 23, 190
  and Prussian, compared, 230
  and redefinition of gentility, 118, 121
  rise of, 121–22
  social origins of, 227–28
Professionals, Prussian, 137–38, 228, 230
Property, relation to, and social stratification, 20, 29

Prussia, 2, 4, 6, 7, 38. *See also* Admin-
    istration, Prussian; Aristocracy,
    Prussian; Education, Prussian;
    Examinations, Prussian; Land
    tenure, Prussian; Middle class,
    Prussian; Patronage, Prussian civil
    service reform in, 126–66,
    224–27, 230
    civil service reform and educa-
        tional reform, 155–66
    crisis of the aristocracy, 137–45
    rising middle class, 145–51
    Stein-Hardenberg reform memo-
        randa, 127–37
    historical background, 3, 13, 23,
        37–90, 224–26, 230–31
    historical pattern, 38–45
    militarization and its conse-
        quences, 46–54
    from patronage to limited compe-
        tition, 54–81
    social structure of education,
        81–90, 228–29
Prussia, Duke of, 39
Psychology, sociology and, 24
Public Health Act of 1848, 174
Public schools, English, 194, 223, 227
    attendance at, as mark of gentility,
        109
    growth of, 113
    reform of, 183–85
    social composition of student body,
        115–18, 115 table, 116 table, 119
        table, 120 table
"Public school tradition," English, 236

Quality-performance dichotomy, 15
Quarterly Review, 195, 196

Ravensburg, Count of, 39
Reader, W. J., on professional reform,
    189, 191–93
Reading School, 118
Referendar, 152, 153, 156
Reform Act, First, 107–8, 178
Reform Act, Second, 219, 221–22
Reformation, decline in status of clergy
    and, 111
Regierungen

crown-estates control over, 54, 57
    in Prussian civil administration, 43,
        44
    social composition of officeholders,
        66, 164
    Stein's reform of, 135
Registered Medical Practitioner, crea-
    tion of position, 190
Representative government, Prussian,
    131–33, 146–47
Retrospective determinism, 9, 11–12,
    23
Revolution of 1688, 94
Rice, Stephen Spring, 208, 209
Ringer, Fritz K., on Prussian examina-
    tion system, 163
Romilly, Edward, 180, 212
Rosenberg, Hans
    and administration in Prussia, 58,
        61, 66–67, 80
    on Cocceji's reforms, 71, 72–73
    and crown-estates power struggle,
        57
    on education as defining characteris-
        tic of new status group, 154
Rothblatt, Sheldon, on English univer-
    sity reform, 121, 123, 186
Royal College of Physicians, 190
Royal Commission, 186, 190
Royal Military Academy (Woolwich),
    202, 205
Rugby School
    as model for public school reform,
        183–84
    social composition of student body,
        115, 115 table, 116 table, 184
Russell, Lord John, 98, 187, 206, 215,
    233
Russia, 28, 92, 140

St. John's College, Cambridge, 110
St. Paul's School, 118, 119 table, 120
    table
Schleiermacher, Frederick, 149
Schmoller, Gustav, 236
Schoen (influencer of Stein), 132
Schroetter, Minister von, 135
Schwerin, von, 63
Secondary schools, Prussian, reform of,
    160–62, 165, 231

Select Committee on Civil Service Expenditures, 222
Select Committee on Medical Education, 190
Select Committee on Sinecure Offices, 103
Selection methods, pattern variables as, 13–23
Septennial Act of 1716, 95
Serfdom, Prussian, abolition of, 126, 128, 135
Seven Years' War, 85, 141
Sinecures, English, 103, 104
Smelser, Neil J., on principle of selection, 13, 14
Smith, Adams, influence of, in Prussia, 129, 146, 157
Social honor (Weber), 32, 239
Socialization, of pattern variables, 15–16
Society of Apothecaries, 189
Sociology
  historical sociology, ix–x, 2, 10, 11, 24, 26
  and history, compared, x
  psychology and, 24
  sociological theory and empirical relations, 23–24
Somerset, England, 111
Spearman, A. Y., 212–13
Specificity-diffuseness dichotomy, 15–16, 19–20
Spectator, The, 206
"Spoils system," U.S., 105
Staatsdienst, höherer (upper-level administration), 162
Stände, decline of, 92
Status, and status groups, 2, 5, 12, 23–36
  assimilation strategies of, 30
  and classes, 25–36
  and manipulation of educational requirements, 9–10
  in Parsons' pattern variables, 20
  and social honor, 32
  as tendencies of group formation, 32–33
  as units of analysis in conflict-group approach, 10
  Weber's definition of, 2, 27, 34–35
Status groups, English, 97, 121
  and education, 109–11, 122

linkage of, through universities, 122, 227–28
  and pressure for reform, 182–83
Status groups, Prussian, 46, 50–51, 228
  abolition of state monopolies and, 128–29, 131
  bureaucrats as, 155
  education as boundary of, 153, 154
  Hegel on universal status group, 159, 231
  revision of status order in General Code of 1794, 155
Status society (Weber), 27–28
  class society and, 29, 30
  predominant in traditional society, 30–31
Stegmann (influencer of Stein), 132
Stein, Freiherr vom, 59, 129, 142
  on characteristics of lower-level administrators, 152
  Nassau memorandum, 132–33
  reforms of, 132–33, 134–36, 137
  separates judicial from civil administration, 156
  social background of, 132
  and Stein-Hardenberg reforms, 126, 127–45
Stein-Hardenberg reforms, 126, 127–45
Stone, Lawrence, on educational reorientation in England, 108, 247
Stratification process, 27–29
Superannuation Act of 1859, 218
Svarez (Prussian administrator), 157

Tauton Commission, 114
Taylor (English administrator), 177
Teachers, Prussian, state control over, 159–60, 163
"Tendential" approach (Weber), 34–36
Textile industry, Prussian, state regulation of, 145
Tharau, Friedrich-Karl, 86
Theology, examinations for, 187
Thirty Years' War, 39, 41, 42, 61, 82
Thomasius, Professor, 61, 244
Thompson, W. H., 187–88
"Tide Barnacles" (English aristocracy characterized as), 179

Times, The, 194, 206, 216
Tocqueville, Alexis de, 4
Traditional administration (Weber's ideal type), 34
Traditional society, status-group formation in, 30
Tradition-modernity dichotomy, 13–23, 25, 27, 30–32
Treasury Department, English, 177, 206, 220
    patronage in, 95, 96, 102
Trevelyan, Sir Charles, 98–99, 168–73, 187, 195, 217, 221, 236, 245
    on examination levels, 210
    exchange with O'Brien, 203–4
    and Indian civil service reform, 203–4
    and need for permanent administration, 176–77
    and opposition to his reform plans, 203–4, 206, 212, 213–16
    on patronage, 99, 232
    on purpose of reform, 183
    reforms advocated by, 176–78, 182, 196–97, 200, 205–11, 233
    on social composition of reformed administration, 203–4
Trevelyan-Northcote report, 100, 124, 167–73, 175, 197, 199, 232
    academic community and, 187–88
    commissioning of, 174
    reform views articulated after publication of, 182
    submission to Gladstone, 200
Trinity College, Dublin, 195
"Tudor despotism," and house of Tudor, 92, 93
Tutoring, in Prussian society, 149–50

United States
    civil service reform in, 197
    modern value orientation in, 19–20
    rising educational qualifications for jobs in, 9–10
    social biases to admission to education, 18
    "spoils system" contrasted with English patronage, 105
Universalism-particularism dichotomy, 15, 16, 17

Universality, in American value orientation, 19–20
Universities, English, 227. *See also* Cambridge University; Oxford University
    cost of, 123
    and redefinition of gentility, 118, 121–25
    reform of, 121, 183, 185–88, 197–98, 231
    social composition of student bodies, 110, 123, 223
Universities, English and Prussian, compared, 122–23, 230
Universities, Prussian, 78, 165. *See also* Frankfurt/Oder, University of; Göttingen, University of: Halle, University of
    and expansion of liberal ideology, 145–46
    reform of, 87–90, 126, 160–63, 231
    state's role in, 87–88, 159
University College, London, 185
University Commission of 1850, 188
University Reform Bill, 188
Urbanization, and redefinition of gentility in England, 118, 121
Utilitarianism (Bentham), 180–81, 164

Value orientation (Parsons), 20, 238
Value pattern, dichotomous classification of, 22–23
Vaughan, Dr. Charles, 195, 199
Victoria, Queen, 212
Vidich, Arthur J.
    on contrast of traditional and modern lifestyles, 32
    on interinstitutional cliques, 239
Vincke, von, 135

Walford, Edward (*Country Families*), 118
Wartensleben, Count von, 61
Weber, Max, x
    on bureaucratization and exams, 11, 12
    on classes
        class societies in modern society, 31–32

class stratification by status,
26–27
conceptualization of, 2
formation of, 27
and Marx's concept of, 26–27
overlap with status groups, 30
and status groups, distinguished,
25–36
concept of "party," 239
on dynamic aspect of formative
process, 32
on education as family related, 18,
231
ideal types, "tendential," 5, 23–36
danger of dichotomizing, 21–22
institutional, 34
of society, 27
as tools, 233–34
on limits of functional analyses, 11
"mass behavior" concept, 33
on "politics of notables," 55
on purpose and cause, 237
"social honor" concept, 32, 239
on status groups
and classes, distinguished, 25–36
conceptualization of, 2
formation of, 27
overlap with classes, 30
status societies in traditional society, 30–31
and units of analysis in conflict-
group approach, 10

Weinberg, Ian, on English boarding
school education, 113
Welfare, Prussian, for families of aris-
tocracy, 142, 143
Welfare system, English patronage sys-
tem as, 96–100
Wellesley, Lord, 198
Wellington, Duke of, 107
Westminster College, 199
Westminster School, 198
White, Morton, characterization of an-
tiformalism by, 18–19
Williams, Charles Wenburg, 47
Wilson, P. A., 189
Wolfe, Christian, 88
Wolfenbüttel, noble academy at, 84
Wood, Sir Charles, 197, 198, 199
Woolwich, Royal Military Academy at,
202, 205
Wright, Maurice, 197, 222
Wylich and Lottum, Imperial Knight
von, 61

Yorkshire, education of gentry from,
111
Young, Michael, on principles of selection, 13, 14

Zemskii sobor, decline of, 92